D1068665

ALSO BY LARS ANDERSON

Carlisle vs. Army

The First Star

The First Star

RED GRANGE

AND THE BARNSTORMING TOUR

THAT LAUNCHED THE NFL

Lars Anderson

RANDOM HOUSE
New York

Published in the United States by Random House,
an imprint of The Random House Publishing Group,
a division of Random House, Inc., New York.

RANDOM HOUSE and colophon are registered
trademarks of Random House, Inc.

Frontispiece: (detail) Wheaton College (Ill.) Special Collections
Title page: (detail) Getty Images

LIBRARY OF CONGRESS CATALOGING-IN-PUBLICATION DATA
Anderson, Lars.
The first star : Red Grange and the barnstorming tour
that launched the NFL / Lars Anderson.
p. cm.
ISBN 978-1-4000-6729-9 (alk. paper)
eBook ISBN 978-1-58836-894-2
1. Grange, Red, 1903–1991.
2. Football players—United States—Biography.
3. Football—United States—History.
4. National Football League—History.
I. Title. GV939.G7A64 2009
796.332092—dc22
[B]   2009023084

Printed in the United States of America on acid-free paper.

www.atrandom.com

2 4 6 8 9 7 5 3 1

FIRST EDITION

Book design by Mary A. Wirth

For Rosanne Jane Anderson Bratz
and Gordy

Not the victory but the action;
Not the goal but the game;
In the deed the glory.

—HARTLEY BURR ALEXANDER

CONTENTS

The First Star

1

AN AMBITIOUS PLAN

Carrying *a polished walking stick,* he strode through the chill of the Chicago night, moving under the bright lights of the Madison Street marquee of the Morrison Hotel. He pushed through the lobby doors, a Lucky Strike cigarette dangling from his thin lips, and passed the marble front desk and richly paneled walls that rose twenty-eight feet. The plush high-rise hotel was the center of Chicago's business and social life, housing the Boston Oyster House restaurant and Terrace Garden dinner theater. Now, on the evening of November 22, 1925, this forty-five-year-old man had his own business to take care of.

He reached the elevator. After making sure he wasn't being followed, he stepped inside. He wore a black overcoat, a double-breasted charcoal-gray suit, spats, a silk tie with a diamond pin, and a fine derby hat. With his dapper outfit reflecting in the mirrors of the elevator's three walls, he told the red-capped operator that he needed to go to the seventeenth floor. The sparkling golden doors shut.

The man had a thin, neatly manicured mustache. His dark but graying hair, which was immaculately trimmed nearly every day, was slicked back with pomade. He cut the figure of a smooth, fast-talking salesman, which he was. As the elevator rose through the skeleton of the forty-five-story hotel, he puffed on his Lucky and stood by the mirrored wall in silent contemplation. His mind was afire with possibilities, because he believed he was on the cusp of making history, of negotiating a deal that would change forever the landscape of professional football in America.

The elevator doors slid open, and Charles C. Pyle stepped forward, a rippling line of smoke rising from the red-orange ember of his cigarette. He looked to his left, to his right. No reporters. Walking down the thickly carpeted hallway, he stopped in front of room number 1739, where he'd been told the clandestine meeting would take place. He rapped his fist on the door. Moments later it swung open. Pyle walked inside, his chest thrust forward as usual, and extended his hand to the man he was meeting for the first time.

Outside the windows of the newly opened hotel, darkness fell and a bitterly cold winter's night enveloped the city. Pyle shed his overcoat and settled into a high-backed chair at a table, and took measure of the man that sat opposite him: George Stanley Halas, the head coach and owner of the Chicago Bears, a National Football League franchise that was on the verge of bankruptcy, just like nearly every other team in the NFL. Pyle, the son of a preacher, was blessed with a golden smile and a silver tongue. He could talk to anybody about anything—and he also could convince anybody to *do* most anything. For a few minutes, the two made small talk.

Lighting another Lucky and drawing long on it, Pyle finally launched into the subject he had come to discuss: money. Pyle, the first agent in football history, wanted to broker a deal for his client, a football player who had just dropped out of the University of Illinois and who days earlier Pyle had boldly promised to make the richest young athlete in America. Not only that, but Pyle had guaranteed that he could turn him into someone as famous as baseball's Babe Ruth, as beloved as the thoroughbred Man o' War, as iconic as pugilist Jack Dempsey. The young man's name was Harold E. "Red" Grange, and Pyle had an ambitious plan for him: He was going to make him the NFL's first star.

Like all originals in business, the underworld, and sports, Grange already had a nickname: the Galloping Ghost. It was a lyrical, apt so-he was in real life, because their herky-jerky nature created the illusion that he moved faster than he really was; the illusion that maybe he actually was a ghost.

Grange particularly captured the hearts and hopes of fans in the lower classes of society and those who had been away overseas. Thousands of immigrants who came to America in the 1890s and those who had endured the battles of world war were now flocking in droves to the fields of sport. The economy was booming, jobs were plentiful, and people who had struggled to make ends meet just a few years earlier now had "extra" money for the first time. Transportation was affordable. Model Ts rolled off the Ford assembly line at a rate of one every ten seconds and cost only $290. People had more leisure time, too, as most Americans no longer had to work seven days a week. Boxing was immensely popular with ethnic fighters generating pride among new Irish-Americans, German-Americans, Italian-Americans, and Jewish Americans. Baseball also flourished. Tickets were cheap, and many of its stars, like Ruth, looked and acted like nine-to-five guys getting dirt underneath their fingernails while making a living.

But many in the lower and middle classes had viewed football—both the college and pro games—differently. In the early 1920s, college football was considered by the lower classes to be a snooty game played by rich kids from the East Coast in front of rich girls waving pom-poms. It was a sport dominated by the likes of Harvard and Yale and Penn, and sports fans across the middle and lower classes of America struggled to identify with any of the players on those elite teams. But soon that dynamic would change. Soon one of their own would rise and charge the imaginations of farmers and factory workers and foot patrolmen all across the country.

Professional football in 1925 was a game largely managed by low-level hustlers looking to make a quick dollar, and it attracted little public interest. Its franchises were located mostly in out-of-the-way towns like Pottsville, Providence, Rock Island, and Green Bay. On a good day, an NFL game would draw a few hundred people; on a bad briquet, because it instantly conveyed what made him so special c the football field—how, from his halfback position, he ran with never-before-seen mixture of speed and power and elusiveness; ho he seemed to see holes in the line before they actually opened; how h threw thunderbolts with his stiff arm at defenders who tried to tak him down; how his hips swiveled in a flourish to sidestep and juk defenders and leave them lying on the ground along his zigzag trai how he made them feel as if they were trying to corral a phantom.

Grange, age twenty-two, even looked somewhat ghostlike Standing five foot nine and weighing 170 pounds, Grange had deep set, haunting gray eyes. It was as if a shadow were always falling ove his eyes, yet when he gazed at you, those same eyes projected such ; liquid intensity—a narrow beam of brightness—that it made peopl feel like he was looking through them, not at them. He was classi cally handsome: His nose was straight and powerful; his lips wer full, a little like those of a poster girl but slightly downturned in a continual frown; and his jaw was square and rock solid, like that of a Roman centurion. Everything about Grange—from his angular fea tures to his granite-sturdy build that had been sculpted by hauling one-hundred-pound blocks of ice in his youth—suggested fitness and hard work.

Short film clips of Grange's games at the University of Illinois were frequently shown in movie houses across the country before the feature show. There on the big screens, in black and white, moving at sixteen to eighteen frames a second, audiences saw the feats of Ruth, Dempsey, and Man o' War. But in the closing days of 1925— the high point of the golden age of sports in America—it was Grange who especially held moviegoers and sports fans spellbound.

By '25, nearly three-fourths of Americans went to movie houses at least once a week, and what played on the big screen greatly shaped popular culture. Sitting in the cool darkness of "picture palaces"—as the most grandiose theaters were called—moviegoers from New York to Los Angeles marveled at Grange's exploits. Watching him perform up on the flickering screen, audiences were mesmerized by his improbably fluid shifts and feints, by his jazzlike improvisation on the field, by his absurdly long touchdown runs. The fluttering clips even made Grange look more spectacular than day, only a few dozen curious spectators gathered along fence lines or in rickety bleachers.

The league had been created five years earlier during a meeting in August 1920. Called by Jim Thorpe, who was the league's first president, the meeting of sixteen men took place in Ralph Hay's Jordan and Hupmobile showroom, a car dealership in Canton, Ohio. When they emerged from the showroom, the American Professional Football Association had been formed. Two years later, at the prompting of Halas, it was renamed the National Football League. This was a misnomer, because the league had no teams west of Chicago or south of Washington, DC, but Halas wanted a more regal-sounding name in order to give the league additional legitimacy.

In the league's first few seasons, more than twenty franchises folded. Most players held full-time jobs outside of football and had trouble fitting in time to practice. A few who had special and rare skills, like kickers or speedy halfbacks, offered their services to the highest bidder and floated among teams, sometimes earning as much as $100 a game. But others were paid far less—and less frequently too—and often failed to show up for the weekend contests. Even coaches sometimes were absent at kickoff, and nearly all the contests had the unorganized feel of a pickup game at the local park or on a pasturelike field. Not surprisingly, the press largely ignored the fledgling league. Sometimes there was a paragraph or two of coverage on page three of the sports section, but often there was no mention of NFL action. That all changed, though, in the fall of 1925 when Grange became the first college player to quit school early in the hopes of turning pro.

Pyle and Halas negotiated through the night, floating offers and counteroffers at each other in ping-pong fashion. Halas needed Grange, the college game's biggest draw, to save his franchise. Pyle needed Grange to fill his own bank account.

Pyle did most of the talking. He was the sports version of P. T. Barnum—a carnival barker and promoter who during his life would organize bicycle races, boxing matches, tennis matches, hockey games, and a cross-country foot race dubbed the "Bunion Derby." He even tried to sell the public on a newfangled idea of a domed sports stadium that featured a retractable roof, escalators, and magnifying glasses that could be cranked up and down in the seats farthest away from the field. His mind was a small factory that churned out ideas and schemes, as he was constantly dreaming up new ways to push along the boulder of evolution in the field of sports—with the hope, at the same time, of getting rich quick. But nothing would be more seminal in Pyle's career than what would transpire in this hotel suite.

The two went back and forth all night, arguing passionately about what Grange was worth. They took periodic breaks, each man smoking a cigarette and gazing out the windows at the city below, where the yellowish glow of the gaslit streetlamps threw circles of light onto the pavement. But neither man would budge. It was turning into a battle of wills.

As the first blush of sunlight filled the morning sky, sending shafts of winter light into the smoky room, the high-stakes negotiating finally wound down to its end. Soon the most important contract in the history of the NFL would be signed. Soon Halas would have his man. Soon Red Grange would be a Chicago Bear.

2

SOMETHING NOT SEEN IN
FOOTBALL BEFORE

Thirteen months earlier . . .

The caravan of Model Ts snaked through the autumn dusk, their headlights forming a river of radiance against the night. The column of cars—there were hundreds of them—stretched for more than a mile and hummed along at forty miles per hour across the flats of the upper Midwest, cruising past the fields of wheat and corn that sandwiched the two-lane road of Highway 24. It was October 17, 1924, and thousands of fans and students from Ann Arbor, Michigan, were trekking 350 miles to Champaign, Illinois, on the eve of what was being hailed by many sportswriters as "the game of the century"—a term that had only recently been coined expressly for this University of Illinois–University of Michigan contest.

The previous season, the Fighting Illini and the Wolverines had tied for the Big Ten Conference Championship, but because of a scheduling quirk, the two teams didn't play each other. Many sportswriters crowned Illinois national champions and pegged Michigan as the number two team in the country in 1923. (The first formal poll rankings, conducted by the Helms Athletic Foundation, wouldn't be released until 1936.) The Wolverines hadn't been defeated in twenty games, and their 1924 team was widely considered one of the best teams in the fifty-year history of college football.

Illinois entered the game on a ten-game winning streak of its own—during which it outscored opponents 185 to 36—but was considered a slight underdog. The game attracted even more attention because the Fighting Illini were celebrating their homecoming, and on this day, Memorial Stadium was officially being dedicated to the 124 Illinoisans who had lost their lives in World War I.

The demand for tickets was unprecedented. Sixteen special trains of the Illinois Central Railroad left Chicago on the morning of the contest. Chicago radio station WGN dispatched announcer Quinn Ryan to Champaign to broadcast its first-ever football game. (Ryan had experience with live-event radio; that summer he covered the Scopes trial—the first live broadcast from a trial in U.S. history.)

WGN executives expected tens of thousands of people up and down the Midwest to gather around radios at high school football stadiums, gas stations, and in living rooms to listen to Ryan's play-by-play description of the events. And because of the dedication ceremony and the expected record crowd for an athletic contest in the Midwest, more regional newspapers than ever before sent reporters to cover the game. It was the college football event of the year, and even University of Notre Dame coach Knute Rockne acknowledged it. "The eyes of the Middle West turn to Urbana [Champaign] Saturday for the Illinois-Michigan game," he said. "The game is sure to be nip and tuck . . . [Michigan] will build a special defense for Grange and will stop him most of the afternoon. This lad is resourceful, though, and may pull one at any time."

Six days before kickoff, reporters asked legendary Michigan athletic director Fielding Yost (who was still in charge of the program, though the Wolverines were technically coached by George Little) about Grange. In the first three games of 1924, the Illinis' triple-threat tailback had been a running and passing machine, virtually unstoppable. In the season opener against the University of Nebraska, he played all sixty minutes—halfback on offense, defensive back on defense—and ran for 116 yards in addition to completing six passes for another 116 yards in Illinois's 9–6 win. A week later, in a tune-up game for Michigan against an overmatched Butler University team, Grange ran for 104 yards, passed for 30, and scored two touchdowns in the 33–0 victory—in just 14 minutes' playing time.

Grange was relatively unknown outside of the Midwest, but Yost knew that he was the engine that powered the Illinois team, so during the previous few months, Yost drilled his players on how to stop the Illini tailback. "Mr. Grange will be carefully watched every time he takes the ball," Yost told reporters. "There will be eleven clean, hard Michigan tacklers headed for him at the same time. I know he is a great runner, but great runners usually have the hardest time gaining ground when met by special preparation."

Reading these words in the local Champaign newspaper fired up not only Grange but also his coach, Bob Zuppke. Shortly after his boys left campus in June for their summer vacations, Zuppke started sending them letters. Nearly every morning, seated at his desk, he would remind his players in careful, steady handwriting that Michigan expected to "romp over us" and that the upcoming game against the maize-and-blue would be the touchstone of their season. When the players returned to campus in late August, they excitedly strapped on their leather helmets and began getting ready for Michigan in earnest at nearly every practice, no matter their next opponent.

Two months later, on the day before the game, the team worked out at the Champaign Country Club. As he walked around his players during the light practice, Zuppke constantly reminded them that Michigan was taking this game lightly, that the Wolverines were overconfident, and that this made them vulnerable. Zuppke was personally insulted by Yost's claim that Grange would be stopped, because Grange was like a son to him. Zuppke had discovered Grange, who hadn't even planned on playing college football, and now Zuppke pulled every motivational trick he knew to rile up his boys and get them to play the game of their lives against their rival. The coach shouted his most beloved aphorisms: "Victory in football is forty percent ability and sixty percent spirit!" . . . "In times of stress, leaders rise!" . . . "Prepare not to lose!"

The Michigan team stayed at the Urbana Country Club, and Yost presided over its final practice looking like a man without a fear. At age fifty-three, Yost already was a college football legend. In 1900, when he was at Stanford University, he became the only man in history to coach four teams in one year: the Stanford varsity and freshmen teams, a local high school team, and the squad at nearby San Jose Teachers College. He began coaching at Michigan the following season. At his first practice, Yost noticed that his players weren't performing the drills at the pace he wanted. "Hurry up! Speed it up!" he yelled. "Let's hurry now. Hurry up there. If you can't hurry, make way for someone who can!" After that first practice, Yost was branded with a nickname that would stick for the rest of his life: Hurry Up Yost. In his first season in Ann Arbor, Hurry Up's team outscored its opponents 555–0.

Unlike most coaches of the day, who preferred to play straight-ahead, power football on offense, Yost designed plays that relied on quickness, speed, and agility; he often told his boys to "go where the defenders aren't." Yost favored rapid play and runs to the outside. His system was unlike any other coach's in the country; when one of his backs was tackled on offense, he had his players rush back to the line of scrimmage and hike the ball right away. Beginning with his first Michigan team, Yost's boys piled up a dominating 55-1-1 record from 1901 to 1905. During that stretch, the Wolverines outscored their opponents 2,821 to 42, and because of their ruthless, quick-strike ability to score touchdowns, Yost's teams became known as "Point a Minute" squads. By 1924, he had won three national championships with players who were lighter than most. On the '24 squad, not a single player topped two hundred pounds.

But Yost's talents as a coach were nearly matched by the size of his ego. When he applied for the Michigan job, he mailed to the school several boxes of reference letters and newspaper clippings that detailed his success; the boxes weighed more than fifty pounds. At the same time, Yost rarely shied from talking himself up. One time Ring Lardner, a famous sportswriter in Chicago, was asked if he'd ever chatted with Yost. "No," Lardner said. "My father taught me to never interrupt."

Yost's larger-than-life personality made him a reviled figure on the Illinois campus. And his offhand comment about shutting down Grange made the game personal to the Illinois halfback, who normally was reserved, almost placid. Now Grange had something to prove.

. . .

The morning of October 18 dawned bright over Champaign, promising a golden Indian summer day. At just past nine o'clock, a Pullman car carrying the Michigan football team rolled into the Urbana depot. The night before, at the Urbana Country Club, Yost had barely slept. He had spent the dark hours—just as he had spent the nights of the past several weeks—pondering one question: How do we best stop Grange? Sitting in his compartment on the train, sucking on a cigar as he examined his reams of notes, Yost concluded that his boys needed to punish Grange, to hit him sledgehammer-hard every time he touched the ball. Yost had attended Illinois's game earlier in the season against Nebraska, and he noted that the Cornhuskers smacked Grange around better than any other team, causing Grange to wear down as the game wore on and limiting his effectiveness in the fourth quarter. If Grange was hit hard on every play, Yost believed, his speed would slip away. He would become ordinary. And so before the coach exited the train, he told his boys as they sat in their railcar that now was the time to unleash holy hell on Grange, that today was the day to treat him as if he were their mortal enemy. It was a simple strategy, but Yost believed that the best way to stop Grange was to have him hauled off the field on a stretcher.

As soon as Yost stepped off the train, he was surrounded by a group of reporters. "Coach Yost, what about Grange?" they shouted.

"I know Grange is a great runner," Yost replied, "but we've got eleven good men who are going to stop him."

"How are you going to stop him?" a reporter asked.

"There are eleven good tacklers on this Michigan squad, and those eleven good tacklers are going to be after Mr. Grange all afternoon. Anything else you want to know, gentlemen?"

By nine o'clock the temperature had risen to above seventy. Special traffic police from Chicago were already in place at the giant brick-and-steel horseshoe stadium to handle the standing-room-only crowd of seventy thousand—the biggest crowd to attend any football game in 1924. By ten, the streets of Champaign were clogged with cars. Special trains snaked into the tiny Champaign depot, arriving every thirty minutes, their Pullman cars bursting with charged-up Illini fans dressed in orange and blue. Just north of the stadium, a grass field covering several acres was turned into a parking lot; one reporter estimated that there were more autos in Champaign on this day than in all of Europe. And the fraternity and sorority houses on the leafy campus were festooned with colorful streamers and decorations to celebrate the school's homecoming. Everywhere on campus, there was anticipation in the air. By noon, the temperature was over eighty degrees.

An hour later, long lines of people stood at the entrance gates around the stadium, which was faced with red brick and white Bedford stone. A throng of fans surged along the two great memorial colonnades that were lined with one hundred pillars of stone, each one dedicated to an Illinois soldier who had lost his life in World War I. The fans then made their way inside to the two decks of seats, all made of concrete. By one-thirty, the bleachers were nearly full.

More than twenty thousand people had unsuccessfully tried to obtain tickets, and those who couldn't get in now began gathering around their radios throughout the Midwest to listen to the pregame dedication ceremonies and the game itself. As the players watched from the sidelines, Illinois's president, David Kinley, delivered a dedication speech. His voice, carried by dozens of loudspeakers, pierced through the noise of the crowd as he proclaimed that this venue would now be known as Memorial Stadium in honor of the state's World War I veterans. Moments later, a parade of veterans walked onto the grassy field—it was the emerald green color of a well-manicured golf course—prompting a thunderous roar from the crowd. At the end of the ceremony, a bugler blew taps for the fallen. The crowd fell silent for the last time.

The two teams then retreated to their respective locker rooms. In the Illinois quarters, Zuppke paced back and forth through the cramped, musty room, his arms folded like a philosopher deep in thought. While many of the players talked quietly, Grange stood off to one side, alone, imagining what he was about to do out on the field. Though Grange was one of the quietest players on the team, he was also one of the most intense. In the moments before kickoff, he always liked to be by himself, willing his adrenaline to rise with every heartbeat.

Then Zuppke quit pacing. He ordered his players to remove the cotton stockings that stretched from their feet to above their knees— a standard part of their uniform. Realizing the unseasonably high temperature outside, Zuppke didn't want his players to overheat. A few players objected, saying they didn't want their shins to get cut by the cleats of the Michigan players, but Zuppke was adamant. "Without those heavy socks, you'll feel a lot fresher and cooler," he said.

The Fighting Illini then ran out into the warm, sunny afternoon. As soon as they emerged from the portal in the southeast corner of the stadium, the crowd cheered so loud that the thunder of noise could be heard a quarter mile away. But something wasn't right, and this caused the crowd to rise in confusion: Why were the players' lower legs bare? They had always worn stockings that protected their legs, but now the sweat on their white limbs glistened in the sunlight.

The Michigan players were jogging through their warm-ups on the field when the Illinois players appeared. In an instant, the Wolverines stopped what they were doing and stared across the field. They had never seen a team play without stockings. Yost was sure that Zuppke was trying to play a trick on his team, especially since the Illini players had been wearing the stockings during their pregame warm-ups. Yost ran to the referee and asked if there was anything in the rule book against this; the referee said no, the move was perfectly legal.

Yost was furious. He and Zuppke had been coaching against each other for a dozen years, and neither trusted the other. Even though the scheduled kickoff time had passed, Yost ordered his team captain, Herb Steger, to go over to the other sideline and inspect every Illini player to see if they had grease on their legs, which would make them harder to tackle.

Steger trotted over to the Illinois side of the field. With the perplexed crowd watching intently, he ran his fingers over the legs of every player, inspecting them closely. He found nothing but hair on their legs and reported this back to Yost, who then reluctantly sent

Steger back onto the field for the opening coin toss. Like all coaches, Yost despised surprises, and this certainly wasn't a situation he had envisioned. He continued to protest furiously with the officials, but they merely shook their heads and said there was nothing in the rule book against bare legs.

At midfield, Steger shook hands with Illinois captain Frank Rokusek, an end. The referee flipped the coin, and the Fighting Illini won the toss. As was common at the time, Illinois elected to defend the north goal, hoping to go on defense first. But Yost ordered Steger to kick off. Yost's defense had surrendered only four touchdowns in the last two years, and he believed this game was going to come down to a battle of field position. If his defense could hold the Illinis on downs deep in their own territory—as Yost believed it would—then after a Fighting Illini punt, Michigan would most likely get the ball for its first offensive possession in Illinois territory. It was a strategy that coaches all over the country employed, but it played right into Zuppke's hands: He wanted Grange to touch the ball as soon as possible.

The crowd rose. Grange, standing on the sideline, buckled his flaming orange leather helmet and loped onto the field, his blue number 77 jersey already dripping with sweat. On the Michigan sideline, Yost gathered his team around him. "Kick off to Grange!" he yelled above the crowd noise. "Let him know he hasn't gotten us worried! Hit him and hit him hard! See that he stays hit!"

Grange stood on the 5-yard line between the goalposts, ready to receive the ball. Steger, like the rest of the Wolverines, had read newspaper accounts of Grange and his greatness during the past year, and now Michigan's captain was eager to put Grange to the test. Steger approached the ball with straight-on strides and lofted the pigskin in Grange's direction. The game of the century was on.

The ball turned over and over against a sun-drenched, baby blue sky. The crowd noise at the newly minted Memorial Stadium fell a few decibels, as if everyone felt the sudden need to be quiet so as to focus his or her entire attention on what was about to transpire. These were the true believers in Grange, after all, and as soon as he cradled the ball at the 5-yard line and began charging up the field with gathering speed, his knees kicking high, a piercing roar erupted. This was what they had come to see: Grange versus the vaunted Michigan Wolverines; the up-and-coming star laying it on the line against a team that few outside of Illinois believed could be beaten. A perfect team, some had called the Wolverines.

Grange darted up the center of the field, across the 10-yard line to the 20. The first Michigan defender approached, but he was taken off his feet by a jarring block from Wally McIlwain, the other deep back. Grange then cut sharply to his left, dodging a tackler. Earl Britton, a blocker on the kick return team, then pasted a Wolverine player who was flying at Grange, driving the would-be tackler to the ground with a ferocious hit.

Then a cluster of Wolverines zeroed in on Grange. He ran to his right, spun, stiff-armed a player, powered through another, then peeled back around to his left, darting upfield and charging through three tacklers. In a blink, Grange had broken five tackles. By the time he reached the 40-yard line, he had emerged from a scrum of Michigan players and was sprinting toward the Wolverines' side of the field.

It was all happening so fast, it was so unexpected, and the crowd noise rose even higher as Grange crossed midfield. Grange's stride lengthened, and he sprinted across the Michigan 40-yard line, the 30. Grange was pulling away from everyone on the field similar to the way Man o' War did whenever he neared the finish line of a money race.

Near the 20-yard line, a Michigan safety lunged at Grange. He had come from the other side of the field and had the angle on Grange, but his dive fell short as Grange blew by him. Grange crossed the 10-yard line, the 5, and finally slowed to a canter into the end zone. The return covered 95 yards, and in the twelve seconds it took Grange to run from one end of the field to the other, it was clear that the game of the century would belong to no one else. Just past the goal line, he laid the ball on the ground.

At gas stations in Chicago, at the Wheaton High field in Grange's hometown of Wheaton, Illinois, and in thousands of homes across the Midwest, people sat around radios and listened to WGN's crackling play-by-play account. As Grange burst into the end zone, scores of radio listeners leapt into the air and screamed as if they were actually perched on the 50-yard line. Over the airwaves, Grange was even more magical than he was in person, because in the imagination he could be even bigger, stronger, faster than he actually was, and in this world, the world of radio, Grange was now coming off as a kind of supernatural athlete, so mythical did the run sound over the airwaves.

Quinn Ryan, WGN's announcer, frantically searched for adjectives to draw verbal pictures of what had just happened: *unbelievable, incredible, the best play of all time.* Ryan's attempt to put into words what Grange had just accomplished only burnished Grange's burgeoning legend, because it was clear that try as he might, Ryan couldn't accurately verbalize what he'd just seen. Then again, nobody could. The country had found heroes in baseball and boxing, but so far the Roaring Twenties had yet to produce a football player who could capture the imagination the way Ruth and Dempsey had. Could Grange be that once-in-a-generation athlete who commanded the attention of the sporting public by the sheer force of his grace and power and gilded play on the gridiron?

In the press box, more than one hundred sports reporters who were hunched over their typewriters began banging at their keys the moment Grange crossed the goal line. A reporter for the *Chicago Tribune* wrote:

> Grange had torn Michigan to pieces before the game had gone more than fifteen seconds. . . . Right then and there Michigan knew it was up against something it hadn't seen in football before.

Grange was just getting started.

After *Illinois's Earl Britton* kicked the extra point to give the Illini a 7–0 lead, Michigan opted to kick off again, hoping to pin Illinois deep in its own territory, another common practice at the time. Steger booted the ball, and Grange fielded it at his goal line. This time, though, Grange bobbled the ball and it tumbled onto the grass. He quickly scooped it up and scampered 20 yards before he was brought down. Illinois was flagged for illegal use of hands, a penalty that put the ball back at the 10-yard line. On first down, Illinois quarterback Harry Hall handed the ball to fullback Earl Britton, who gained 3 yards. Given his team's poor field position and not wanting to risk a fumble, Zuppke ordered his team to punt on second down—yet another common tactic. But Britton flubbed the kick, and it traveled only 23 yards. Michigan took over on offense with the ball on the Illini 36-yard line.

Steger, playing quarterback, passed to James Miller, Michigan's left end, for 9 yards on first down. On the next play, Miller took the ball and pushed forward for 2 yards and a first down. After an incomplete pass, Yost ordered his team to line up in field goal formation, even though it was only second down, because he didn't want to take the chance of turning the ball over. But he had a trick up his sleeve: Yost, who invented the fake field goal, told Steger to run the famous play. The coach knew that the game's momentum was on Illinois's side because of Grange's stunning touchdown return, and he thought that a sleight-of-hand trick could flummox the Illini and tie the game. The plan backfired: The holder fumbled the snap from center. An Illinois player jumped on top of it at the 30-yard line, prompting another outburst from the stadium.

On first down, Wally McIlwain, a back, ran into the center of the line for 1 yard. The next play, Grange lined up as the deep tailback in what Zuppke called the "Grange formation." In this alignment, the Illini had seven linemen crouched in three-point stances along the line of scrimmage. Grange, with his hands on his knees, stood 5½ yards directly behind the center. Illinois's Harry Hall lined up a yard behind the right tackle, and McIlwain knelt in a three-point stance a yard behind Hall.

In the standard "Grange play," the center hiked directly to Grange, who then immediately ran to his right. With Hall, McIlwain, and Britton, who lined up as the right wingback a yard behind the right tackle, leading the way, Grange would wait for their blocks as he charged around the end. He had the option of cutting inside or outside depending on how the defense reacted, and it allowed Grange the freedom to do what he did best on the football field: improvise.

On second down and 7 from the 31-yard line, with Grange lined up as the deep back in this special version of the single-wing offense, the ball was snapped to number 77. Instead of bolting right, which was what Grange usually did, he cut to his left. Hesitating a moment to allow Hall and Britton to get out in front of him, Grange bided his time as he jogged to his left. But when his two backfield-mates engaged their blocks, he took off up the field, his legs pumping hard. He darted around the left end for nearly 15 yards, untouched. When a Wolverines defender closed in, Grange cut sharply to his right to evade him, then charged up the middle of the field. By the time he reached midfield, it was clear to everyone in the stadium that no one was going to catch him.

He pulled away from every other player, blazing down the field like fire across oil, past the 40, the 30, the 20. When he crossed the goal line to score his second touchdown in less than three minutes of play, no one was within 20 yards of him. It was an arresting run, an explosion of speed, and it whipped the crowd into a roiling froth. Britton kicked the extra point, and suddenly the Illini held a 14–0 lead.

Yost, pacing the sideline, decided to stick with his pregame strategy and kick off again. This time the maize-and-blue stopped Grange after a return of 20 yards. Two plays later, Illinois punted, but Michigan failed to move the ball after two offensive plays and kicked it back to the Fighting Illini, giving Grange another chance to touch the ball.

On second down on the Illinois 44-yard line, Grange, lined up 5½ yards deep in the formation that had been named for him, took a handoff from quarterback Harry Hall and began running to his right. He sprinted to the outside, into open space, trying to outrun the aggressive pursuit of the Michigan defenders. They took the proper angles of direction, but they overpursued Grange, just like they had on his previous touchdown run. Skimming just inside the sideline, Grange suddenly cut back sharply and moved with lightning speed diagonally across the field. In the previous two seasons, he had rarely cut back; instead he allowed himself to get tackled or pushed out of bounds. But now he sharply changed directions, and the well-coached Michigan defenders, who had studied Grange's running pattern, weren't prepared for his sudden cutback. Once he reached the Wolverines' 45-yard line, his stride lengthened and again he broke away from the Michigan defense. He bolted up the field, passing the 30, the 20, the 10. Yost couldn't believe what he was seeing, and he raised his arms to the sky in disbelief. Grange reached the end zone, capping a 56-yard touchdown run. It was his third touchdown in less than eight minutes of play against the nation's top defense.

Britton missed the extra point. Then Michigan's Steger kicked off for the fourth straight time, booting the ball into the Illinois end zone. On first down from the 20, Grange took a pitch from his quarterback and was thrown for a 5-yard loss. Zuppke ordered a punt, and Britton unleashed a towering kick. Michigan's return man fielded it cleanly, but as soon as an Illini defender hit him, he fumbled. Illinois's team captain, Frank Rokusek, recovered the ball at Michigan's 44-yard line.

A murmur of expectation once again rose from the stadium as Grange lined up in the backfield. On first down, he took a pitch from the quarterback and again charged to his right. With a wall of blockers in front of him, Grange angled toward the right sideline. After he had gained 10 yards, Michigan defenders had him surrounded. But in a blur of twists, spins, and stiff-arms—the moves were instinctual, coming as natural to Grange as musical notes did to Gershwin— Grange broke free from four potential tackles and cut back sharply to his left toward the center of the field. He'd done it again. Zipping away from an exhausted Michigan defense, he glided into the end zone for his fourth touchdown in less than twelve minutes. After Britton's extra point, Illinois led, 27–0, over a team that hadn't lost in two years.

A few minutes later, the Illini called a timeout. When trainer Matt Bullock ran onto the field with a bucket of water, he went straight to Grange, who was hunched over with his hands on his knees. "I'm so dog tired I can hardly stand up," Grange told Bullock. "Better get me out of here." Bullock relayed Grange's request to Zuppke, who then signaled for Grange to come out of the game and rest on the bench.

As Grange jogged off the field, the overflowing crowd rose to its feet and serenaded the tailback with a spontaneous ovation that would be talked about for years to come. For more than five minutes, everyone in the crowd stood—including twelve-year-old John Wooden, the future UCLA basketball coach, who had made the trip from his hometown of Centerton, Indiana—and wildly cheered Grange, who had just put on the greatest twelve-minute show in the history of college football. Not even the legendary Jim Thorpe, a star for the Carlisle Industrial Indian School in Pennsylvania fifteen years earlier, had ever authored a quarter of football like this. Grange had scored four touchdowns, covering 95, 67, 56, and 45 yards. In total, he had gained 303 yards in the first quarter, more yards than the Michigan defense had given up in the last year. The newspapermen in the press box knew they were witnessing something historical. Many searched the ends of their vocabularies trying to put into prose what Grange was doing on the football field, dropping words like *preternatural, otherworldly,* and *sublime.*

But Zuppke didn't want Grange to think he couldn't do better. So when Grange reached the sideline, the coach told his player, "Shoulda had another one, Red. You didn't cut right on that one play."

Grange listened to his coach's analysis, then took a seat on the bench. He needed a rest.

Zuppke didn't put Grange back into the game until the third quarter. When Grange loped back onto the field, he was given a hero's welcome, as the crowd rose again to salute its newest star. Midway through the quarter, Grange scored on a 12-yard touchdown run, busting around the right end again and cutting back to the center of the field. Then, late in the fourth quarter, he tossed an 18-yard touchdown pass to Marion Leonard. At the end, the game of the century had become the blowout of the century: Michigan 14, Illinois 39.

Roughly *850 miles* to the east of Champaign, Grantland Rice was sitting in the press box at the Polo Grounds in Manhattan. Rice, a columnist for the *New York Herald Tribune,* was covering the Army–Notre Dame game. In a few hours, after the Fighting Irish had upset the Cadets, 13–7, he would pen what would become the most famous lead in the history of sportswriting:

Outlined against a blue-gray October sky the Four Horsemen rode again. In dramatic lore they are known as famine, pestilence, destruction and death. These are only aliases. Their real names are: Stuhldreher, Miller, Crowley and Layden.

As Rice was making music on his typewriter in his customary dramatic fashion, the news of Red Grange's exploits in the middle of the country filtered into the Polo Grounds press box. Who was this Red Grange? Where did he come from? What made him so good, so dominant, so seemingly magical? To Rice—and to the rest of the country—Grange would soon become an obsession, a virtual mythical figure that arose out of the wheat fields in the country's heartland, a player of such appeal that even men, women, and children who didn't care for sports wanted to see him play. After this day was over, after Rice had banged out his milestone story, the most acclaimed sportswriter of his time made a silent vow: He had to cast his own eyes on this Red Grange kid.

Grange *was mobbed* as he trudged across the field toward the locker room. Fans, teammates, even opposing players and opposing coaches wanted to shake his hand. He had scored six touchdowns and turned in the best performance of his career in his biggest game. Now even the newspapers on the East Coast couldn't ignore what Grange had done. Sports editors in cities like New York, Boston, and Philadelphia had repeatedly dismissed college football in the Midwest as second rate, calling it "Western football." But the next day, the *New York Times* carried a detailed Associated Press story of the game on the front page of its sports section, something the paper rarely did for contests played in the heartland. Overnight, Grange was introduced to readers across the nation.

The timing couldn't have been better for Grange, because the country was hungry for a new sports hero. Babe Ruth had been typically spectacular in 1924—leading the league in batting average (.378), runs (143), and home runs (46)—but no other baseball player in America had transfixed the public in '24. Jack Dempsey wasn't fighting; instead he was acting in Hollywood. Golfer Bobby Jones had won the '23 U.S. Open, and tennis player Bill Tilden had just captured his fourth consecutive U.S. Open singles title, but neither Jones nor Tilden participated in a sport that was accessible to everyday Americans. Golf and tennis were games of the wealthy; baseball, boxing, and football were games of the everyman.

And now here was Grange, a fresh-faced Illinois football player who was running his way into the national sporting consciousness. He was something new, and soon everywhere he went, reporters and fans would follow in his shadow, trying to learn all they could about this quiet kid in the Midwest.

By *the time* Grange reached the locker room, the celebration was in full swing. Players whooped and hollered, slapped one another on the back, and together reveled in their unexpectedly easy triumph. As soon as Grange appeared, he was swarmed by reporters, all wanting to know how he had shredded the Michigan defense with such élan and ease. Grange wasn't used to all the attention and wasn't naturally long winded, so his responses were cryptic and stammered, but he did the best he could, giving credit to his teammates for their blocking. *I couldn't have done it without them,* Grange said. *I'm just one player on the team.*

After speaking to reporters for about forty-five minutes, Grange finally retreated to the showers. The locker room was nearly empty by the time he got dressed. He slowly walked out of the locker room alone, carrying his duffel bag. He strolled back across the cleat-marred field, where just hours earlier he had left the crowd awestruck. He didn't hurry, as if trying to absorb the moment before it was gone. In the distance, Grange could hear Illinois fans singing and celebrating the team's victory in the half-light, but he felt most comfortable here, alone on the field, alone with his thoughts.

The long line of Model Ts and Durants and Roamers headed back to Ann Arbor, full of disappointed fans. They had witnessed a historic performance, but it wasn't the kind of history they were hoping for. As Yost, Michigan's athletic director, sat in his railcar for the trip home, he was already planning to fire Michigan coach George

Little and reappoint himself to the position so that he could exact revenge on Grange and Illinois next season.

Grange continued to walk leisurely through the dusk, wearing a cap and sweater, his hands in his pockets. He finally left the field, passing fans in anonymity as he strolled back to his on-campus fraternity house, Zeta Psi. When he ambled through the door, he was greeted like the big man on campus he was. An impromptu celebration had broken out at the house—dozens of students and fans crammed into the fraternity—and Grange was the guest of honor. But Grange didn't relish the partying, so after a few minutes of talking with some friends, he slipped into his room, changed clothes, and, with a friend, sneaked out a back door and headed to a small downtown restaurant for dinner. Afterward the two went to a movie at Champaign's Virginia Theatre.

By the time they returned to their fraternity around ten-thirty, the party had moved on to another location, which suited Grange just fine. By eleven, on the biggest day of his athletic career, on a day that would change the course of his life, Red Grange was fast asleep.

3

A HARD LIFE

The *Red Grange hype machine* started to hum the next day, as newspapers around the country launched their love affair with the reluctant hero. The newspaper business had changed dramatically in the early 1920s, and that helped pave Grange's path to fame. Instead of giving abundant space to society news, editorials, and letters to the editor, which had filled the papers in the 1900s and 1910s, newsmen shifted their focus, devoting more space to sporting news. This included using three-column photographs of game action shots as well as large illustrations that explained the intricacies of different sports.

The changing landscape of America precipitated the shift. World War I was over, the economy was soaring, people were driving automobiles in ever-increasing numbers, and Americans were enjoying more free time than ever before. Where did their attention turn during these heady times? Largely to sports, as newspaper readers grew increasingly hungry for athletic headlines and heroes. Sportswriters such as Grantland Rice and Damon Runyon fed this growing appetite by waxing lyrically about athletes like Ruth and Dempsey, describing their feats in grandiose expressions and elevating them to near-mythic figures. But in 1924, at the height of the golden age of sports—a time when the country, anxious to bury the memory of World War I, longed to find larger-than-life heroes on the fields of play—college football was becoming the fastest-growing sport in the nation, and editors filled their pages with news of this up-and-coming game.

Some twelve hours after he scored his final touchdown against Michigan, Grange was romanticized in newspapers across the country. The *Herald Examiner* in Chicago reported, "They'll have other great ones, to be sure, but the memorial columns of the stadium will be so much dust before they'll ever see another young man run the opposition as dizzy as Red Grange did here today." The *Detroit Free Press* raved, "When histories are written on the feats of red-headed warriors, Grange must be given his place with those old heroes Richard the Lion-Hearted, Frederick Barbarossa, and Eric the Red." And the *Chicago Tribune* wrote:

> With Red Grange on the Illini, it is doubtful if a team in the country could beat the Zuppke machine. . . . He stamped himself as one of the greatest football stars of all time, East or West.

But the most vivid words—and the most enduring phrase—about Grange would spring from the typewriter of Grantland Rice. Though Rice didn't even see the game, he had heard the accounts of the young player's breathtaking runs while he was at the Polo Grounds in New York covering Army versus Notre Dame. Rice was so taken with Grange—with his seemingly limitless ability to dodge tacklers even when he was virtually within their grasp—that he would soon write a story about him for the *New York Herald Tribune,* the nation's largest and most influential newspaper. Employing his flair for the dramatic, Rice referred to Grange using the three words that would follow Grange for the rest of his life; three words that eloquently summed up what made him so special on the football field; three words that would become, in all of sports history, one of the greatest nicknames of all time: the Galloping Ghost.

Grange also did something to Rice that few athletes could: He moved Rice to poetry, inspiring a poem that began with his calling Grange:

A streak of fire, a breath of flame
Eluding all who reach and clutch;
A gray ghost thrown into the game

Within weeks of the conquest of Michigan, reporters from across the country descended on Champaign to dig for nuggets about this ghost. Who was he? Where did he come from? What made him tick? The nation's first true football star, a player whose biography would one day be known from the Carolinas to California, from the Dakotas to Texas, was about to be born.

At the turn of the twentieth century, Lyle Grange was as tough and country strong as any man in Forksville, Pennsylvania, a tiny hamlet of 190 located in the thick of the Endless Mountains in the northeastern corner of the state. He stood six foot tall, weighed just over two hundred pounds, and had a lumberjack's muscular, toned physique. Like most men in town, Grange, who was of Scottish-Irish descent, worked from dawn until dusk cutting trees, which was a thriving industry in the Northeast. One day in the early 1900s, he fought another man to determine who would be the foreman of their crew. For six hours, according to Grange family lore, the two men raised their fists and battled in the woods of the rolling, green mountains. Always charging forward, Grange pounded the bigger man, over and over, making a bloody mess of his face. The opponent eventually fell to the ground, unconscious. Grange, the taste of blood in his mouth, his face scowling, stood over him like a victorious heavyweight, daring anyone else to step forward. No one did. After this display of strength and bare-knuckled determination, none of the other lumberjacks disputed the promotion he'd given himself.

On June 13, 1903, Lyle's wife, Sadie, gave birth to their third child, a redheaded boy they named Harold. Even at a young age, he showed natural athletic ability. One of his favorite games was played with his dog Jack. He would lead the dog into a corner of their fenced backyard. Trapped, the dog would try to bolt past little

Harold, darting to the left, then to the right. Harold would lunge at the dog, trying to wrap his arms around him, but the dog almost always squirted away. Yet Harold closely studied Jack's movements, committing them to memory. This was the beginning of Grange's education in the art of open-field running.

Like most small boys, Harold was constantly on the run in his early childhood. He played in the shallows of the creeks that poured out of the mountains and babbled through Forksville. He chased his friends around town in games of follow the leader, passing places like the one-room schoolhouse where grades one through eight were taught, and the general store where locals gathered to exchange town gossip and make predictions about the weather. In winter he went sledding in the mountains, and in summer he enjoyed trekking to the county fair and watching the adults play baseball and compete in track and field events. Red, as his friends called him because of the color of his hair, was particularly intrigued with the pole vault. The spectacle held his eyes every time a vaulter put his pole in the box and lifted skyward. In his mind, the vaulters could fly.

Grange was so fascinated that he wanted to do it himself. One day he broke off a branch from one of the towering hemlock trees that sprouted throughout the area. Holding the branch, he raced across the grass in his backyard. As soon as he reached full speed, he planted the branch into the ground to catapult himself upward and hurl himself into the air. But the branch snapped in half, and he tumbled to the ground, hard and awkward. As he fell, the splintered branch drove into his side like a stake being hammered into the earth. When he landed, he felt the air escape his lungs. Eventually he regained his wind and discovered that he had broken two ribs—the first sports injury of his life.

In the winter of 1907, tragedy blew like a tornado into the Grange household: Sadie, Red's mother, died suddenly. After having a tooth pulled, she hemorrhaged. The bleeding was so profuse that she bled to death before her husband could rush her to the nearest doctor several miles away. The event triggered an earthquake in Red's life, and its aftershocks would be felt for years. The already quiet kid withdrew from everyone and everything for months after his mother passed away—from his brother and sisters, his dad, his friends, and even sports. He rarely talked, and when he did, it was in clipped answers to questions: "no sir," "yes sir," "no thank you." Over the years, Grange would have little to say about his mother, and he never publicly explained the circumstances of her death, but she was never far from his thoughts. Her death would not only have a profound influence in shaping the person he would become, it would also one day help ignite his passion for sports. Because out on the fields of play, Grange could forget, however briefly, about the heartache he suffered when he was just a five-year-old boy.

A *few months after* Sadie Grange died, Lyle loaded his family into a car and drove 680 miles to Wheaton, Illinois, the town where he had grown up and where his four brothers and sister lived. He needed their help in raising Red, older daughters Norma and Mildred, and their little brother, Garland, who was two years younger than Red.

The move to Wheaton in 1908 brought the Granges into a vastly different world from the one they had left behind. Located thirty miles west of Chicago, Wheaton was founded in the 1830s as an agricultural community. But a few years later, after a local railroad company laid tracks that cut through the heart of town, it underwent a growth spurt. By the time Lyle and his family arrived, Wheaton had a population of some four thousand and was becoming a bedroom community of Chicago.

The Granges moved into a small house, and Lyle took a job with his brother Sumner, who owned a house moving company. But after several months, Lyle realized he couldn't keep the family together. Worried that his daughters needed a strong female figure in their lives, Lyle put them on a train back to Pennsylvania to live with their maternal grandparents. He arranged for his sister, Bertha, to care for his boys during the day while he worked. But she soon moved to New York State, forcing Lyle to hire a woman to be part nanny and part housekeeper. All the while, Red continued to retreat into his own world, becoming increasingly reticent.

His father tried to make up for the loss of his mother, but Lyle—ever the lumberjack, the brawler, the man of few words—simply was incapable of being a truly nurturing figure, of guiding by quiet counsel, empathy, and putting his big arms around his boy's shoulders. Rather, he taught verbally, by rudimentary axioms: *Work hard. Don't show off. Talk with your actions, not your lips. Never back down if you are wronged, even if you lose the fight. Always do the right thing, even if it's the hard thing.*

In fact, for much of his early life, Grange would find it difficult to relate to women. But if the lack of a mother figure haunted him when away from the fields of sport, on them it would make him an undeniably stronger athlete. Because his will, forged at the knee of his father, was as resolute and forceful as his dad's right-handed haymakers that could knock flat the toughest of characters.

Lyle *struggled to earn* a living. In the course of the next few years, he and his boys moved several times in Wheaton. They stayed in the house of Luther, another of Lyle's brothers, who was an unmarried attorney in town. Later, when Red was in eighth grade, Lyle and brother Garland moved into apartment 113 over a store on Wheaton's Front Street, but Red went to live on a nearby farm owned by another uncle, Ernest. For about a year, Ernest worked Red tirelessly on the farm. Red would usually rise at five o'clock, put on his clothes, and trudge to the horse and cow barns. There he'd feed hay and oats to the five horses and milk the four cows—tasks that took about an hour. After a quick breakfast of eggs and bacon, he'd return to the barn to water the horses, hitch two of them to a wagon, and put bottles of milk in it. Then, with a crack of a whip, he'd drive the wagon into town and leave the bottles at the dairy. Finishing that, he'd go back to the farm, put the horses in their stalls, change into his school clothes, hop on his bicycle, and ride several miles to school. By the time the first bell rang, Grange had already logged four hours of hard labor.

When school was over, the work resumed. First he had to clean the barn, then get the hay down from the hay mow for the next morning, and, finally, feed the horses and milk the cows one last time. Grange never complained about anything to his father—he was too proud and tight lipped and afraid to do that—but Lyle could see that his son was being overworked. It was affecting his schoolwork; Grange had trouble keeping his eyes open in class. So after a year, Lyle allowed Red to move into his second-story, five-room apartment on Front Street, which was lined with several establishments, among them a bank, a small restaurant, a gas station, and an agency for the Cable Piano Company.

This had been an important year in the life of Red Grange. Out on the farm, during the predawn mornings and the after-school early evenings, Grange learned the value of hard work. *Anything can be done,* his uncle preached to him, *if you put heart and time into it.* Though Red didn't enjoy his months on the farm, he began to believe in the benefits and the power of a strong work ethic. Years later that ethic would become a major part of his allure to fans across the country. Because not only did he have an abundance of natural athletic skill, he was also the hardest worker on the field. At this time in America's history, work was a badge, an identifier of a class—especially of those in shops, mines, fields, and factories. At his core, Grange was an everyman, kin to every average toiling guy in the country.

The same year that Lyle Grange moved to Front Street, the Wheaton Police Department hired him as the assistant to the town marshal, a man named Emil Ehinger. Lyle was a natural for the job. Tough, physically imposing, and possessing a no-nonsense demeanor, Lyle cut a menacing figure as he walked the streets in his uniform, wielding a baton. In May 1914, Ehinger was promoted to county sheriff, and Mayor H. Ward Mills appointed Lyle the new marshal. His salary was bumped to $100 a month, the most he'd made since his lumberjack days in Pennsylvania.

Lyle was on duty for as many as twenty hours a day, which meant that Red and Garland were often alone during their teenage years. Wheaton couldn't afford to hire another police officer, so Lyle patrolled the city by himself, and he had plenty to keep his eyes on.

Con men and career thieves who made their livings in Chicago were discovering Wheaton when Lyle took over as marshal. They'd ride the train into town and prey upon unsuspecting business owners and citizens, who generally were as trusting as the typical midwesterner. Lyle didn't want the corruption of mob-infested Chicago to infiltrate his town, so he'd spend most nights on the streets, patrolling for characters with knives in their pockets and sin on their minds.

His father's dedication to his beat further deepened Grange's sense of isolation. At school he often kept to himself, and around girls he was as bashful as any boy at Wheaton High. Grange told his friends that he didn't go on dates because he didn't have nice clothes and money, but that wasn't the whole truth. Once, after a basketball game in the school gym, three girls approached the locker room, hoping to speak with Grange. When told of their presence, Grange panicked. Not wanting to talk to the girls—he always grew embarrassingly tongue tied in such situations—he opened a window at the back of the locker room and leapt out to escape.

At home, though, Grange couldn't hide from anything. Because of his unusual family structure, he had to grow up faster than most kids in Wheaton. His father weighed his older son down with heavy responsibilities—responsibilities that would have belonged to Grange's mother had she lived longer. The two boys initially divided the tasks in the evening. Red prepared the meals, Garland did the shopping, and they both did the dishes. The evening meals usually did not include Lyle. But ultimately, because he was older, Red assumed responsibility for the entire household.

To Garland, Red was equal parts brother, father, and friend. To Red, Garland was his number one responsibility. Red was robbed of his childhood, but his living situation made him the most dependable young man in all of Wheaton. It also caused him to covet one thing he didn't have: money. This singular desire, formed during these long days of struggle, would shape his most important decisions in the upcoming years.

One woman did figure in Red's young life, however. Emma

Dollinger, the wife of Charles "Doc" Dollinger, who owned a corner drugstore in town, was literally the neighborhood mother. She often doled out free sodas and ice-cream cones to kids in town and frequently had Red and Garland over to the Dollinger house for supper. Those and other small acts of kindness—like making sure that the boys had gloves and boots before winter set in, and treating their ailments and many cuts and scrapes—made their lives a bit better.

It was Red who frequently needed first aid, because he played sports during his every free moment. During basketball season, he played pickup games at the farm of his friend Lawrence Plummer. In a barn, Red and his buddies dribbled an old basketball on the hay-strewn plank floor and shot it at a hoop they fastened to a wall. In the summer, Red pedaled his bicycle all around town, through open fields and along dirt roads, trying to find mischief or a game, whichever came first. Sometimes he'd stop at a friend's house and ride horses; other times he'd head to a local candy store and pick out his favorite sweets. The highlight of his summers, though, was the annual church picnic, which featured games of baseball—one of Red's favorite sports—and several races for the kids. The first time Red ran a race, he was eight years old, and he won his age group; instead of a trophy, he received a baseball. From then on, Lyle told his son that he would give him a quarter for every race he won, and that was all the incentive Red needed. Over the next several years, he always crossed the finish line ahead of his competition, and his dad always stayed true to his word.

But Red's favorite sport was football. In junior high, Red tagged along with older boys who, after the final school bell had rung, would walk to a vacant lot on the eastern edge of town. A high hill bisected the lot, with fifty yards of field on each side of the rise. Red was often the deep back on the kickoff, and he couldn't see the ball until it had crested the arcing hill. When he cradled the ball into his arms, he'd charge up the field like his hero George "Potsy" Clark, the quarterback who led Illinois to undefeated seasons in 1914 and '15.

Wearing a homemade uniform of old pants that he'd cut off at the knees and a stocking cap stuffed with socks for padding as a makeshift helmet, little Red ran with a fearless abandon that impressed even the older boys. But because he was much smaller than the other players—at age thirteen he was about five foot one and 105 pounds, whereas many of the other kids were five inches taller and 30 pounds heavier—he often absorbed violent hits that, on occasion, knocked the wind out of him. He once suffered a deeply bruised spine due to a kick in the back, and couldn't sit for two weeks. After practically every game, he'd come home with bruises or a black eye or a gash that required stitches. One day he told his dad that he was thinking about giving up football for good; that he'd rather be doing something less hazardous like shooting marbles. But his father, in his blunt way, told Little Red to keep at it, to never give up, no matter how much pain he was in. *It will make a man out of you,* Lyle said to his oldest son.

So Red kept playing. On many days after school, he'd head to another vacant lot adjacent to the house of the town's only black family. The only white kid there, Grange dazzled the other boys with his speed and agility. Grange was always impressed with the play of the black kids—he said later in his life that they taught him more about football and how to succeed in the sport than anyone else. Once he started dominating these games, he had his first inkling that, perhaps, he could someday play on the Wheaton High varsity team.

Grange also began to develop a mean streak on the playing field, which stood in stark contrast to the passive and genial nature he displayed in every other facet of his life. Sports were becoming his outlet, his diversion from his hard-luck life. When he was in a game, he could be the person he wasn't in everyday life: someone who was aggressive, tough, even downright violent. The way he attacked the game of football, it sometimes seemed as though he were running from demons. Grange even fought others on the field when he was in junior high. Because the boys he battled were usually older, Grange often ended up bloodied and beaten. When he told his father that he was tired of getting, in his word, "whipped," his dad reminded him that it was more honorable to lose fairly than to sucker punch someone and win. Lyle Grange uttered these words without the slightest trace of sympathy, because fighting, to him, was as natural as breathing. The only thing that mattered once the fists were raised was not winning or losing but how one fought. It was Grange's first lesson in sportsmanship.

But it was Grange's health, not his fights, that jeopardized his athletic career. When he was eight, he developed a severe cold, and a doctor was called to the house. His diagnosis was a virtual death knell: Grange had a heart murmur, and he could no longer participate in anything that raised his heartbeat, which obviously included football, basketball, and baseball. Obeying the doctor's orders, Lyle forbade Red to play sports ever again.

At first, Grange followed his father's command, afraid that he'd get the paddle if he were ever caught. But after a few weeks, Grange, unable to let sports go, started sneaking out of the house after school and joining his friends in the neighborhood games. He'd return home before his father walked through the door after another long day at work, and for a while, Grange's secret life of sports was safe.

But then one afternoon he injured his back playing in a sand-lot football game; afterward, his face twisted into a mask of agony whenever he bent over. When Lyle saw that his boy was in pain, he demanded to know what had happened. If Red had learned one thing from his father, it was to always tell the truth, so he confessed that he'd been playing football with his friends. Grange expected that his butt would soon meet the paddle. But instead of forbidding Red to play sports, Lyle, without even consulting the doctor, said to go ahead and participate, the physician's orders be damned. The father may not have been outwardly affectionate, but he did recognize that sports fostered a special connection between himself and his oldest son. It was the one great love they shared. He understood that the rewards of his boy playing were far greater than the risks.

In August 1918, Grange entered the ninth grade at Wheaton High School and underwent his first physical exam since his heart scare six years earlier. Not only had his heart condition disappeared—

it was likely a temporary problem that Grange had outgrown—but he was also pronounced perfectly fit to try out for the Wheaton High varsity football team. After years of playing pickup games on dusty neighborhood lots and on rock-strewn fields, Red Grange would finally have his chance to show his stuff on a real athletic field.

4

THE WONDER OF WHEATON

O*n April 6, 1917,* the United States entered the world's first great conflict, and a year and a half later, when fifteen-year-old Red Grange ambled through the doors of Wheaton High for the start of ninth grade, the war was on everyone's mind. In fact, it was causing a surge in the popularity of high school athletics across the country. Physical education experts viewed football as an ideal athletic endeavor to strengthen the body, a way to prepare young men for the rigors of battle. An alarming number of prospective soldiers were failing their draft physical examinations—in some states it was as high as 40 percent—and as a result, the nation's top military brass encouraged high school principals to push their students into sports such as football. Grange didn't have to be asked twice.

A few days after school began in 1918, he tried out for the football team. After the final bell rang, he walked a mile and a half to an apple orchard, where the practice field was located. Standing five foot seven and weighing 138 pounds, Grange was one of the smallest kids to show up on that first day of practice. Grange, his heart jackhammering, timidly approached the coach, Roy Pucky, who also served as Wheaton's manual training teacher and was the school's only male instructor.

"What position do you play?" Pucky asked.

"What positions are open?" asked Grange.

Pucky told Grange that the only position not filled by a returning starter was right end. Grange, hoping to play immediately, told Pucky that he happened to be a right end, even though he'd rarely played the position in the sandlot games. Pucky immediately anointed Grange his right end—a position Grange would play his entire freshman season. He rarely touched the ball in practice, but because he was the only player to volunteer to play that position, he was a starter.

Before Wheaton's first game, played on a Saturday morning in early September, Grange and the other freshmen were assigned a task: clear the field of apples that had fallen from the trees. Carrying baskets, the players spent twenty minutes picking up apples from the ground, and as they were cleaning the field the crowd began to arrive. Though there weren't any bleachers, about two hundred people usually showed up for the games. While a hat was passed around for requested donations of 25 cents to 50 cents per person for the Wheaton High athletic fund, the crowd followed the action on the field by walking up and down the sideline to get as close to the line of scrimmage as possible. Upon seeing the crowd for the first time while scooping up apples, Grange grew anxious. He'd never played football in front of spectators before, and now, just minutes before he made his high school debut, he wanted to run away.

Though he had starred in the neighborhood pickup football games, this was different. He didn't have a mother to encourage him, and his dad rarely praised him—two factors that caused his self-esteem to be unusually fragile. But at least his dad, dressed in his police uniform and keeping a watchful eye on the crowd, was now on the sideline, and that had a soothing effect on Grange. Lyle may not have been good with words, but his devotion to his son would be evident over the next four years on every football Saturday in the fall. In fact, his dad wouldn't miss a single football game during his son's high school career.

Just seeing his dad—so powerful, so in control—cranked up Grange's courage, and he trotted onto the field for the opening kickoff. The school provided uniforms that consisted of bulky cotton shirts with numbers on them, football knickers that stopped just above the knee, and socks. But the athletic fund didn't have enough money to provide cleats and helmets. Grange saved his pennies to buy these items, and he begged his dad for a few extra nickels. But money being scarce for the Granges, it had to go toward food and school clothes, not luxuries like football accoutrements. So Grange cut a deal with a player who'd graduated a year earlier and bought his tattered leather helmet at a bargain-basement price; then he convinced one of his teammates to loan him a pair of his extra cleats. Although the cleats didn't fit—in fact, during his freshman season, Grange would never wear cleats that matched his actual shoe size— he kept his sore feet a secret.

Wheaton won its first two games, though Grange never touched the ball. But late that fall, Coach Pucky saw something on the field that would dramatically change the team's fortunes in the upcoming years—and would ultimately change the course of the history of the sport. He saw Red Grange run with the ball.

As his freshman season wound down, Grange desperately wanted to become involved in the offense. He hadn't had a single pass thrown his way or had a chance to return a kickoff or punt the entire season, but in Wheaton's second-to-last game, on a cold November morning, Grange finally got his opportunity. Midway through the game, Wheaton's opponent kicked off. Grange, who was lined up as a blocker on the return team at about the 20-yard line, expected the ball to be booted deep to one of his team's return men. But the kicker didn't make good contact with the ball, and it bounded into Grange's hands around Wheaton's 25-yard line.

This was the moment he'd been waiting for all season, and Grange, his legs driving like pistons, his right arm clutching the ball, blasted up the field. He dodged tacklers, ran over a defender, pushed another aside with his left arm, and cut so sharply that others simply slid by as if on ice. The slack-jawed fans on the sideline marveled at Grange's bursts of speed, his nimble feet, his changes of direction, and the fluidity of his every move as he galloped into the end zone.

It looked so easy, the way he ran. Some kids picked up playing the piano or recorder without much teaching. Others at Wheaton High could solve math problems with hardly any guidance. These were their gifts; running on a football field, it was clear after one play, was Grange's.

Before the start of the next season, at the urging of his team-mates, Grange approached the new coach, Bill Castleman. Grange told Castleman that the only reason he had played end during his freshman season was because the team didn't have anyone else to play there, and that his true position was halfback. Castleman then moved Grange to left halfback during a few preseason practice sessions to see if the boy could effectively run with the ball. Nearly every time he touched the football, Grange wowed the coach as he tore through tackles and sprinted away from defenders. Though Castleman had no experience coaching football—he was the manual training teacher—even a novice could see that Grange was a rare player, maybe the best in the state, even as a sophomore. So Castleman quickly penciled Grange in as his starting left halfback—and more. He made Grange the core of the offense. The Wheaton High Tigers, the coach determined, would go as far as Grange would carry them.

By the time Grange was sixteen, his stiff-arm was a lethal weapon. When a defender approached, he could strike him on the forehead with either arm, sending him to the ground in a whirling daze. The power he packed in his arms was developed and built by working as an iceman—a job that, once reporters dug into his background, would one day add another layer of mystique to the legend of the Galloping Ghost.

One morning in the summer of 1919, Red was playing with friends when Luke Thompson, who owned and operated an ice truck, pulled over to speak with the boys. Grange and his gang liked to chase the horse-drawn ice wagon when Thompson came by, hoping to snag a coveted ice chip. Thompson delivered blocks of ice to families all around Wheaton, and when he saw Grange and his friends, he decided to play a joke on them. Thompson offered a dollar to any of the boys who could hoist a seventy-five-pound block of ice onto his shoulder. Grange was intrigued. During the previous few summers, he had ridden on Thompson's ice wagon, and though he didn't lift any ice—his job was to watch the horse while the ice-men delivered to houses and apartments—Grange had silently studied how they used their ice tongs to pick up the cakes of ice and put them on their shoulders. Red had never tried the maneuver himself, but he knew the proper form.

One by one, each of the neighborhood kids tried to lift an ice block onto his shoulder, and, one by one, each failed. Then Grange stepped forward. Almost nonchalantly, he grabbed one of the two handles of the S-shaped tongs, stuck the sharp picklike end of the tong into opposite sides of the ice block, and, in a graceful move, lifted it on his shoulder. It was as if he had been doing it his entire life. Thompson was astounded. He'd never dreamed that this scrawny Grange boy—who then weighed no more than 120 pounds—could hoist an object that was more than half his weight. It was a feat of strength reminiscent of what Lyle Grange routinely did back in Pennsylvania as a logger lifting more logs than anyone in his outfit. True to his word, Thompson handed over a silver dollar to Grange and asked him if he'd like to work for him during the summer at a weekly wage of $37.50.

Grange happily nodded his head. His family needed the extra income, and he knew that the news of his acquiring a job would be met with the smiling approval of his father—something Grange always sought. So sixteen-year-old Red Grange became an iceman.

His first day on the job at L. C. Thompson and Company, Grange rose out of bed at four-thirty, put on his work clothes—overalls, T-shirt, socks, work boots—and strode into the still, dark morning. By five o'clock, he met Thompson. Grange hopped into the ice wagon, Thompson gave his horse a lash, and they began clip-clopping down the dirt roads of Wheaton. Every morning two-hundred-pound blocks of ice would arrive in Wheaton on a railcar from Wisconsin. Grange and Thompson would cut the blocks in half, lift them into the wagon, and begin making as many as forty deliveries. At each stop, the pair would inspect the customer's ice card to see how many pounds of ice were wanted—it could be any-where from twenty-five to one hundred—and then either Grange or Thompson would haul a hundred-pound block on his shoulder to the customer's icebox, where he would cut the block to the pound quantity ordered for that day. Then one of them would raise the remaining cake of ice back up on a shoulder and move to the next apartment or house. Some fourteen hours later, Thompson would drop Grange at his home. The next day, at four-thirty, Grange would repeat the routine. He was an iceman for eight consecutive summers.

The work was strenuous. Grange often had to climb several flights of stairs to make his deliveries. He also walked alongside the ice wagon for tens of miles a day, preferring that to riding in the back and constantly jumping on and off at each stop. On occasion, the ice blocks in the wagon shifted and mashed his fingers, or a block slipped from his grasp and landed on his feet. He also had an ice pick puncture his skin several times—a common accident among icemen when the pick went in the wrong direction while breaking the cakes into smaller chunks. And sometimes his skin got stuck to the chilled tongs.

Then, too, in his years as an iceman, Grange became involved in a few confrontations with his customers. One time after making a delivery, a woman scolded him for leaving muddy footprints on her kitchen floor. Grange apologized profusely, but the woman said that if her husband ever caught up with him, he'd teach Red a lesson with his fists. The next time Grange dropped off ice at their house, the wife loudly implored her spouse to "teach the young punk some manners."

Grange stood his ground. He looked at the husband and guessed that he outweighed the man by thirty-five pounds. The husband, a small man, wanted nothing to do with Grange but figured he had to put on a show for his wife. So as he approached Grange, he winked to indicate that he wasn't going to do anything serious, then he grabbed Grange by the shoulders and shook him as if he were scolding one of his own kids, telling him in a loud voice never to dirty his floors again. Grange played along, keeping his mouth shut as the man berated him. Later that day, the husband stopped his automobile alongside the truck and apologized to Grange for the charade, thanking him for "making me look so brave in front of the old lady." He then handed Grange a $5 bill.

Despite the difficult customers, the long hours, and the hardships Grange endured as an iceman, it provided him with two benefits, one intended, one not: It filled Grange's pockets with much-needed money, and it proved to be an ideal summer workout regimen for a budding football player. Not only were his arms thickened by the repetitive motion of lifting and carrying heavy blocks of ice, but his legs—which would be the real secret to his future gridiron success— were also strengthened by the demands of the job. Grange's legs were naturally long and slender, like stilts made of two-by-fours. As a kid, he never lost a footrace to a boy his age, and even kids who were three and four years older rarely beat him in a sprint. But Grange's ice hauling increased the power in his legs. Indeed, at the end of his first summer on the wagon, Grange's body was transformed. Though just sixteen, he now looked like the kind of young man you wouldn't want to tussle with, not in the alley behind Front Street or anywhere else.

In *preseason practices* in the late summer of 1919, Grange lined up at left halfback for the first time in his high school career. Right away, Castleman couldn't take his eyes off Grange, who seemingly changed directions quicker than a cornered rabbit every time he had the ball in his hands. And not only could Grange outmaneuver and outrun the other boys, he steamrolled over them with his high leg lifts and pounded them to the ground with his vicious stiff-arms. After Grange scored a touchdown nearly every third carry in these scrimmages, Castleman vowed to put the ball in Grange's hands as much as possible during the season.

It was a wise plan. Though Grange was only a sophomore, he quickly became the talk of DuPage County. Despite playing most of the season with a sprained ankle, he led the Tigers to a 5-1-1 record. Competing against other schools in the Chicago suburbs, he scored 15 touchdowns and kicked 9 extra points. He was so impressive that he garnered his first press attention. The *Wheaton Illinoian* named Grange to its all-county team, calling him "the star of the selection" and noting that he often "spilled three to seven men" on runs with his stiff-arm.

After he finished his sophomore year, Grange returned to work- ing on the ice wagon, enjoying the paycheck as much as the physical labor. For the first few weeks of the summer, he slipped back into his work routine: up at four-thirty, deliver ice for fourteen hours, walk home, cook dinner for himself and Garland, then fall into bed bone tired around nine o'clock. Six days a week, the schedule rarely changed.

One morning in early July, Grange went to work as usual. After making a few deliveries, he approached the Ford Formatruck that Thompson had purchased to replace his horse-drawn cart. The driver on this morning, Herman Otto (who was also a Tigers team-mate), turned the ignition key and started pulling away as Grange neared the vehicle. Grange enjoyed leaping onto the side running board of the truck while it motored down the street. He'd grab a handle that was affixed to the cab and then stand on the running board as the truck rolled on to its next delivery stop. Grange did this nearly every day, and he'd never once misjudged his jump or fallen off the truck.

But now, as Grange made his great leap and reached for the handle, it snapped off, causing him to lose his balance. In one of the most ungraceful moments of his young life, Grange fell backward and landed on the dirt road. Otto couldn't stop the truck, which was loaded with three tons of ice, fast enough. The right rear wheel rolled over Grange's left leg slightly above the knee.

White-hot pain shot through his leg. He rolled around on the ground in agony, in despair, in panic. One of his first thoughts was that he might never play football again, that his playing career would be over before it had really gotten started. Moments later, he feared the very worst: that he might not even walk again, much less play football.

Otto stopped the truck and ran to Grange, who was clutching his left knee with both hands, then cradled him in his arms and hoisted him into the cab. Otto quickly slid behind the driver's wheel and floored the gas. The truck whipped up a trail of dust in its wake, and he sped to the doctor's office. Otto carried Grange inside.

After a cursory exam, the doctor told Grange that it appeared that his left knee might be crushed and would require amputation. Grange was destroyed. He wasn't so much worried that his day-to-day life would become a struggle if he lost part of his left leg; rather his thoughts were wrapped around football and how much he'd miss the game, the thrill that he experienced every time he had the ball in his hands and ran free in the open field. As Grange lay on the examining table while the doctor conducted a more detailed examination, he was cold with fear.

The doctor continued to press and poke around his knee, asking Grange if this hurt, if that hurt. After several minutes, the doctor determined that the wheel had rolled over the leg one inch above the knee joint. That one inch, he told Grange, likely saved his leg. He wouldn't need an amputation, but there was only a fifty-fifty chance that he'd recover completely. And without a complete recovery, his athletic career was over.

Back at home, Grange lay in his bed with his leg elevated in a sling. His father cared for him as much as he could, but Garland spent the most time with Red during his convalescence, cooking him food and keeping him up to date on all the town gossip. His friends frequently stopped by, but Red rarely smiled. Even if he recovered, he feared his speed—the secret to all of his athletic success—would never be the same.

Luke Thompson, the owner of the ice truck, felt responsible for Grange's accident. The doctor bills could have bankrupted the Granges, but Thompson covered all of the expenses, and he continued to pay Grange his weekly salary of $37.50 while he recovered.

After nearly a month in bed, Grange started to walk. First a few steps, then around the block, then for long strolls, then for a jog. By the end of the summer, his leg had healed completely, which surprised even Grange. His leg felt so good, in fact, that he reported to opening day practice in late August. The school doctor gave him a physical. The boy was 100 percent healthy and ready to play, he declared to Grange and his new coach, Charles "Dink" Weldon. It was the best news Grange had received all summer.

I*t was his speed* that caught everyone's eye. In the first days of practice, Grange seemed to possess as much quickness as anyone at Wheaton had ever seen. He was always naturally fluid when he ran with the ball, but now there was something different about him: He could pull away from the fastest defenders with apparent ease, as if he had an extra gear of speed that no one else had. By September, the injury he'd suffered was truly a distant memory. Not only had his leg healed well, his long convalescence seemed to have produced a wellspring of energy.

Grange was already a track star. In his sophomore year, he was named captain of Wheaton's track team, as he was its top runner. The high school didn't have its own track, so Grange and his teammates would jog two miles to Lawson Field at Wheaton College. Red would practice his best events: the 100-yard dash, the 220-yard dash, and the broad jump. At all of these he was, simply, a natural. As in football, he didn't think when he competed; he just ran, letting instinct—and his legs—take over.

Earlier that summer, before he had injured his leg, Grange had hauled ice in the morning and competed in a track meet in the afternoon. He participated in six events—and won all of them. His friends often asked him what his secret was, but Grange could only shrug his shoulders. Before he graduated from Wheaton High, Grange would win state titles in Illinois's class B—the state's second largest class—in the 100, 220, and the broad jump. And he didn't just win these events, he obliterated the field. His fastest time in the 100-yard dash was just over eleven seconds, which in 1921 was a few hundredths of a second slower than that of the world record holder, Charlie Paddock, a sprinter from California.

No one was more impressed with Grange's speed than Coach Weldon, who had played quarterback on Wheaton's first-ever football team in 1910. Weldon became Wheaton's athletic director and first full-time coach the summer before Grange's junior year. He had served as a marine in World War I and before that played football at Western Michigan College. He had an eye trained to spot talent, and it took only a practice session to realize that the best way to win games would be to give Grange the ball and let him run wherever he wanted.

Weldon moved Grange to a new position, quarterback. Lining up four yards behind the center in the single-wing formation, Grange would receive the snap and usually cut to the right or the left. The plays were so rudimentary that they could have been drawn up in the dirt: When he ran left, the blockers on the line simply tried to push their men to the right, and vice versa. Grange would follow the tailback and fullback around one end and patiently wait for his blockers to engage defenders before he ignited his afterburners and flashed up the field. The genius of Weldon's coaching was that he didn't complicate things or interfere with Grange.

In preseason practice, Grange concentrated on improving his ability to cut sharply in the open field. The key was to throw his hips from one side to the other when changing direction, and nearly every day after practice, as the last glimmers of light shot across the open fields of Illinois, Grange could be seen alone on the field with a football in his hands, dodging and faking out imaginary defenders. Grange's unwavering passion to get better could be seen nearly every evening as August turned to September in 1920, his junior year.

The first game of the season was against nearby Wauconda High. As the crowd gathered in the apple orchard, there was a greater sense of anticipation than in seasons past. Stories of Grange had spread throughout the state, as if pushed by a prairie wind, and people from neighboring communities were now coming to see Wheaton and Grange play. Before the opening kickoff, the freshmen on the Tigers squad followed tradition and cleared the field of fallen apples. Lyle Grange paced the sideline with his sidearm in its holster. Though no one was keeping an eye on the town jail, nothing was going to keep Lyle from watching his boy.

Grange's reputation grew just minutes into the game. Operating at quarterback, he ran plays to his right, to his left, and up the middle. No one on the Wauconda team seemed to be able to get a clean shot at Red, the way he twisted and cut and stiff-armed. By the time the game was over—his white jersey covered in splotches of red from being tackled on a few of the apples that the freshmen had missed—Grange had rushed for over 300 yards and scored three touchdowns in Wheaton's easy 41–13 victory.

After wins like this, Grange and a few of his teammates would hop in the back of Doc Dollinger's Buick, and he would ferry the boys to his corner drugstore. Still wearing their uniforms, the boys would sit on the high one-legged stools with their elbows plunked on the counter and be treated to sundaes and sodas. Grange especially enjoyed these winning Saturday afternoons, because he felt he had extended his family. And his first free soda was his first fringe benefit of his rising stardom.

Although Wheaton lost the next game, 39–0, to LaGrange High in Chicago, Grange still rushed for 259 yards. LaGrange was annually one of the strongest teams in the state, its student body outnumbering Wheaton's seven to one, but even the best team in the Land of Lincoln couldn't stop Grange, who seemed to gain confidence and power every time he touched the ball.

After that game, Grange would go on a seven-week tear never before matched in Illinois high school football history. In leading his team to seven straight wins, the phenom scored a total of 33 touchdowns and booted 33 extra points. At the start of the winning streak, Coach Weldon moved Grange to right halfback and inserted Vic Gustafson, a freshman who would eventually become an all–Big Ten player at Northwestern University, as the team's left halfback. With Gustafson blocking for him, Grange simply overwhelmed the opposition more than ever; at the end of these games, the volunteers who agreed to keep the statistics needed several sheets of paper to calculate Grange's final numbers. Against Batavia High, for instance, he scored 52 points and rushed for 504 yards on 21 carries. Later in the season, against Naperville, he tallied 59 points in a decisive Tigers victory.

With each hard-to-believe performance, the press began to take longer and longer looks at Grange's young career. To reporters, his story almost sounded like a fable, one that began with the words *Once upon a time,* so unreal did the statistics he was putting up seem. Even though he still had one season of high school football left, a reporter for the *Wheaton Illinoian* declared that Grange already was "the greatest player Wheaton has ever had." But the paeans in print were just starting; soon college football coaches would read all about this kid from Wheaton.

Grange *went back* to work on the ice wagon again in the summer of 1921. On Sundays he'd often enjoy a respite. He and Garland would pedal their bikes to the Wheaton depot and take a train to Chicago. There the brothers would go see silent movies like *The Kid,* Charlie Chaplin's first feature, and *Seven Years Bad Luck,* starring Max Linder, a French comedian whose style would one day influence the Marx Brothers and Abbott and Costello. During other trips, they'd take in a vaudeville show or watch the Chicago White Sox at Comiskey Park. Rabid Sox fans, the Grange boys even skipped school a few times to make the trek to Comiskey.

Grange was a gifted baseball player himself. Though Wheaton High didn't have a diamond, the school fielded a team every spring, and for four years, Grange was one of its best players. In vacant lots that served as makeshift baseball diamonds around Wheaton, Grange threw and hit right-handed. He packed a lot of power at the plate—hauling ice in the summers had thickened his arms and chest—and he could throw the ball as far as anyone on the squad. He played every position, but his favorite was first base, the same position once played by one of his baseball idols, the Cubs' Vic Saier. Red was a good player, but his prowess on the diamond didn't approach his performances on the football field. There was no other high school player like him in the entire state of Illinois, and he would prove that again during his final season at Wheaton High.

Playing right halfback in the single wing, Grange was the focus of attention of every opponent. Teams all across the state had heard about that Grange kid in Wheaton. Newspapermen were already speculating in print that Red Grange could be the most talented high school player to ever come out of the Midwest; that when he had the ball, he was nearly as unstoppable as the great Jim Thorpe. It was rare for a high school player to generate this kind of attention, but instead of intimidating opponents, it motivated them. And at least one team, Scott High in Toledo, Ohio, resorted to dirty tactics to stop Grange.

Early in the game, a Scott player punched Wheaton's Charles Moore after the whistle had blown. But the aggressor quickly apologized to Moore when he realized that he'd hit the wrong player. Minutes later, Grange caught a pass and ran upfield. After he was tackled and was lifting himself off the ground, out of nowhere, a Scott player reared back and kicked Grange in the head, sending him sprawling with a thud back onto the grass field. Grange's world went dark.

The Wheaton players and coach tried to wake Grange, sprinkling water in his face and shouting at him, but his eyes remained shut. The blow had knocked Grange unconscious. A few of his teammates carried his motionless body to the sideline, but no matter what anyone did—slap his cheeks, shake him, sprinkle more water on his face—Grange didn't respond. This was his first serious football injury, and it would be forty-eight hours before he regained consciousness. No permanent damage was done, but something changed permanently for Grange the moment that foot thundered into his forehead. Grange was now a wanted man.

Scott beat Wheaton, 35–0, the Tigers' sole defeat in 1921. Grange returned to the field the following week, and he powered Wheaton to a 7-1 overall record and its second straight DuPage County title. For the season, Grange scored 23 touchdowns and kicked 34 extra points. In three years of play at Wheaton High, Grange set state records for touchdowns (75) and points in a career (532). But Grange didn't like to talk about his accomplishments, and he didn't understand why anyone would think he was extraordinarily special because of what he'd done on the football field. He simply told people that football was just a game, even as it provided an escape for him, an avenue for him to express all that he couldn't whenever he stepped outside the chalk lines.

With the close of football season, Grange put on a basketball uniform, just as he had during his freshman, sophomore, and junior years. Because of all the time he had spent practicing in the hayloft of his friend's barn during his childhood, Grange was an excellent shot, the team's best. He started at center in his first three seasons, but now he switched to forward. He was Wheaton's top scorer, launching shots from all over the court that swooshed through the net, and he was named to several all-sectional teams during his high school days. Though Red felt that basketball was his best sport, he never played in an organized league again after finishing Wheaton High.

When basketball season was over, he captained the track team. He had become one of the state's top sprinters. Everything about him looked so graceful when he ran—the way his arms and legs churned in perfect harmony, the way his head remained steady, the way he glided down the track. Ever since he ran races as a child at the country fair back in Pennsylvania, he'd been a natural at running. His legs were the fundamental source of all of his athletic success, and now his father insisted that those legs should carry him to college. The question was, which·one?

The first time Grange shook hands with a college coach was late in his senior year during a track meet at Wheaton High. Carl Johnson, a track coach at the University of Michigan, traveled with several alumni 350 miles from Ann Arbor to meet Grange and tell him why he should attend their school. Not only could he run track at Michigan, Johnson told Grange, but he could also play football. Athletic scholarships weren't given to high school kids during this era, but the group from Michigan emphasized to Red all of the school's positives: that Michigan offered a top-flight education, that its football team was annually among the best in the nation, and that the school's campus was as pristine as any in the Midwest. Grange was flattered by the attention, but he told Johnson and the Wolverines alums that he didn't think there was any way his father could afford to send him to Michigan because of its higher-priced out-of-state tuition.

In fact, Grange didn't care to attend college at all. Despite his intelligence, he struggled in the classroom. Schoolwork never fired his imagination—or his work ethic. He passed his courses in high school, but his grades were rarely above average, and he applied himself only because the thought of being academically ineligible to play sports scared him into studying. Reporters who probed into Grange's life would erroneously conclude that he was an academic lightweight and a borderline country rube. While Grange didn't possess much intellectual curiosity—he preferred to read about sports rather than dive into the classics—he could quickly solve real-life problems like caring for his little brother or helping his dad make ends meet. It didn't surprise any of his friends when, after graduating from Wheaton High, Grange just wanted to work full-time on the ice wagon and lead a nice, quiet, simple life in the town he called home.

His father felt differently. Lyle was adamant that his oldest boy continue his education and be the first Grange to go to college. Lyle didn't give his oldest son an alternative; he *would* go to college. Within a few weeks of meeting with the Michigan people, the choice of where he would attend was essentially made for him.

University of Illinois coach Robert Zuppke had read newspaper stories about Grange, about how he was gaining 200 and even 300 yards in a game. *I need to meet this kid,* Zuppke told himself, but he didn't want Grange to know that he'd been admiring him from afar. Zuppke had already won two national championships and was too proud a man to openly fawn over an eighteen-year-old boy. Plus, Zuppke considered it beneath himself to personally ask young men to play for him, especially kids in the state; he believed they should want to wear the orange and blue of Illinois for the honor of representing their school and their state. So in late May 1922, Zuppke walked over to the state track meet that was taking place on the Illinois campus, intent on talking to Grange—though he wanted the meeting to appear accidental.

Grange was spectacular in the state track finals, winning gold in the 220-yard dash and bronze in the 100-yard dash. After Grange had finished those events, Zuppke approached him.

"What's your name?" the coach asked.

"Red Grange."

Over the next few minutes, Zuppke and Grange walked around the leafy campus. As they strolled through the fresh spring air, Zuppke put the hard sell on Grange, detailing how, ever since he came to Illinois in 1913, he'd built the football program into a winner, telling Grange that the Illini had won four of the previous nine Big Ten Conference Championships. As they continued to walk and talk, Zuppke, who was born in Berlin, Germany, grew more personal with Grange, tagging him with a nickname: *Granche,* which was the German pronunciation of Grange's surname. It was a little thing, but it heightened the connection between the two. Zuppke may have eschewed talking directly to young prospects, but when he did, he combined the soft approach of humor and the hard approach of a car salesman. This pet nickname was one of his ways to try to lure Grange onto his football team. He knew that if Grange felt comfortable with him, if he trusted him, there was a good chance that he'd show up in Champaign the coming fall.

Near the end of their walk, Zuppke told Grange, "I think you have a good chance of making the football team." Grange was flabbergasted. He genuinely believed he was too small to play major college football, and the thought of lacing up the cleats in college had never seriously crossed his mind. But Zuppke was insistent. Grange was as fast and as quick as any high school football player he'd ever seen, and Zuppke believed that with some coaching and sculpting, Red could one day mature into a truly special player.

When Grange returned to Wheaton and told his dad about his encounter with Zuppke, it didn't take long for Lyle to issue the order: Red would go to Illinois. There was no further discussion. The school was only 150 miles from Wheaton, and, at only $400 in total annual expenses, it was more affordable than Michigan or any other out-of-state Big Ten school. One of the Granges' neighbors, George Dawson, played for the Fighting Illini, and he frequently told Lyle that Red should try to play ball for Zuppke. Now that the elder Grange had learned that even the coach at the school wanted his son, there seemed no reason in the world why Red shouldn't enroll at the University of Illinois. And so he did.

5

A MARKED MAN

R*ed Grange dragged* a beat-up, secondhand trunk behind him and carried a duffel bag atop his shoulder as he boarded the train at the Wheaton depot. He had said his good-byes to his father and brother—there were never any tears among the stoic Grange men—and then lifted the trunk that his father had given him into the rack above his seat. The Pullman clacked and wheezed to life, steaming toward Champaign in August 1922, and Grange peered through the window. He waved to the two most important people in his life, who now stood on the platform alongside men in bowler hats and fedoras and women who flashed white handkerchiefs above their heads. Then he was gone.

Grange's confidence was shaky, just as it was for many eighteen-year-olds leaving home for the first time. But he had been popular among the boys in his class, and he had no reason to believe that he would have a hard time making friends at the University of Illinois. And while he usually felt a little awkward around women—he just never could find the right words when they were near—he hoped it would be easy to avoid the gentler sex once he stepped onto the school's large campus.

Grange was feeling a mixture of excitement and trepidation. He couldn't predict what the next day would bring like he could in

Wheaton, but there was something thrilling about this, something intoxicating. There were so many things he didn't know: What would classes be like? How much studying would he have to do? How dearly would he miss his father and brother? But he did know this: There was no way on God's green earth he was going to play football at Illinois. True, he had no peer on the football field in high school, but those games were played mostly against plodding farm boys from small towns across the state. Grange considered himself nothing more than a small-town wonder, and he didn't believe that his football skills were any match for the young men who had played at big high schools in front of big crowds. He wanted to try out for the Illini basketball and baseball teams, but at five foot eleven and 166 pounds, he figured he'd be steamrolled on the practice field by the giants who played football at Illinois. Yes, he had the support of Zuppke, who was a towering figure at the school, but Grange feared that he'd end up in the infirmary once defensive tacklers seventy-five pounds heavier than him started clobbering him.

The train squealed to a stop at the Champaign station. Carrying his duffel bag and lugging his trunk, Grange made his way to the Zeta Psi fraternity house. Grange's neighbor in Wheaton, George Dawson, was a brother there, and he helped Red make arrangements to follow in his footsteps at the fraternity.

Grange moved in and quickly learned that, as a pledge, he didn't rank very high in the fraternity's caste system. He was ordered by the upperclassmen to choose a sport or two in which he would participate. With Zeta Psi's reputation on campus as an athletic house, its members wanted the incoming pledge class to carry on the tradition. Grange reported that his best sports in high school were basketball and track and that he planned to try out for both varsity teams. He purposefully didn't mention football; he had no desire to get injured in a frat game, and he didn't want to raise speculation about playing varsity football.

Grange's white lie didn't do the trick. Many in the fraternity knew about his accomplishments on the football field at Wheaton High, and the senior members of Zeta Psi commanded him to report to the football field for freshman tryouts. They told Grange that football was the most prestigious sport at the school, and, given his background, he could make all of the Zetas look good if he made the team. Grange stood his ground, saying he was too small. But the fraternity brothers didn't back down. They issued an ultimatum: He could either try out for the team or join a different fraternity.

Reluctantly, Grange agreed to try out. But on the first day of freshman practice, he was overwhelmed by what he saw: The players were even bigger in real life than in his imagination. Grange figured he was one of the lightest players to show up for the tryouts. As he stood in line to receive a jersey and equipment, he continued to look around, to take stock, gazing at about 150 boys who all looked like they could lift a Model T with little effort. Before he was handed a jersey, Grange made a snap decision: He wasn't going to play. *I'll never make this team,* he thought to himself as he walked away from the locker room. *I'm just a yokel from Wheaton.*

Grange returned to his fraternity house and broke the news to his brothers. "They're too big," he said.

But Grange's pleadings only angered the older Zeta Psis. One of the brothers fetched a large wooden paddle and told Red to bend over. There was a price to pay for disobeying the older brothers, and that payment was now due. But before Grange bent over to take his beating, he looked around and told his brothers with a nervous smile, "Football makes a lot of sense to me."

The next day Grange grudgingly returned to the practice field. He may have been one of the lightest players on the squad, but he quickly discovered that he was one of the fastest, if not *the* fastest. Grange played halfback, just as he had at Wheaton, and whenever the ball was in his hands, the defenders had trouble catching and tackling him. It took Grange only a few days to realize that he could do this; that he might be able to make the freshman team after all. After a week of tryouts, the freshman coach trimmed the squad from 150 to 60. Not only did Grange make the cut, but when the depth chart was posted, he was on the first string.

Days later the freshman team scrimmaged the varsity. This was designed to be nothing more than a tune-up session for the varsity players, a chance for them to beat up on the younger guys and gain confidence before their first game against Butler University. As Zuppke watched intently from the sideline, a whistle draped around his neck, the varsity squad lined up in punt formation. Grange was the freshmen's deep man, ready to receive the punt. As he waited on the 40-yard line in his leather helmet and orange practice jersey, his heart thumped with excitement; this was his first chance to impress the varsity coach.

The ball came down into Grange's waiting arms. He ran up the field, cutting here, twisting there, using his powerful forearm whenever a defender lunged at him. His knees rising high, he broke one tackle after another and eluded several defenders with sharp cuts right and left. In an instant, he crossed the 50, the 40, the 30. As Red ran toward the end zone, Zuppke couldn't take his eyes off him. The coach had never seen a player with his quickness—his "pickup," he called it—and his ability to change directions so adroitly, so seamlessly. Grange trotted into the end zone. The way he ran, the way he slicked through the entire varsity punt return defense, astonished Zuppke. He knew that Grange had been a good high school player, but he never imagined what he had just seen: that Grange would step on campus and make a mockery of the talents of the older and experienced players on his varsity team.

After the scrimmage, which the varsity narrowly won, 21–19, the coaching staff deemed Grange a "made" player, meaning that he was a lock to be on the freshman team in 1922. When the final cuts were announced, the players were awarded their game jerseys. Grange stood near the end of the line to receive his gear and number. The player in front of him was given number 76; the player in back of him was issued number 78. Grange was handed jersey number 77—a number that would one day be as famous as Babe Ruth's pinstriped number 3.

During the 1922 season, the freshman team scrimmaged the varsity twice a week—and the freshmen, led by Grange, almost always won. The eighteen-year-old emerged as the team's top back as the temperature cooled and summer gave way to fall. Zuppke soon was telling his friends that he had more talent on his freshman squad than on his varsity team, which struggled to a 2-5 record, so he began spending more practice time with the freshmen than with the varsity—and, specifically, more time with Grange. This was the dream player that Zuppke had been waiting for ever since he started coaching at Illinois in 1913, a gift delivered to him from football heaven, and he spent hours schooling Grange on how to play halfback. Grange had a tendency to use his speed to run to the outside on every play; Zuppke wanted him to control his speed, to not be afraid to cut back into the center of the field.

The head coach also liked the toughness and roughness his young players showed on the field. One time, during a freshmen-varsity scrimmage, several of the freshmen had grown tired of varsity guard Roy Miller's merciless insults and sharp-tongued taunting. On one play, to teach Miller a lesson, all eleven players from the first-year squad piled on top of him, breaking his nose. The insults stopped that day.

The freshmen squad, playing other freshmen teams in the Midwest, finished undefeated. After the football season was over, Grange ran intramural track for the Zeta Psi fraternity. His dominance was total: In the final meet of the season, Grange entered six events and took first place in all of them. Behind his strong performance, the Zeta house won the intramural cup. Grange's athletic gifts were making him one of the most popular freshmen in his fraternity, and his brothers were always asking him to go out with them to dinner or for a soda. But Grange preferred to stay in his room, content to be by himself and quietly read his schoolbooks.

In the spring, Zuppke held a nine-week training camp for his football team. Zuppke was the first college coach in history to conduct spring football practice, and he believed these extra training sessions were crucial to developing his players. His first move was to elevate Grange to the varsity. Every weekday afternoon, Grange worked tirelessly to improve his running, and Zuppke liked what he was seeing. He planned to make Grange the centerpiece of his offense in the coming fall. The coach believed that, in Grange, he had a player who singularly could transform an average team into an elite team. To that end, he was going to put the ball in Grange's hands as much as possible.

After the school year was over, Grange returned to Wheaton for the summer. It would be his last as a relatively anonymous young man. He moved back into the apartment with his dad and his brother and resumed his job on the ice truck. After lugging ice as much as fourteen hours each day, Red and Garland would often go to a nearby vacant lot with a football. Together they'd play catch, run different drills aimed at improving their speed, and chase each other around. They'd stay out until the stars filled the sky, then trudge back to the apartment, where Red would cook dinner. By ten, he'd be fast asleep. At four-thirty, his alarm would be ringing again.

Though his father rarely expressed it, Lyle was deeply pleased with his oldest boy. He was making something of himself at the university, and this was something no Grange man had ever done. In the few instances during the summer when the father sat with his sons at the dinner table, he would lean back in his chair and listen to Red describe what his freshmen football season had been like. His father still worried that Red might get hurt playing the game, but football, in a way, had brought them closer. The Granges never vocalized their feelings, yet the father's curiosity about his son's gridiron exploits said it all: He was proud of Red. And for one of the first times in his life, Red knew it. The game had become their silent bond.

When Grange returned to Champaign at the end of the summer, he was in ideal shape—iceman shape. On the first day of summer practice, he was handed his number 77 jersey and told by Zuppke that he was now the team's first-string right halfback. Grange responded by tearing off spectacular runs in every preseason scrimmage. Word began to spread around campus that a sophomore named Grange was shining on the Illinois football team. And before the first game of the season against Nebraska, the reigning Missouri Valley Conference champions, the Urbana-Champaign Courier wrote that "the debut of Zuppke's new back will be anxiously awaited. Harold Grange has trotted through the freshmen ever since practice opened."

On October 6, in the locker room at Illinois Field, which would soon be replaced by Memorial Stadium, Grange was so nervous that he had trouble breathing. During pregame warm-ups, he'd gazed across the field at the Nebraska players and saw corn-fed specimens that were so big they seemed to blot out the sun. He guessed that their linemen all weighed at least two hundred fifty pounds, and he shuddered when he thought about what it would feel like to have a couple of those beefcakes tackle and fall on him. In the locker room before kickoff, as he sat alone to the side, Grange was in a kind of shuddering reverie. He looked at his hands: They trembled.

Even though he'd been the talk of the preseason camp, even though he knew he was faster than anyone else wearing a football uniform, Grange still didn't believe that he belonged on the field with these other college players. So now, as he jogged onto the field and looked up into the sun-soaked stands filled with eighteen thousand fans, he was petrified. He'd never played in front of such a large crowd before, and he momentarily felt like running away—just like he did before his first varsity game at Wheaton High.

Before kickoff, Zuppke strolled out to midfield, where he met Nebraska coach Fred Dawson. As the two stood in the bright late-summer sunshine—each wearing a bowler hat and dark suit—they made small talk about the game. Before they parted ways, they shook hands. "Let's make it a football game," Dawson said to Zuppke.

"That suits me," replied the confident Illinois coach.

In the opening quarter, Grange was so flustered by the enormity of the moment that he had trouble remembering the plays. And when he did recall the correct play, he'd lean in the direction the run was supposed to go before the ball was snapped, which the Nebraska defense quickly clued in on. At the end of the first quarter, with the score 0–0, Zuppke called Grange to the sideline and shouted, "You're leaning, Red, and giving away the plays!" Grange nodded his head and jogged back onto the field. It was all the coaching he'd need.

Playing right halfback in Zuppke's single-wing offense and no longer signaling the direction of each offensive play, Grange took over the game. He ran through the Cornhuskers' defense, scoring one touchdown on a 35-yard sweep around the right end and another on a 60-yard gallop of zigs and zags and jarring stiff-arms. When the final gun sounded, Illinois won, 24–7. In his first varsity game, Grange had rushed for 202 yards and scored three touchdowns. Now he knew he belonged on the field with the big boys. He was even better than the hype that surrounded him, and by the time the sun set in Champaign that evening, his celebrity on campus had officially been born. Soon nearly everyone in the region, even those who didn't follow football, would know his name.

The day after the game, referee Walter Eckersall, a former All-America quarterback at Chicago, penned a story in the *Chicago Tribune*. He wrote that Grange's performance had been "a spectacular piece of work, the sort expected of a player with the speed of the former Wheaton star who has all the earmarks of developing into a wonderful player. His activities today will make him a marked man in all the remaining games of Illinois's schedule."

G*range felt more comfortable* in his second year at Illinois, and it wasn't just because he was succeeding on the football field. Garland was now attending the school. The Grange boys were constantly together when they both had free time, heading out to ice-cream parlors and greasy spoons, playing catch in an open field together like they did back in Wheaton. Garland was an excellent football player himself. A few weeks into the season, he'd already impressed the coaches on the freshmen team. He was a starting tailback and the squad's best player. Like his older brother, Garland possessed outstanding speed; it was their genetic link. He wasn't as elusive or as powerful as Red, but the varsity coaches believed he would be an integral part of the varsity team during the following season of 1924.

Garland had watched in awe from the bleachers as his brother ripped through the Nebraska defense. But the Red Grange show was just beginning. The next Saturday against Butler, he scored two touchdowns in the 21–7 win. The following week, the Illini traveled to Iowa City to play the University of Iowa, the defending co–Big Ten champions. It was homecoming on the Iowa campus, and that morning a parade of floats and bands streamed down the street that ran in front of the Jefferson Hotel, where the Illini team was staying. Zuppke summoned his players to a team meeting at the hotel before the squad left for the stadium. But when he called the roll, one player was missing: fullback Earl Britton, who was Grange's lead blocker on most of the running plays.

Zuppke dispatched his team captain, left tackle Jim McMillen, to find the six-foot-three, 240-pound Britton. McMillen asked an elevator operator if he'd seen a burly young man who looked like a football player, and the operator directed McMillen to the hotel roof. McMillen found Britton with a devilish smile on his face. Britton had taken a ream of hotel stationery up to the top of the building, written the words "To hell with Iowa" on each sheet, then folded the pieces into paper airplanes and slung them over the side of the roof and down onto the street that was lined with parade-watching Iowa fans. When Britton finally joined the team meeting, he told Zuppke and the other players of his stunt, which caused the room to break out in laughter. Even Zuppke was impressed with Britton's ingenious display of school spirit.

Relaxed and loose while playing in front of thirty-five thousand screaming fans, Britton put Illinois on the scoreboard first by kicking a 53-yard field goal. But the remainder of the game turned into a defensive battle; for three quarters, Iowa was able to do what no other team had done in 1923: contain Grange. Though Red would rush for 175 yards, he wasn't able to break free for one of his customary long touchdown runs. With less than five minutes left in the final period, Iowa led, 6–3.

Illinois took over possession at its own 19-yard line. Realizing that his running game was struggling, Zuppke ordered his offense to start passing the ball—to Grange. On first down, the ball was snapped to quarterback Harry Hall, who handed off to Britton, one of the team's best passers. Britton then rifled a forward pass to Grange, running down the right sideline. Grange caught the ball and sprinted up the field to the Illinis' 48-yard line before being tackled. On the next play, he caught another toss from Britton, this one for 2 yards. The play after that, Britton hurled another pass at Grange, who cradled the ball in his arms and ran for 22 yards. The Britton-to-Grange combination was working in perfect synchronicity. The two connected again, and Grange ran the ball to Iowa's 2-yard line. With the crowd in full throat encouraging the Iowa farm boys to hold their ground and not let Illinois score, Grange took a handoff and barreled into the end zone with under a minute left on the clock. The touchdown sealed the 9–6 victory, and that final drive proved to Zuppke that Grange wasn't just a gifted runner, he could also catch the ball as well as anyone on his team. All those hours spent tossing the ball back and forth with Garland in the summer twilight were now paying off.

The next Saturday, the Illini traveled to Chicago to play Northwestern at Cubs Park, home of Chicago Cubs baseball. Though Northwestern had lost its first two games of the season, the Wildcats drove the ball down the field early in the first quarter. Then Grange made the game-changing play. Playing defensive back, Grange intercepted a Northwestern pass at the 10-yard line and sprinted 90 yards, scoring the first touchdown of the afternoon. But it wouldn't be his most spectacular play of the game. In the second quarter, Britton threw a pass in Grange's direction. A Wildcats defender covered Grange tightly. The two rose together high into the air in a virtual pirouette, and Grange wrestled the ball away. He then broke from the defender and ran nearly 80 yards for his second touchdown. Grange played only nineteen minutes in the 29–0 win, but he accounted for 247 yards, a career high. For the first time, the *New York Times,* which rarely devoted space to football games in the Midwest, mentioned Grange's name in print after his stellar all-around performance. The foundation of nationwide fame was being laid.

Every day for the next six days, University of Chicago head coach Amos Alonzo Stagg repeated one phrase over and over to his team: "Stop Grange." The Maroons were to travel to Champaign the following Saturday for the opening of the new Memorial Stadium. Although construction of the $2 million structure wasn't finished, Illinois officials wanted to play Chicago in the new stadium in order to accommodate the soaring demand for tickets. A capacity crowd of fifty-five thousand was expected at the renewal of the Illinois and Chicago rivalry, which dated back more than a quarter century. Police estimated that more than twenty thousand cars would carry fans to the game. To deal with the crush of people and cars, twenty traffic officers and scores of plainclothes officers from Chicago would be brought in to direct traffic and patrol the stadium, mainly to try to prevent petty crimes such as pickpocketing.

This game was especially important because Illinois, Chicago, and Michigan were each undefeated in the Big Ten, and Michigan wasn't scheduled to play either university. So the Illini-Maroons game was the de facto conference championship—as long as the game's winner went on to win the rest of its games. Stagg, one of the top coaches in the country, knew that slowing down Grange was the key to victory. He had his freshman team simulate the Illini offense, often deep into the night. Practicing under newly installed arc lights, which bathed Chicago's practice field in an eerie glow, Stagg marched up and down the field and loudly reminded his boys over and over that Grange was a talent the likes of which they'd never seen before, and that they had to hit him hard whenever he had the ball. It would take a total team effort, Stagg told his players, to stop Grange and beat Illinois. To prevent Grange from taking over the game, Stagg had his defensive ends line up farther to the outside than usual. At the snap of the ball, they were to charge forward and force Grange to stay in the center of the field, between the defensive tackles. Grange's forte was running to the outside, and Stagg was determined to keep him from doing that.

On the morning of the game, a bank of storm clouds rolled over Champaign-Urbana. Rain started to fall from the gray sky, but that didn't dam the flood of Illini fans who trekked to the campus to celebrate this homecoming game in a new home. For over a year, Illinois supporters had talked about and clamored to get into the new stadium, and now their excitement level was amped up even more because Grange would be on the field. Many towns in Illinois arranged for special trains to carry fans to Champaign, and papers across the state, and as far away as St. Louis, published maps of the Urbana-Champaign area and described the best route to the stadium.

Officials at radio station KYW in Chicago, sensing the spiking regional interest in the game, decided to broadcast the contest, the first over-the-air broadcast of an Illini football game in history. The station sent a technical crew of more than thirty and a play-by-play announcer to the stadium to call the game. KYW reached a larger audience than all but two other radio stations in the country, and that translated into a first-ever opportunity for all the players, especially Grange. Because now, for the first time in the players' careers, people outside of the stadium could follow the game in real time, in the moment. For the first time, thousands across the state and the region would be able to hear the exploits of Grange and be able to let him run ghostlike across their imaginations.

By one o'clock on November 3, the stands were already full—an hour before kickoff. A total of 60,632 people streamed through the gates, making this the largest gathering in the history of Illinois for anything—sporting event, political rally, even the state fair. As the rain picked up in intensity, fans pulled over their heads slickers that they had fashioned from various colored oilcloths: red, yellow, blue, and orange. When the players ran out of their locker rooms just before two, the field had already become saturated. The slick, muddy conditions didn't favor Grange; he relied on solid footing to make his impossibly sharp cuts.

The first two quarters of the game were little more than an ongoing pushing match, as each team simply tried to slam the ball straight ahead on running plays. But then, as quick as a magician's hand, Grange seized control of the contest. Taking pitches and running around both the left and right ends, he cut, twisted, and stiff-armed his way to runs of 20 yards, then 25, then 42. But all of Grange's efforts were undone by his two fumbles. Near the middle of the third quarter, the game remained scoreless.

Then, late that quarter, Grange came alive again. With the ball on the Illinois 35-yard line, he found good footing and dashed around the right side on a sweep. Seeing that there was a line of defenders in front of him, he switched directions, sprinting to the other side of the field that was now pocketed with mud holes. For a few moments, no Chicago defender could catch him. After gaining 28 yards, he was finally pushed out of bounds by a Maroons player at Chicago's 23-yard line. On the next play, Grange sloshed around the right end for 15 more yards to the 8-yard line. He was single-handedly wearing down the Maroons defense. Two plays later, he launched his body into the end zone, scoring the only touchdown of the game. As his teammates mobbed him and the crowd thundered its approval, Grange simply dropped the ball at the end line and walked back to the huddle.

At game's end, the final tally on the new scoreboard at the still-undedicated stadium read in white block letters and numbers: Chicago 0, Illinois 7. As Grange slowly walked off the soggy field and through the misty late afternoon, the soaking-wet crowd showered him with applause and cheers. Grange, his helmet in hand and his uniform splattered with mud, kept his eyes trained straight ahead with not even a trace of a smile on his face. Student reporter Ralph Cannon observed the scene.

"Here was a moment fitted for the climax of a novel, the finale of a human life," wrote Cannon in the campus newspaper. "Here was Grange, the idol of his fellow students, at the supreme pinnacle of collegiate fame, and if he had come off that field of honor with just the least little hint of a strut or a swagger, could he not have been excused? But he did not! Grange walked stoical and satisfied, like a businessman coming home after a day's work. Just four or five steps; he took them easily, confidently, unembarrassed by his glamorous achievement— a man submerged in his game, oblivious to its exterior."

In the locker room, Zuppke tried to explain to reporters what made Grange so good, so workmanlike. "Grange has absolutely no lost motion," Zuppke said. "He doesn't take an unnecessary step. He is the fastest man I have ever coached. He has the ideal football physique: stocky thighs, long, muscled calves, and man-sized feet that enable him to keep his balance when he is hit hard."

As Zuppke spoke, Grange shed his wet uniform quietly in front of his locker. He soon slipped out of the locker room door and walked to his fraternity house. There Grange was greeted by dozens of frat brothers, friends, and neighbors, waiting for him on the cinder driveway. For more than an hour, in the falling mist from the ever-darkening sky, Grange shook hands and engrossed the gathering crowd with tales from the game. He was the only one who didn't have an umbrella, but still he entertained everyone with his words. Grange never liked to be the center of attention, to be fawned over, but these were his most ardent fans, and he didn't want to disappoint them by disappearing, even though he wished he could. It was a small sign that he was growing up and feeling more comfortable with what he was becoming: a sports star.

Grange eventually enjoyed a quiet dinner at an out-of-the-way restaurant with one of his friends. While the rest of the campus celebrated the win over the school's archrival, Grange was back in his room before ten. Near his bed were several boxes filled with candies, cake, nuts, and cookies that had been sent to him by fans, but Grange rarely indulged in a late-night snack. Instead he shared the goodies with his fraternity brothers—one more reason why he was now the most popular Zeta in the house.

The *story broke* a few days after Illinois defeated Chicago, and it made headlines in papers across the Midwest: Red Grange had played pro football in Green Bay in 1922. If the facts were accurate, it meant that Grange was ineligible to play college football, but both Grange and Zuppke vigorously denied the allegation before Illinois hosted the University of Wisconsin. Grange was so distraught over the story that he had to fight back tears when he first heard about it.

"I have never played football anywhere except in high school at Wheaton and at Illinois," Grange told reporters. "If anyone thinks differently, I welcome an investigation. I hope one is made at once."

"The story is absolutely baseless," Zuppke added. "It is a shame that anyone should have suggested it. It looks as if somebody did his best to stir up trouble between Wisconsin and Illinois."

Indeed, someone with ties to the Badgers had fabricated the story, but charges of having played pro football would dog Grange for the rest of his days at Illinois. And nothing could tar a college player like this allegation, because across the nation, pro football was considered unseemly and corrupt, a league run by scam artists who were only looking to make a quick buck at the gate. "Keep away from professionalism," Zuppke often told Grange. "Football isn't a game to play for money." Virtually every college coach in America shared this sentiment.

Grange wasn't interested in being part of a professional league— not yet.

The *false rumor* that Grange had played pro ball angered the Illinois players. They saw the effect it had on Grange, and it caused their intensity level to redline against the Badgers. Grange was friends with every player on his team. His skills on the field were admired, naturally, but so was his comportment off the field. He was quiet, polite, good natured, humble, and never had a bad word to say about anyone. A sophomore, Grange was a little brother to the upperclassmen.

Early in the first quarter, with the ball on Wisconsin's 28-yard line, in front of twenty-five thousand fans at Illinois's home field, Grange took a pitch and veered around the right end. The Badgers tried to employ Chicago's defense, lining up their defensive ends out wide to push the play inside, but the scheme didn't slow Grange. With the ball tucked tightly to his side, he stiff-armed a defensive end, pushing him to the turf, and sprinted toward the sideline. From there he cut up the field. He was in the clear. But near the 10-yard line, out of the corner of his eye, he spied a defender rushing at him from the other side of the field, and he had the angle on Grange. A collision appeared imminent. But just before the Badger clawed at Grange's number 77, Grange stopped as abruptly as if he'd hit a brick wall. The defender whizzed by without laying a finger on Grange, who cut to the inside of the field and waltzed nonchalantly into the end zone.

The run caused the stadium to explode in noise. This was exactly what the paying fans had come to see, and now Grange had given them another indelible memory. It was the only touchdown of the game. In the second quarter, Grange was knocked in the head so hard that he became dizzy. Not wanting to risk a serious injury to his star, Zuppke removed Grange from the game and didn't let him off the bench until the final whistle blew in the fourth quarter. Illinois won, 10–0, to stay undefeated.

Grange didn't play the next week against Mississippi A&M, an undermanned team that put up little fight in the Illinis' 27–0 victory. Zuppke also rested many of his other starters in anticipation of the season's final game in Columbus, Ohio, against the Buckeyes of Ohio State University. With a win, Illinois would clinch at least a tie of the Big Ten championship. Michigan, also undefeated, would host the University of Minnesota Gophers on the same day that the Illini faced the Buckeyes.

Ohio State had sent a scout to watch a few of Illinois's games. Based on what he saw, he wrote a report on the Illini that the Buckeyes coaches and players used to prepare for the game: "The Illinois offense is built around Red Grange and Earl Britton. Grange carries the ball practically 75 percent of the time and [runs] short and wide ends runs, off tackle, and cut backs. His end running attacks are successful due to two things: one, a wonderful superman who uses all the tricks of a good halfback's stock and trade; and two, some extremely effective interference and blocking ... They block with much more vigor for him than any other Illinois back.

"If the Illinois end-running attack of Grange is stopped, they will resort to their desperation passes from Britton to Grange like they did in the Iowa game. And there again, this man Grange becomes a nightmare. Against Iowa, Grange cut across the back line of the defensive team and took passes on the dead run high over his head. Down the field under long passes and short passes over the line, he consistently went up in the air and caught the ball although surrounded by three or four Hawkeyes ... Grange has shown remarkable speed, dodging, hip shift, stop up, change of pace, and other abilities, yet when he is caught by several tacklers, the man simply puts on steam and drives and whirls in an even better manner than Earl Martineau, the great Gopher, and leaves a wake of would-be tacklers strewn in his path behind him."

After reading these words, the Buckeyes players were filled with anxiety. How in the world, after all, do you stop a "superman"?

Playing on a wet field, Illinois started slowly against Ohio State. Neither team could move the ball effectively on offense, and after three quarters, the score remained 0–0. Before the start of the final quarter, Zuppke, dressed in his bowler hat and dark suit, reminded his boys that the Big Ten title was now in their grasp; they needed to fight like soldiers to bring the conference crown back to Champaign. The words struck a chord with the players. Just a few minutes into the final quarter, Britton booted a 38-yard field goal. And on the Illinis' next possession, Grange took a handoff from the quarterback at Ohio State's 32-yard line, busted through the middle of the line virtually untouched, and sprinted down the heart of the field into the end zone. His score iced the game for the orange-and-blue, 9–0.

With the victory, Illinois finished its season with a perfect 8-0 record and secured its first Big Ten title and first national title in four years. But it didn't win the conference championship outright, as Michigan also earned a share of the crown by shutting out Minnesota, 10–0, the same day. The Illini players and coaches immediately talked about wanting to play the Wolverines next season.

A few days later, during a meeting of Big Ten officials and coaches to set the schedule for the following fall, Zuppke and coach George Little of Michigan agreed to play each other in Champaign in 1924. It would be the game that would mark the dedication of Memorial Stadium. As the two coaches shook hands in front of several photographers to informally confirm the deal, Zuppke told the Michigan coach, "I'll squeeze your hand on this, and I'll squeeze your hand harder next fall." Zuppke laughed, while Little remained stone faced. The buildup to the Game of the Century had begun.

A*fter the season was over*, Grange received the ultimate compliment: He was named to Walter Camp's All-America squad. The father of American football had spent most of his sixty-five years on the East Coast. He was Yale's team captain in 1878 and '79, and he served as a longtime advisor to the Yale football team. Although he held a full-time job at the New Haven Clock Company, Camp revolutionized the game of college football with his writings and opinions. He was largely responsible for introducing the seven-man offensive front line, which became the standard offensive formation in the early 1900s. He published thirty books on the sport and wrote dozens of articles in magazines such as *Harper's* and *Collier's Weekly*. His writing helped spread the gospel of the game across the country, and every year at season's end, players, coaches, and fans eagerly awaited the names of the players he would put on his prestigious All-America team.

Camp, like most football fans in the East, had an eastern bias toward college football. He rarely traveled to see games in the Midwest, and in his thirty-four years of compiling his All-America team, he selected only a handful of players from the region. But he couldn't ignore Grange. Although he'd never personally seen Grange play, the reports he'd read of Grange's exploits were simply impossible to overlook. So, at left halfback on the first team of his 1923 All-America squad, Camp named Grange. He wrote:

> Red Grange of Illinois is not only a line smasher of great power, but also a sterling open-field runner and has been a great factor in the offense of Illinois through the middle west conference.... [Grange is] one of those runners who always seems destined to get loose at the psychological moment.

Get loose at the psychological moment. With those words, Camp perfectly summed up Grange's gridiron brilliance. Grange made plays on the field when it mattered most, not when the game was a blowout. He had the timing of a seasoned Broadway actor. When the crowd was itching to see something spectacular, something unique, Grange seemed to make it happen as easily as snapping his fingers. This, more than anything, was what his growing fame was built on, and why fans across the country were now wanting to see for themselves this Red Grange kid. Grange was often asked what made him so good, but all he could do was shake his head and point to three things: his speed, his instinct—which allowed him to sense when defenders were coming at him, even from behind—and his love of physical contact. Grange would end his explanation by saying, *I'm blessed.*

And his selection by Camp signified a major shift. He was no longer just some small-town wonder on a high school field. In one varsity season, he was a national sensation.

6

THE EDUCATION OF GEORGE HALAS

The *young man sat* behind his cluttered desk in his cramped apartment at 4356 West Washington Boulevard in Chicago and worried. He worried about how he was going to put food on the table for his wife and newborn child. He worried about how he was going to pay the rent and keep the heat on. But mostly, in the fall of 1924, George Stanley Halas, age twenty-nine, worried about how he was going to save the National Football League team he owned, the Chicago Bears, from spiraling into bankruptcy.

Like every other owner in the NFL, Halas had enough financial problems to give him night sweats. At the start of the 1923 season, the NFL fielded twenty franchises. But just a few months into the campaign, several teams had quietly folded, unable to pay their players even $50 a game. Halas's Bears were one of just eleven teams to survive the '23 season and play again in '24.

Just three years earlier, in August 1920, the founders had high hopes when forming the league. About a dozen men had gathered in Canton, Ohio, at Ralph Hay's Jordan and Hupmobile showroom to discuss the potential of an organized professional football association. Semipro teams dotted the Midwest, and the meeting included owners from four Ohio-based teams: the Akron Professionals, the Columbus Panhandles, the Canton Bulldogs, and the Dayton Triangles. Semipro football had existed since 1895 in small towns in Pennsylvania, Ohio, New York, and Indiana, but the sport had never been officially organized. The players typically had full-time jobs outside of the game, and the crowds rarely swelled to more than 150. To get paid, in the early days, the players passed a hat through the crowds, usually earning only a few dollars each per game.

Owners often pulled extravagant stunts to entice fans to the games. In 1922 Walter Lingo, the owner of the Oorang Indians of LaRue, Ohio, a town of nine hundred, staged lavish halftime shows. One featured a live bear wrestling one of his Native American players and another re-created a World War I battle scene that included Red Cross dogs and U.S. Indian scouts. But in spite of the thrilling halftime acts that were nearly as elaborate as vaudeville shows, the Indians failed to draw large crowds. The team disbanded after the 1923 season, and owner Lingo returned to his mail-order puppy business.

Surrounded by a few buckets of cold beer, the owners sat down in Hay's showroom in late summer 1920. They discussed several issues: how to deal with escalating salary demands of star players; how to prevent players from jumping from one team one week to another the next; how to dissuade college players from using fake names and playing in professional games; and the potential threat of other growing pro teams in different areas of the country. They eventually agreed to pitch in $25 each and create the first American Professional Football Association. The following day, the *Canton Evening Repository* summarized what had transpired during the meeting.

> The purpose . . . will be to raise the standard of professional football in every way possible, to eliminate bidding for players between rival clubs and to secure cooperation in the formation of schedules, at least for the bigger teams . . . members of the organization reached an agreement to refrain from offering inducements to players to jump from one team to another, which has been one of the glaring drawbacks to the game in past seasons. Contracts must be respected by players as far as possible, as well as by club managers. The move to abolish competitive bidding for star players

is a matter of self-protection for the magnates, as they have been facing a steady upward trend in the price demanded by players of ability, especially those who have acquired big college reputations.

As news of the meeting spread across the country, several other owners of semipro teams in different states grew intrigued with the APFA. A month after the first meeting, another one was held in Hay's automobile showroom. This time representatives of ten teams from five states (Ohio, Illinois, Indiana, New York, and Wisconsin) were present, including George Halas, who was on hand for the Staley Starchmakers, based in Decatur, Illinois. The men agreed to each pay a $100 franchise fee to become members of the league. They then voted Jim Thorpe, who was part owner of the Canton Bulldogs, to be the league's first president.

Thorpe was as famous as any semipro player in the nation, with a name that was known around the world. He had starred at the Carlisle Industrial Indian School in Carlisle, Pennsylvania, from 1907 to 1912 while playing for coach Glenn "Pop" Warner. The Indians barnstormed across the country taking on the top college teams of the day—Army, Harvard, Yale, Penn—and Thorpe, who also won two gold medals in the 1912 Summer Olympics in Stockholm, Sweden, generated more ink in newspapers from 1910 to 1912 than any other athlete in America. In 1915 he signed to play for the Canton Bulldogs for $250 a game, by far the highest salary paid to any football player in the country. The investment by Canton owner Ralph Hay was an immediate boon: At Thorpe's first game, a crowd of eight thousand turned out to see him play, then the largest gate for a semipro game in the short history of the sport. Naming Thorpe president five years later was intended to give the APFA instant credibility and a shot of adrenaline. Still, the league struggled to attract fans in its first few years.

From its start, the venture was an organizational disaster. The league had no schedule, as many of the APFA teams played against nonmember teams. No records were kept, making it easy for players to move from team to team in order to make as much money as possible. And many college athletes played under assumed names in order to keep their amateur eligibility intact. On top of those problems, Thorpe was often drowning in the bottom of a bottle, as he was battling a serious alcohol problem. The future of pro football did not hold much promise in the early 1920s.

In *February 1920*, six months before the APFA was born, George Halas was hard at work designing bridges for the Chicago, Burlington and Quincy Railroad for $55 a week. Only twenty-five years old, Halas still pined to play the favorite game of his youth: football. Born in Chicago, he had attended the University of Illinois, where he had laced up his cleats for coach Bob Zuppke. Halas wasn't a particularly gifted player, but his tenacity was the stuff of a coach's dream. Playing backup right end as a sophomore in 1915, he first caught Zuppke's eye during a midseason scrimmage. A varsity player intercepted a pass with nothing but open field in front of him. As he sprinted up the field, every junior varsity player quit chasing him except Halas. After 60 yards, Halas lunged and caught the player's leg. When the varsity player fell to the ground at the 3-yard line, his heel violently smacked Halas in the face, breaking his jaw. Zuppke loved this kind of hustle, this kind of determination, and the coach soon promised Halas a starting position the following season.

But during preseason drills in 1916, Halas limped from the field near the end of a practice session. He thought he had suffered either a deep bruise on his leg or a pulled muscle. But the next day, the pain was worse. When Zuppke saw him hobbling around the field, the quick-tempered coach accused him of faking an injury in order to get out of practice.

"Halas, stop loafing!" Zuppke screamed. "Get in there and hit."

These words lit the wick of Halas's temper. Halas, who was holding a football, reared back and threw it with all his strength at his coach. The ball zipped over Zuppke's head, missing the coach by inches. "I'm not loafing!" Halas yelled. "If I am not getting in there and hitting, it's because I have a painful leg!"

"Leave the field," Zuppke demanded.

Halas limped away. He eventually met with the trainer, who examined him and then took him to the hospital. An X-ray revealed that Halas had suffered a broken bone in his leg, which was put in a cast. After being stuck in a hospital bed for five days, Halas returned to classes and, on crutches, hobbled up and down the sideline during practices, carefully studying every word that Zuppke uttered, every move the coach made.

Feeling sorry for his young player, Zuppke put Halas in charge of the team's supply room and paid him $300 a semester. During his entire junior season, Halas was never far from Zuppke. The injured player was also a budding entrepreneur, and he hired an assistant in the supply room for $150 a semester, an investment that allowed him to spend more time near Zuppke. He wanted to learn as much as he could from Zuppke, who was becoming his coaching mentor.

At the end of the season, after Zuppke let Halas travel with the team to Minnesota to watch Illinois upset the Gophers, 19–14, the coach spoke at the team's annual banquet. The words that flowed from his lips would stick with Halas for the rest of his life. "Just when I teach you fellows how to play football," Zuppke said, "you graduate and I lose you."

Sitting in his chair at the banquet, Halas was struck by an idea. *What if,* he thought, *college players had somewhere to play after their eligibility was exhausted? What if there was a legitimate pro league?*

One *afternoon* in January 1917, days after the banquet, Halas was studying in his fraternity house when Ralph Jones, Illinois's head basketball coach, knocked on the front door. He needed an agile, fleet-footed player to fill one of his roster spots, and he wanted the six-foot, 170-pound Halas, who had played guard at Crane Technical High in Chicago. "George," Jones said, "I want you at basketball practice tomorrow."

Halas replied that he had recently broken his leg. But this didn't deter Jones, who had traveled with the football team to Minneapolis for the season finale.

"I saw you throw the crutches into the air when we beat Minnesota," Jones said. "You can manage. Be there."

The next day Halas joined the basketball squad. He was as rough as any player on the Illinois roster. In his first game, he committed four fouls—in less than three minutes. Halas enjoyed the contact, even coveted it. But he eventually settled down, and by late in the season, he developed into one of the team's top players, helping lead the Illini to the brink of the Big Ten title. With thirty seconds left in the championship game against Wisconsin, the Badgers held a one-point lead over Illinois. Only seconds remained when the ball was tipped to Halas. He took a few dribbles and then, from just past midcourt, stopped and launched a two-handed set shot. Just as the final buzzer blew, the ball zinged through the net, handing Illinois the Big Ten title. For one night, Halas was the king of the campus.

Halas played football for Zuppke again in his senior year. He returned punts and kickoffs but otherwise had an unremarkable season as Illinois went 5-2-1. Yet he could often be found in Zuppke's shadow, watching, studying, listening to his coach. No detail was too small for him to capture, whether it was Zuppke's jaw-clenching comportment on the sideline or the tender way in which he talked to troubled players. For Halas, this was his education.

The United States entered World War I on April 6, 1917. Halas, like many of his classmates, was immediately struck with war fever. He was twenty-two years old and knew that he would soon be drafted. But he didn't want to wait to join the battle, so in January 1918 he enlisted in the navy. University administrators agreed to waive the final six hours Halas needed to finish his degree in civil engineering. With degree in hand, he left school. The navy ordered him to report for officer's training at the Great Lakes Naval Training Center near Waukegan, Illinois.

Commissioned an ensign in the spring of 1918, Halas hoped to experience action at sea. But instead of being ordered aboard a ship, he was assigned, along with a few of his athletically gifted teammates from Illinois, to the sports program at Great Lakes. The sports teams at the training center were deemed important by Halas's superiors for two reasons: They were tremendous recruiting tools, because whenever they competed against university squads, the Great Lakes players and coaches would tout the navy and the need for young men to enlist; and the squads were also morale boosters for the entire naval force, as navy men around the globe would follow with pride the various Great Lakes teams.

But Halas had been stirred by the winds of war, and he told his mother that he thought he'd be wasting his time playing sports at Great Lakes. "Son," she responded, "the navy knows much better how to win the war than you do, so be a good boy and do as they say."

Halas did. He first played on the Great Lakes basketball team, then on its baseball team. But it was on the football field where Halas would make his greatest impact. The training school commander, Lieutenant C. J. McReavy, doubled as the Great Lakes football coach. But McReavy had little free time to spare, causing him to frequently miss practice. Realizing this, the always ambitious Halas approached McReavy with a proposition: He and two of his teammates would coach the team. McReavy agreed, stipulating that he'd show up on Saturdays to coach from the sideline. Though McReavy was there for kickoffs, everyone on the team knew who was really in charge.

This was Halas's first coaching job, and he made the most of it. The majority of his players had played college ball at schools in the Midwest, and with his guidance—his style was already a carbon copy of Zuppke's—the team emerged as one of the nation's finest in the fall of 1918. In the Sailors' season opener, they beat the Iowa Hawkeyes on the road, 10–0. A week later, Great Lakes and North-western played to a scoreless tie. The following Sunday, the Sailors traveled to Champaign to face Halas's mentor and friend, Zuppke. Halas, playing end for the Sailors, got the best of the man he modeled himself after: Great Lakes beat Illinois, 7–0.

The next opponent was Notre Dame, whose first-year coach was Knute Rockne. The Fighting Irish didn't intimidate Halas and his boys; the final score was 7–7. After beating Purdue University, 27–7, and Rutgers University, 54–4, to run their record to 4-0-2, the Great Lakes players traveled by rail to Annapolis, Maryland, to take on the Naval Academy Midshipmen. Three trainloads of sailors followed the Great Lakes squad on its long-distance journey, eager to see this intra-navy battle for gridiron supremacy in what was one of the most anticipated games of the season.

The armistice to end World War I had recently been signed, and the patriotism that surged across the country filled Thompson Stadium at kickoff. Early in the game, Navy marched down the field and had the ball inside Great Lakes's 10-yard line when Midshipmen fullback Bill Ingram took a handoff from the quarterback. Ingram barreled ahead, but just before he crossed the goal line, he fumbled the ball. The pigskin bounced once on the ground and then straight into the hands of Dizzy Eilison, a Great Lakes defender. With Halas blocking and clearing his path, Eilison darted up the field. By the time he reached midfield, it was clear that no Navy player would catch him.

"Tackle him, tackle him!" shouted Navy coach Gil Dobie from the sideline.

Dobie's words prompted action. One Midshipman, who had been on the bench, shot onto the field and tackled Eilison with a violent hit—a blatant violation of the rules. The next few moments were chaotic. Halas and his Sailors teammates vehemently protested to the referee, arguing that Great Lakes should be awarded a touchdown. Coach Dobie claimed there was no precedent for that in the rule book and that the referee should simply assess a penalty on Navy and not give Great Lakes a touchdown it didn't actually score. The official agreed with the Navy coach; he penalized the Midshipmen and didn't award Great Lakes any points.

But that didn't end the controversy. After several more minutes of bickering, Captain Edward Walter Eberle, the superintendent of the Naval Academy, left his seat in the bleachers and walked onto the field. Eberle announced that the referee had made an error and that the honorable thing to do was to give Great Lakes a touchdown. When the official said this change violated the rules, Eberle stood his ground. "I said it was a touchdown," Eberle told the official. "I run this place, and a touchdown it is."

Because of Eberle's act, Great Lakes eventually won the game, 7–6. It was an incident that contained within it a great lesson: Integrity matters. But this wasn't a lesson that made any great impression on Halas, as he would later prove.

After Great Lakes toppled the Naval Academy, officials at the Rose Bowl invited the squad to play in Pasadena, California, on New

Year's Day 1919 against another service team, the Mare Island Marines. In front of twenty-seven thousand fans, Halas played at his highest level in the most important game of his young football career. He scored on a 10-yard reception from Paddy Driscoll, and he also returned an interception 77 yards to the Marines' 3-yard line. (That a defender caught Halas from behind on the interception would bother him for years—the play would haunt his sleep—and once he became a professional coach, he would tell his players that if they were at the 3-yard line, they should dive into the end zone, not merely jog across the goal line as he tried to do against Mare Island.) Great Lakes won the game, 17–0, and Halas was named the Most Valuable Player of the Rose Bowl—the only time that he would ever be the most dominating player on the field.

After spending a day walking around Hollywood, Halas and his teammates took a train back to Chicago. The news of his stellar performance had reached his mother, who read about her son's exploits in the newspaper. But she was appalled. She didn't want her son playing what she believed was the most dangerous sport ever invented. When Halas told her that he knew how to avoid getting hurt, she replied, "Well, if that is so, how did you happen to break your jaw and leg at Illinois?"

Halas didn't have an answer. He soon pledged that his football days were over. And, for a while, they were. When he returned to Great Lakes after his leave was up, he played baseball, basketball, and served as the base recreation officer. In March 1919, he was discharged from the navy. Not wanting to give up his dream of playing sports for a living, Halas hopped on another train, this one bound for Jacksonville, Florida, where the New York Yankees were holding spring training.

The Yankees contacted Halas in his junior year at Illinois, when a scout invited him to attend their spring training camp. Halas deferred, saying he'd try out once his college career was over. The war had further delayed his plans, but now, like many former servicemen searching for jobs in the big leagues, he showed up in Jacksonville with dreams of being the next Ty Cobb, his favorite baseball player.

Though he struggled to hit a curveball, Halas made the team as an outfielder. Early in the season, the Yankees traveled to Detroit to play the Tigers, who were led by Cobb. Halas was on the bench when Cobb strode to the plate. A veteran on the Yankees team, catcher Truck Hannah, was sitting next to Halas in the dugout, and he told the young outfielder to throw some verbal stones at the irascible Cobb, to razz him and tell him that he had no chance of connecting with the ball.

Halas went along with Hannah's suggestion, unleashing a river of foul language at Cobb, who dropped his bat and marched over to the Yankees' dugout. "Punk," Cobb yelled at Halas, "I'll see you after the game! Don't forget, punk!"

Not wanting to appear scared, Halas replied, "I will look for you."

But Halas was mortified. Cobb was his baseball idol, the man he'd looked up to for so many years. Aware of Cobb's legendary surliness, Halas figured that Cobb probably wanted to do his talking with his fists. So Halas took an extra long shower after the game, hoping that the Georgia Peach would grow tired of waiting for him. But when Halas left the locker room, there was Cobb, who was just leaving the Tigers' locker room.

Halas was terrified, but Cobb simply extended his hand, telling the young player, "I like your spirit, kid, but don't overdo it when you don't have to."

Halas would never forget that admonition. It taught him another lesson: Don't let passion get the best of you. Halas wasn't an elite athlete, but his enthusiasm for sports was as boundless as anyone's. He always worked himself into a fever whenever he stepped onto the fields of play, and he was slowly learning that he had to harness his eagerness in order to maximize his ability. This was something he would impart to his players at a job he would soon hold: head football coach of a semiprofessional team.

In the summer of 1919, Halas appeared in twelve games for the Yankees, and in 22 at-bats he had two hits, which translated into a .091 batting average. After the season ended, he returned home to Chicago, believing that his athletic career was over. It was time for the twenty-four-year-old to grow up and work nine to five in an office. At least, that was what his overbearing mother said.

Halas reported for work in September 1919 as a bridge designer for the Chicago, Burlington and Quincy Railroad. Armed with his degree in civil engineering, he spent his days studying the stresses that trains impose on bridges, and each week he brought home $55. His mother couldn't have been happier. Finally, her boy was making good in the real world.

But Halas was still hooked on football. He missed so much about the game: the fellowship of teammates, the rush of delivering a bone-jarring hit, the thrill of testing himself against other men, the satisfaction of outwitting a rival coach. As Halas sat behind his desk and worked in the quiet of his office, he would vividly recall Zuppke's lament, "Just when I teach you fellows how to play football, you graduate, and I lose you." Halas didn't want to lose the game. One day that fall, he arrived at a decision: I will play football again.

Halas knew that there was a semipro team based in Hammond, Indiana, only twenty-five miles south of Chicago. A doctor, A. A. Young, owned the team, which played other semipro outfits from around the Midwest and in the Rust Belt. His club consisted mostly of former college players who practiced only once a week—on Thursday nights after work—and were paid $100 a game.

Halas hatched a plan. He would take a train to Hammond each Thursday afternoon and return home after practice. On Saturday mornings, he would then train back to Hammond—or to wherever the team was playing—for the real action. This meant that Halas would spend at least four hours a week on the train, but to a football zealot like him, that was a small price to pay.

When Halas arrived in Hammond for the first time, he conferred with Young and then headed to the practice field. He was surprised to discover that the team was a who's who of former college stars. There was Doc Hauser, who had been an All-America tackle at Minnesota; there was Shorty Desjardien, a former All-America center at the University of Chicago; there was Bert Baston, a one-time All-America end at Minnesota. And there was Paddy Driscoll, who had played with Halas at Great Lakes and was one of the team's top players. Halas had something in common with all of these men: He couldn't let go of the game.

There were thirteen players on the Hammond Pros, as the team was called, and Halas joined the squad for six games in the autumn of 1919. The highlight of the season was a game against the Canton Bulldogs, who were led by the mighty Jim Thorpe. Halas marveled at the sight of the thirty-one-year-old Thorpe, who stood six foot one, weighed 220 pounds, and looked like he could yank an oak tree out of the ground. Because Thorpe was on the field, several thousand fans showed up to see the former Carlisle Indians star put on a show, and Thorpe delivered. One time he hit a Hammond player so hard that Halas swore that his teammate "sailed three feet into the air, all 230 pounds, and came down with a thud." Even though Thorpe bashed his head on the bench while being tackled out of bounds by a Hammond defender, causing blood to bubble from Thorpe's forehead, a trainer stitched him up, and the muscular Indian stayed in the game.

The crowd was awestruck by Thorpe. Late in the game, Canton lined up in punt formation at its own 2-yard line. Thorpe was the punter, and as soon as he received the snap, he took one step forward, then another, then reared his right foot back like a pendulum and connected with the ball. It traveled impossibly high and far, tracing the arc of a giant rainbow. It soared over the head of the Hammond return man and bounced down the field. By the time the ball came to a rest, it had covered 80 yards.

The Hammond Pros lost the game, but on this day Halas learned another crucial lesson, vital not only to his own career but also to the entire future of professional football in America. This game was all about the players, about stars, about men who could attract spectators and leave them thirsty for more action, more hitting, more athletic brilliance. This was the power that Thorpe wielded even as his playing career declined, and Halas would one day realize that he needed a player of Thorpe's stature in his prime to save professional football from bankruptcy.

After the Hammond Pros finished their six-game season, Halas continued to work at the CB&Q offices. As the months crept by, he missed football like a long-lost friend, but he had accepted that his playing career was over. It was time to become an adult and earn some real money. Still, when he glanced at the older engineers in his office, at men who'd been doing the same thing five days a week for several decades, he saw a chilling picture of his own future. That image often reappeared to Halas as he rode a streetcar to and from work, and it demoralized him. There had to be more to life.

One cold morning in February 1920, Halas was in his office examining the drawing of a bridge when his telephone jingled. This was an ordinary day of work, so he anticipated a call related to design or engineering. But the voice coming out of the other end of the receiver identified himself as George Chamberlain, a name that Halas had not heard before. The man explained that he was the general superintendent of the A. E. Staley Corn Products Company in Decatur, Illinois, and that he was currently in Chicago on business.

Halas continued to listen, not really sure where the conversation was heading. Chamberlain said he had an important matter to discuss, and that he'd like to meet Halas after work at the Sherman House, a hotel located near Halas's office in the Loop. Halas, with nothing to lose, agreed to stop by and see what Chamberlain had on his mind.

Soon after five o'clock, Halas walked to the Sherman House, one of the largest hotels in Chicago and one of its most popular nightspots for jazz. He found Chamberlain, and, after shaking hands, the two sat down and began chatting.

Chamberlain cut to the point. He said that his boss, Mr. A. E. Staley, the president and owner of the company, believed that athletics should play an important role in the future of his business. A year earlier, he had formed a semipro football team—named after his company—and now he wanted to hire someone with coaching experience. If the Staleys could win consistently, Mr. Staley believed it would spread the company name to places he never could reach otherwise; it would be advertising gold and increase sales. He also believed that a successful company football team would boost the morale of his entire workforce, because the team would be a rallying point for everyone on his payroll.

Chamberlain continued to talk. He said that officials at both the

University of Illinois and Great Lakes had recommended Halas to Mr. Staley for this new position he wanted to create, a position that Mr. Staley, through Chamberlain, was now offering Halas. The job, Chamberlain said, had several responsibilities. First, from nine to five on most weekdays, Mr. Staley wanted Halas to use his engineering ability to make starch. Then, after the five o'clock whistle blew, Halas would play on the company baseball team in the spring; in the summer and fall he would organize, coach, and play on the football team.

The proposition intrigued Halas. His passion for the game blasted back at him. He was ready for a change, for something new in his life to escape the drudgery of the working world, and this was the perfect opportunity. Though his impulse was to accept the job immediately, Halas coolly demanded a few things. First he wanted to know if he could personally recruit the players. Specifically, he wanted to target both college stars—past and present—and established semipro players currently on other rosters.

Of course, Chamberlain replied, Halas would have the authority to sign any player he wanted. Chamberlain then told Halas that it was, in fact, Halas's background in the game—and his relationships with current players—that initially made him such an attractive candidate to Mr. Staley. The deep-pocketed corn company owner wanted a coach who had credibility with players around the Midwest, someone who could convince them to play on his team. Halas had already earned his coaching bona fides at Great Lakes, and now, Chamberlain told Halas, Mr. Staley was willing to pay him nearly the same salary he was earning at CB&Q to work and coach at the A. E. Staley Company.

Halas still had a few more demands. To recruit players, he wanted to be able to offer them full-time, year-round employment at the company. And if the team performed well, he wanted his players to be able to share a small percentage of the gate receipts. Chamberlain agreed to both.

Then there was the issue of practicing. Though semipro teams rarely held regular practices, Halas wanted to know if he could lead the team in practice every day during the season. Chamberlain nodded.

"Two hours each day?" Halas asked.

Chamberlain was taken aback by the request, which to him seemed as absurd as asking for a two-hour work break each day. But Halas explained that he needed the practice time to mold his team into a winner, and that once he started winning games, it would reflect positively on the A. E. Staley Company. After taking a moment to contemplate the issue, Chamberlain agreed that the team could practice two hours a day. "All right," Chamberlain said. "You are the expert. You will be the boss."

Halas wasn't done. "One more thing," he said. "May we practice on company time?"

Halas was now asking for the moon and the stars; no company-sponsored semipro team had ever used company time to prepare for games. Halas was challenging the depth of Staley's commitment to winning, and he was pleasantly surprised when Chamberlain nodded again.

Halas then agreed to take the job. In two weeks, he would move 185 miles south of Chicago to Decatur, where the company's processing center was based, and start working as an engineer and football coach. The rest of Halas's life was about to begin.

Halas rode the train to Decatur. Toting a suitcase, he made his way downtown, where he rented a room in a boardinghouse. The next day, March 29, 1920, he stepped onto a streetcar and traveled to the A. E. Staley Company corn mill, located on the southern edge of town. As he entered the plant for the first time, he noted the company's playing field next to the factory. There was one grandstand that could seat about 1,500 people, and plenty of space for spectators to watch the action from the sideline. Halas later toured the team's locker room, which included showers, individual lockers, and a small meeting room with a blackboard—a room that would soon become Halas's second office.

Halas went to work. During the day, he inspected and weighed deliveries of corn in the factory. At five o'clock he'd head to the locker room, change into his baseball uniform, and, glove in hand, walk out to the baseball diamond and play for the company team.

But even when he was shagging fly balls or taking batting practice, his thoughts drifted to football and how he was going to build a winner. Then in midsummer, Halas took off on a one-man recruiting trip—the first of its kind in the short history of professional football.

On a piece of paper, Halas jotted down a list of players he wanted to contact. He kept the list with him as he boarded a train and traveled up and down the Midwest, hoping to assemble an A-list roster of talent. He first stopped at towns in Illinois and discussed the possibility of playing for Mr. Staley with many of his former teammates at the University of Illinois and at Great Lakes. In every living room Halas visited, his pitch was the same. He'd tell the player that this was a chance of a lifetime, an opportunity to keep playing the game of his youth—*and* get paid for it. Moreover, Halas told his recruits that they could learn a trade while earning a salary playing football. Halas possessed a salesman's touch, a unique ability to connect with people and empathize with their emotions and dreams. More often than not, when he left the homes of prospective players, they were already crafting plans to move to Decatur.

Halas signed several of his Illinois teammates, including halfback Ed "Dutch" Sternaman and guard Burt Ingwerson. He took a train west to Nebraska to woo the Cornhuskers' former star Guy Chamberlain, who eagerly accepted Halas's offer. He stopped in Wisconsin, where he signed former Badgers All-America tackle Ralph Scott. And he also garnered commitments from former players at Michigan State, Notre Dame, and Washington University in St. Louis, along with current players from Penn and Northwestern.

Halas was building a team; his team. He had a sharp eye for discovering players, a skill he learned from Zuppke. At Illinois, Zuppke had judged his players every day at practice—he constantly noted aloud who was great, who was just good, and who was a goat—and Halas had studied him closely. And now, though only twenty-five years old, Halas was as good as anyone in the game when it came to recognizing, bird-dogging, and developing talent.

Once he assembled his roster, Halas put his boys to work. He taught them the same version of the T formation that he had learned under Zuppke; it called for the quarterback to stand a few feet behind the center, one halfback on each side of the quarterback, and the fullback behind the quarterback. Halas recorded his thoughts in a clothbound notebook. On each page, he diagrammed one play, which he would then write out for his team on the chalkboard in the meeting room. The playbook was Halas's prized possession, and as he stomped around the field during practices, it rarely left his hands. After a few weeks of practice, Halas believed his team couldn't be beaten. His players were experienced, savvy, fearless, and, most of all, as talented as any semipro outfit in America.

Halas was a ruthless coach, schooling his men in the fine art of dirty play. Halas had a history of playing beyond the rules. To make up for his lack of skill as a player, he had seized every opportunity to gain an edge, including inflicting below-the-belt damage after the whistle had blown. He expected the same of his players. Because there would be only three officials calling each game, Halas knew that his players could slyly get away with tripping, hitting after the whistle, punching in pileups, gouging an opponent's eyes, scratching, biting, even throwing haymakers to the groin. Nothing was deemed too violent by Halas, as long as his team didn't get caught. Players wore only minimal padding—leather helmets were optional, no one had had a face mask, and shoulder pads were little more than miniature pillows—and Halas believed that dirty tactics could give his men a competitive advantage; that they could knock out the opposing squad's top players with a few well-timed low blows.

Halas's willingness to bend the rules revealed his intensity, his win-at-all-costs approach to the game. But there was a downside: The prevalence of dirty play in the professional game caused college coaches and newspapermen around the country to decry pro ball as foul, corrupt, and not at all in keeping with the traditional values of fair play and sportsmanship that distinguished other sports, such as college football, pro baseball, even boxing. But Halas didn't care; all that mattered to him were winning, putting on a good show for the fans, and hauling in a boxcar full of cash at the gate.

Yet throughout the summer of 1920, Halas confronted a far different problem, one that had nothing to do with the action on the field. He wrote several letters to coaches of semiprofessional teams around the Midwest asking to schedule games, but the replies he received were noncommittal. Coaches argued over where the games

would be played, when they would be played, and how the gate
money would be divided. Halas grew so frustrated that he eventually
fired off a letter to Ralph Hay, the manager of the Canton Bulldogs,
an organization that Halas considered the elite semipro team of the
day and the best operated. In the missive, Halas argued that professional football needed a legitimate league body that could enforce a
schedule and restrict player movement from team to team one week
to the next. The APFA had lacked the muscle to enforce much of
anything in 1919, and Halas believed that the only way pro football
could survive was to have a truly organized league with a powerful
figurehead who could set the schedule and be the sport's authoritative voice.

Halas asked Hay—who had hosted the original meeting that led
to the birth of the APFA a year earlier—if he could attend the APFA's
preseason meeting. Though the Staley Starchmakers weren't yet a
member of the fledgling league, Hay agreed. So on the morning of
September 17, 1920, Halas and Morgan O'Brien, an engineer who
worked at the corn mill and who helped Halas with administrative
duties for the football team, boarded a train in Decatur and rode
470 miles to Canton, Ohio.

The meeting took place in Hay's car dealership showroom,
which was on the ground floor of the three-story brick Odd Fellows
Building. Officials for twelve teams were present. The showroom
featured several cars—Hupmobiles, Jordans, and Marmons—and
there wasn't enough space for chairs for all the team representatives,
so Halas and a few others sat on the cars' running boards.

Halas was one of the youngest men in the room, but he dominated much of the discussion, arguing passionately about the need
for a strong league and a set schedule. The representatives agreed on
all points, and they eventually added a rule that no team could sign a
college player who still had collegiate eligibility. Halas reluctantly
agreed to the rule—and, in a few years, would violate it.

The meeting lasted two hours. Near the end, every representative agreed to pay the league a franchise fee of $100. Wanting a big-
name president, the officials reelected Jim Thorpe, who was absent.
The league, which was still named the American Professional Football Association, now featured twelve teams.

At the end of the day's business, Halas was as upbeat as he'd been in months. He even boasted to the other representatives about the cast of characters on his team, how he believed he'd assembled a roster that was second to none. That night Halas returned to Decatur full of hope. For the first time, he began to feel that he might be able to make a career out of professional football.

Now *Halas had* everything he wanted: a team full of handpicked players, an owner who met his every demand, and an organized league. But the APFA still didn't keep records, make official decisions, or even codify a set of rules. Many of the teams had so little money that they could afford to travel only short distances, which meant those teams would play only opponents in nearby towns.

The Starchmakers, who would venture no farther than 200 miles to play a game, opened the season against the Moline Tractors, an independent pro team that wasn't a member of the APFA. A crowd of only 1,500 showed up to see the Staleys win, 20–0. There was plenty of side betting going on in the grandstands, but Halas's heart sank when he saw the minuscule crowd. He knew that pro football still had a long way to go if it was ever going to gain a foothold in the American sporting landscape.

But as the season progressed, more fans started filling the stands. After beating the Kewanee Walworths, 27–0, the Starchmakers traveled to Rock Island, Illinois, to play the Rock Island Independents. There was so much interest in the game that more than a thousand Staleys fans in Decatur chartered a train to Rock Island, which was 180 miles away. A crowd of more than five thousand witnessed a savage contest. At one point, a Staleys player, George Trafton, flung Rock Island halfback Fred Chicken into a fence that ran along the side of the field. Chicken smashed into a post, breaking his leg. After the Staleys won, 7–0—generating a windfall for the Decatur fans at the game because most of them bet on their team and won wads of cash—a herd of rock-throwing Rock Island fans chased Trafton off the field. One of Trafton's teammates, Dutch Sternaman, hailed a cab to pick up the fleeing Trafton, but the cab driver refused. Eventually a passing motorist drove Trafton to safety.

The key game of the season occurred on Thanksgiving Day, Thursday, November 25. Halas and his boys rode the train to the North Side of Chicago to face the Chicago Tigers at Weeghman Park, soon to be renamed Cubs Park. Halas had recently heard through the rumor mill that the Tigers were losing vast amounts of money each week. The team paid an exorbitant rental fee to Cubs team president William L. Veeck each time they rented Cubs Park. Even though the games typically drew five thousand to ten thousand fans, the gate receipts didn't cover expenses. Halas expected that the team would fold at season's end.

So Halas, who'd already made dozens of scouting trips searching for talented players, now viewed this game as a scouting trip for a potential new home for his team. While the Starchmakers had been profitable—at season's end, in fact, every member of the Decatur squad would receive a bonus check of $1,900—Halas understood that he would never draw large crowds in Decatur, a town of only one hundred thousand. In his vision for the future, he wanted all the league's teams to move from "tank" towns—small, out-of-the-way places like Akron, Muncie, and Rock Island—to large, booming metropolises like Chicago, where the fan base was larger and would be more affluent. Professional football needed to follow the model of professional baseball, Halas believed, and baseball thrived because its games were played in vast stadiums in the nation's biggest cities.

On this Thanksgiving Day, as Halas trotted onto the field at Cubs Park, he estimated that there had to be some eight thousand people in the stands. *This is it,* Halas thought to himself. *This is the place our team needs to play.* The Staleys won the game, 6–0, but the score was almost secondary to Halas. He had found the perfect place for pro football in the Midwest; now he had to devise a plan to move his team into Cubs Park. (In 1926 the stadium was renamed Wrigley Field after chewing-gum magnate and new Cubs owner William Wrigley.)

Three days later, the 9-0 Staleys journeyed back to Chicago—this time to the South Side—to take on the Racine (Chicago) Cardinals at Normal Park on Sixty-first Street and Racine Avenue. Late in the game, the Staleys held a 6–0 lead when a Cardinals end caught a pass along the sideline. Just as a Staleys defender was about to hit him, several local fans spilled onto the field, providing a shield of blockers for the Cardinals player. He ended up crossing the goal line, prompting the referee to signal a touchdown. Halas loudly disputed the play, arguing that fans had interfered, but the referee didn't overturn his call, afraid that he would cause a riot if he did. Despite Halas's protest, the Cardinals won, 7–6.

Shortly after the game, Halas huddled with Cardinals owner Chris O'Brien. Since both teams had lost only one game to a league opponent, they agreed to a rematch for what they called "Midwestern honors." Because Halas and the Staleys had come to the Windy City for this first contest against the Cardinals, it was agreed that the Cardinals would travel to Decatur for the rematch.

But Halas soon had another idea. The image of those eight thousand fans in the stands at Cubs Park remained seared in his mind. He wondered how many fans would attend a championship-type game at Cubs Park. So when he returned to Decatur, he phoned William Veeck. Halas had one question: Could he rent Cubs Park for one game against the Cardinals? Veeck agreed, as the park was going to sit empty anyway on that day. To Veeck, this was free money. But to Halas, this was his opportunity to test his theory that professional football could make it in a big city like Chicago.

Though the game had been scheduled only a few days earlier, news of the contest spread quickly through the Windy City, and a crowd of more than eleven thousand filled the grandstands. Once again, Halas was dazzled by the size of the crowd, which was the largest ever to watch a professional football game in Chicago. It reaffirmed to him that Cubs Park should be his future home. The Staleys beat the Cardinals in the rematch, 10–0, to claim the unofficial Midwest championship and raise their record to 2-0 at Cubs Park.

Halas still wasn't satisfied. After the game, he phoned the owner of the Akron Pros, who had won the so-called Eastern championship, to inquire about playing a game for the league title the following Sunday. The Pros agreed, and Halas said there was only one place he wanted the game to be staged: Cubs Park.

And so it was. Played on a wet and cold December afternoon, the final game of the 1920 season drew twelve thousand fans—more evidence to Halas that he needed to move his team. Before kickoff,

Halas secretly violated league rules by signing two ringers—players from other teams—for the championship game. But the added talent didn't pay off. Because of the poor playing conditions, neither offense moved the ball consistently, and the game ended 0–0. No official league title was awarded, but Halas proudly told anyone within earshot that his Staleys were the 1920 APFA champions. Halas, in fact, was so confident that his team could beat Akron that he challenged the Pros to a rematch the following week at Cubs Park. Halas saw the potential game as a guaranteed moneymaker; he believed that as many as fifteen thousand people would flock to the park to watch the contest. But Akron officials declined.

After the season ended, Halas resumed his job inspecting corn at the mill in Decatur, and he asked his longtime girlfriend Wilhelmina Bushing, whom he called Min, to marry him, a proposal she accepted. Life was good. His boss, Mr. Staley, had been especially pleased with Halas's effort in his first season as coach. The owner believed that the team had accomplished his goals of promoting his company, boosting employee morale, and increasing sales. Staley planned to keep his football operation hitting on all cylinders for the 1921 season, but the economy slumped that summer. Blue-collar workers all across the country lost their jobs, and by August, it became clear to Staley that he would have to cut costs. Specifically, he couldn't afford to retain twenty-five men whose primary job was to play football. Moreover, those twenty-five men, including Halas, were paid two extra hours a day to practice football. Keeping them on the payroll simply didn't make sense.

After a preseason practice scrimmage against an independent team from Waukegan, which the Staleys won, 35–0, Staley asked Halas to come to his office. It was a rare request, because Staley spoke with Halas only while he was out on the field. Still, Halas believed that the sports programs would be immune from the prospective job cuts that Staley would have to make, because the owner had stated several times that the company sports teams—and his football squad in particular—translated into good business.

Halas took a seat in the spacious office. "George," Staley said, "I know you are more interested in football than in starch. As you know, there is a slight recession in the country. Time lost practicing and playing costs a huge amount of money. I feel we can no longer underwrite the team's losses."

Halas was speechless. For several seconds he sat stone faced, unsure of how to respond. Finally, Staley broke the silence.

"George, why don't you take the team to Chicago? I think football will go over big there . . . Professional teams need a big city base. Chicago is a good sports city. Look at the way the baseball games in Chicago draw profitable crowds."

Halas nodded his head, his mind afire with possibility. He had wanted to move the team to Chicago ever since it played at Cubs Park for the first time, but he didn't have the means to make that happen. But now a new opportunity was arising out of Staley's financial misfortune. As the future possibilities began to percolate in Halas's mind, Staley spoke again.

"I'll give you five thousand dollars seed money to pay costs until the gate receipts start coming in. I ask only that you continue to call the team the Staleys for one season."

Halas was thrilled. The economic recession was the best thing that had ever happened to his professional career. After shaking Staley's hand to cement the deal, he beelined it to his apartment in downtown Decatur and immediately phoned Veeck. He requested a meeting, and the next morning he boarded a train for Chicago where he met with Veeck.

"I am bringing the Staley team to Chicago," Halas told Veeck. "I would like to use Cubs Park as our home, for practice as well as for our home games."

A savvy businessman, Veeck had seen the growing crowds that Halas's team had attracted to the stadium the previous autumn. He told Halas that he liked the idea. He wouldn't charge any rent, but he requested 15 percent of the money earned at the gate and at the concession stand. Considering that Veeck had demanded rent from the Chicago Cardinals football team the previous year, Halas thought this was more than fair. He agreed to the terms.

After leaving Veeck's office, Halas walked to the nearby Blackwood Apartment Hotel and rented ten rooms for $2 a week each. These would serve as his players' living quarters. When he returned to Decatur and informed his team that it would be moving to

Chicago and playing at Cubs Field, only one player refused to go, because he planned to make a career at the Staley Company. But before the team moved, it played its 1921 season opener in Decatur against Rock Island, and the Staleys won, 14–0, in front of 3,600 fans—the largest crowd to ever see a game in Decatur. Afterward Halas and his team packed their belongings and boarded a train for their new home.

Halas *couldn't afford* to run the Staleys by himself. After a few weeks, he judged that Mr. Staley's $5,000 in seed money wouldn't cover the costs of operation for the entire year. Halas approached Ed "Dutch" Sternaman, a Staleys player and a former teammate at Illinois. Halas asked him to be a fifty-fifty partner. They agreed to earn no more than $100 a game if the coffers had money and shook hands on the deal. For all the coaching, recruiting players, promoting games, massaging sore calves, writing press releases, number crunching, and busywork that Halas and Sternaman would do over the next few seasons, the $100 translated into a minuscule hourly salary.

Halas now was in a new city, a new stadium, and had a new co-owner. He craved one more thing: a new star. He understood that the best way to fill the stands was to give fans a player that they simply *had* to see, a player that every sports fan in the nation talked about, a player whose talent and grace left people in wonder. The first star that Halas aggressively sought was Charles Harley, a former halfback at Ohio State University.

Named to Walter Camp's All-America team three times and Ohio State's first consensus All-American, Harley led the Buckeyes to a combined 21-1-1 record in 1916, '17, and '19. (He took a year off from school in 1918 to serve as an Army Air Corps aviator in World War I.) While Harley was playing in Columbus, the Buckeyes' home stadium was tiny Ohio Field, which had a seating capacity of only a few thousand. But Harley had so fired the passions of Buckeyes fans that he had been one of the primary inspirations for a fund-raising campaign to build a new stadium. The campaign raised $1.3 million and led to the construction of the massive Ohio Stadium, which opened in 1922 with 66,210 seats and was referred to as "the House That Harley Built."

Halas was anxious to sign Harley, a Chicago native with film star looks. When he sized up the player, Halas saw him as a marketer's dream. Halas envisioned writing glorified stories about Harley and sending them off to the local newspapers. He would put his picture on leaflets and distribute them around town. Harley would be the franchise's foundation.

Halas met Harley in the lobby of downtown Chicago's Hotel Planters. Harley arrived with his brother, who acted as his manager and had one very large demand: Harley would sign with the Staleys only if the Harley brothers were given one-third ownership of the team, which would make them equal partners with Halas and Sternaman. Halas was so eager to have the collegiate game's biggest name on his roster that he signed a letter of agreement granting the brothers' demand.

When Halas sent out a press release announcing the signing, the news was met with outrage. Sportswriters, college coaches, and editorial boards launched attacks on the pro game, arguing that it was immoral for former college players to earn money to play a game as wholesome as football. On November 2, the *Chicago Daily News* published a story headlined "Stagg Condemns Pro Football Contests." Amos Alonzo Stagg, the well-known head coach at the University of Chicago, was quoted extensively in the article. He warned that gambling might destroy college football, and then added, "And now along comes another serious menace, possibly greater than all other, viz., Sunday professional football."

Halas wasn't expecting a backlash, but the article underscored how far the pro game still had to go before it would be embraced by mainstream America. And almost from the start, the Harley signing was a disaster. After nine games in the 1921 season, Harley underwent a physical. The doctor gave him some life-changing news: He had contracted syphilis. This was a grave diagnosis, because it would be seven years before Alex Fleming discovered penicillin and another twenty before it was used regularly to cure the sexually transmitted disease.

Halas was repulsed. Like his mentor Zuppke, Halas demanded

that his players conduct themselves with class and dignity. Though on the field Halas encouraged his players to be as brutal and merciless as possible toward the opponent—even imploring his players to cheat as long as they didn't get caught—off the field Halas held his players to a high code of conduct. Harley had failed to live up to Halas's expectations. Without giving it a second thought, Halas ripped up the letter of agreement he had signed with Harley and his brother, terminating the deal.

The Harley brothers fought back. Appearing at the preseason league meeting in 1922, they claimed that they were part owners of the Staleys. Halas vehemently disagreed, and then he asked the league members to put it to a vote. The league members favored Halas, 8 to 2. The Harleys then filed a lawsuit, but it was eventually dismissed. Charley Harley never played again, and he spent most of the remainder of his life in a hospital, syphilis having overtaken his brain. He died in 1974.

Halas's first experiment with a big-name college player had been a categorical failure. But he was a daydreaming optimist by nature. He still longed to sign a player who could single-handedly transform professional football from a sideshow to a premier spectacle. Halas believed he'd find that player someday. He just hoped he didn't lose all of his money before then.

The American Pro Football Association was struggling. Before the start of the 1921 season, the league had grown to eighteen teams. But by December, five teams disbanded because of financial problems. The Staleys finished the year 10-1-1 and were declared the official champions of the APFA—the first recognized titleholders in the history of professional football. But all the wins didn't translate into a profit. For the year, the Staleys ended up in the red, losing $71.63.

After the '21 season, Halas wanted to forge his own identity with the team. He was no longer obligated to call his squad the Staleys. Halas searched for a name that Chicagoans could identify with, a name that reminded them of sports in their city. He reasoned that football players were bigger and meaner than the city's professional baseball players, who were called Cubs. So Halas, a longtime Cubs fan, decided that his boys should be called the Bears. It was a one-man decision, and like many that Halas had made in the past, it was based on gut instinct. After switching the name, he reincorporated his team as the Chicago Bears Football Team.

Halas married his sweetheart, Min, on February 18, 1922. He had saved enough money to buy two round-trip train tickets to Tampa, Florida. Even though he was on his honeymoon, his conversations with his bride usually focused on football. Soon after they returned to Chicago, Halas rented a small first-floor apartment on Humphrey Avenue in the Oak Park section of the city. He had one request of the landlord: Always keep enough coal in the building's furnace to keep the couple warm during the cold Chicago winters.

In June the APFA held another owners' meeting in Canton. Halas had always detested the name American Professional Football Association. To him, it sounded second-class, pedestrian, not serious. He wanted a more regal-sounding name, something that people would take notice of and marvel at; a name that sounded credible, strong, and authoritative. At the meeting, he suggested that the American Professional Football Association be changed to the National Football League—the NFL. In a matter of minutes, the owners agreed to Halas's proposal and adopted the name change.

The Bears ended their 1922 season 9-3, finishing second in the league standings behind the Canton Bulldogs. That fall, Halas's wife worked as the team's administrative secretary. She kept the books, fired off letters dictated by her husband, and clipped every newspaper story she could find that mentioned the Bears, storing the articles in a bread box. Meanwhile, Halas continued to write his own stories and press releases about his team, hoping to corral the attention of the local papers in the Chicagoland area. At the end of the season he submitted the first-ever "All-America" professional team to newspapers across the nation. Attached to the roster was a note to editors that read, "It might be amusing to wonder what would happen to college heroes if they had to smack up against this super eleven."

When Halas studied his financial numbers following the '22 season, he liked what he saw. The Bears had turned a profit of $1,476.92.

Still, his mother wasn't impressed. When Halas told her that the Bears' season ended in the black, she replied, "George, go back to the railroad, dear. You'll have steady income there."

Her words rang even truer the following season. The 1923 Bears went 9-2-1 and finished second in the NFL, but lost $366.72. Every team in the league, in fact, struggled to stay afloat. Halas was so concerned about his lack of money that he started selling cars during the off-season. His co-owner, Sternaman, ran a gas station.

Life became even more complicated for Halas when, on January 5, 1923, his wife gave birth to a daughter, Virginia Marion. Wanting to show that he was financially stable, Halas wrote on her birth certificate that his profession was a civil engineer, not an owner of an NFL team. He moved his family to a cheaper apartment at 4356 West Washington Boulevard, where, from an overstuffed office, he ran the day-to-day operations of his Chicago Bears. As 1923 gave way to '24, Halas didn't know how much longer he could stay in the game. The press was largely ignoring the NFL; instead the sports pages were filled with stories about baseball and its star Babe Ruth; about college football and its glamorous coaches like the University of Pittsburgh's Pop Warner and Chicago's Amos Alonzo Stagg. And fans weren't attending pro games like Halas had banked on. In 1923 the Bears' largest home crowd wasn't even 10,000; the Cubs, by contrast, drew over 700,000 that year and had a high crowd of 35,000 for one game against the Giants on July 28.

So as Halas sat in his office and pondered his football future in the autumn of 1924, he was a bundle of nerves. He knew the only way he could save his team—and, likely, the NFL—was to sign that elusive megastar player, one who transcended the game, one who could draw even nonsports fans to Cubs Park. This was why, on November 1, 1924, just two weeks after Illinois defeated Michigan, 39–14, in one of the greatest games in the history of college football, Halas, his wife, and a friend drove 140 miles south to Champaign. There was a young man playing in a football game that day he wanted to see.

7

WORTH COMING THOUSANDS OF
MILES TO SEE

They *cruised over* the back roads of Illinois on a gray but warm Saturday morning in 1924, motoring closer to Memorial Stadium and the player that George Halas wanted to see with his own eyes. Riding in an open-air Hudson automobile, Halas, Min, and his friend Ralph Brizzolara—who had been the best man at their wedding—passed low, rolling fields of recently harvested wheat and corn. Brizzolara had borrowed the car from his father, and he was behind the driver's wheel. This allowed Halas to relax. As he and his wife munched on egg sandwiches that she made that morning, Halas giddily sang his favorite song, "Alice Blue Gown."

> *I once had a gown it was almost new,*
> *Oh, the daintiest thing, it was sweet Alice blue;*
> *With little forget-me-nots placed here and there*
> *When I had it on, I walked on the air.*

The joviality continued for most of the trip. Halas was beside himself; the thought of seeing Harold "Red" Grange caused his spirits to skyrocket. For the last three years, Halas had been reading newspaper accounts about Red and his exploits at Wheaton High and at Illinois. Yet Halas had never personally seen him play, which made Grange seem almost supernatural. Perusing those news stories, Halas had to use his imagination to visualize what Grange was doing on the field. And in the moving pictures of his mind, relying on the florid words that sportswriters employed when describing Grange's feats, Halas envisioned a player who was as golden as the sun, as unstoppable as a freight train. But this was part of the powerful allure of Grange. Because few people actually saw him play in person, his legend grew larger with every story that was written about him, with every dazzling game. Halas was just like nearly every other sports fan in the autumn of 1924: He believed, sight unseen, that Red Grange was the best football player to ever walk the earth.

Halas was determined to eventually sign Grange to play for his Chicago Bears. He'd written several letters to Grange but received no reply. He'd even phoned the halfback at his fraternity house, but the conversation had lasted only a few minutes. Grange hung up without making a commitment or even showing the slightest bit of interest in joining the Bears. Everyone wanted a piece of Red Grange—coaches, teammates, fans, sportswriters, students, teachers, fraternity brothers—but the young man just wanted to be left alone. He was a college football player and a student; that was enough for him.

When the Halases and Brizzolara arrived at Memorial Stadium, storm clouds rolled over the Illinois prairie while cold drops of rain fell from the overcast sky. Halas put on a slicker and trudged toward the stadium. When he took his seat and spotted the redheaded Grange on the field for the first time, outfitted in his familiar number 77 blue and orange uniform, Halas nearly went hoarse cheering.

Grange put on another riveting show. Two weeks after he ran wild against Michigan, when he scored six touchdowns and accounted for 402 offensive yards, Grange carried the ball 37 times against the Iowa Hawkeyes, scoring two touchdowns in the first quarter and totaling 186 yards in Illinois's 36–0 victory. Grange could have run for more yards, but Zuppke pulled him out of the game for the final quarter to rest him for next week's important game against the University of Chicago.

Halas, his voice almost gone, left the stadium contemplating his future plans. Grange had done something that even Halas couldn't believe: He proved to be as good in person as he was in print. *One day he'll be mine,* Halas thought as he walked through the fading light to his friend's car.

A*fter his tour-de-force* performances against Michigan and Iowa, Grange became a staple in the motion picture houses across America. In 1924 an estimated sixty million Americans—more than half the population—attended theaters each week. But it wasn't just the feature films that drew people to the shows. Before each film, theaters would typically run a ten-minute reel of news and sports highlights— "shorts," they were called. And by the mid-1920s, no athlete appeared more often or glowed brighter in these clips than Grange. On the big screen, the action appeared herky-jerky, staccato, but Grange somehow moved with unmatched grace, sprinting in fluid, confident motions past defenders, like a comet across the night sky. He was different from everyone else, that much was certain in these newsreels, and the images of him increased the hunger of fans across the nation to see him live, in the flesh.

More than thirty-two thousand fans crammed into the University of Chicago's Stagg Field to see this rising phenomenon, while thousands more loitered outside the concrete structure, hoping to buy a last-minute ticket. It would cost them: Demand was so great that on game day, $2 seats were selling for as much as $100 on the scalper's market. Before kickoff, several Chicago students climbed a nearby wall, giving them a view of the field. Once the game started, one student, holding a megaphone, shouted a play-by-play account of the action to the students and fans milling about outside the stadium.

With a record of 3-1-1, Chicago was the underdog. But the Maroons started quickly, scoring two early touchdowns to seize a 14–0 lead. Stagg had spent weeks preparing his boys for this contest with a simple game plan: Control the ball on offense by running straight into the heart of the Illinois defense. The Chicago players were bigger, stronger, and slower than the Illini. Stagg believed he could pound running plays between the tackles and slowly advance the ball down the field. This would wear down the Illinois defense and bleed time off the clock, giving Grange fewer opportunities to inflict damage on offense.

The strategy worked beautifully in the first quarter. But after Chicago's second score, Zuppke chose to receive the following kickoff—a rare tactic in this era. A team normally kicked off after the opposing team scored, the belief being that it could hold the receiving team deep in its own territory and force a punt to acquire good field position. But Zuppke scuttled this strategy because he knew the only way he could win was by putting the ball in Grange's hands play after play.

He sent Grange into the game as a return man. A few minutes later, after Grange had broken through the line for several nifty runs and completed a few passes, he took a pitch from the Illini quarterback at Chicago's 4-yard line. He scampered around the right end to score a touchdown. After the extra point, the Maroons' lead was trimmed to 14–7.

The rest of the game seesawed back and forth. Chicago scored another touchdown late in the second quarter to take a 21–7 lead. Then Grange plowed over the goal line from 3 yards out, making the score 21–14 at halftime. As Grange ambled to the locker room, he was already as sore as he'd been all season. The bigger Chicago players hit him hard on nearly every play, often jumping on Grange when he was already lying on the ground. In the locker room, a trainer massaged his body.

In the third quarter, as the Chicago defense started to wear down, Grange came on. He sprinted 80 yards for a touchdown, tying the score at 21. Then, late in the game, Grange fielded a pitch from the quarterback, circled to his left, then blazed up the field in a blur. It was as if a Grange highlight from a film short was coming to life, the way he effortlessly outran the Chicago defenders. He was finally pushed out of bounds by a player who had the angle at the Maroons' 39-yard line after a 51-yard gain, and the Chicago fans fell silent. But an official threw a penalty flag during the run, calling offensive holding. The penalty pushed the ball back deep into Illinois's own territory. Moments later, the game ended. Final score: Chicago 21, Illinois 21.

Grange had rushed for 300 yards and passed for another 150

yards. Walter Camp, who had traveled from his home in New Haven, Connecticut, and watched the action from the sideline, was in awe of Grange's play. "It was worth coming thousands of miles to see," Camp told a reporter. When Camp named Grange to his 1924 All-America team at season's end, he wrote, "Harold Grange is the marvel of this year's backfield. His work in the Michigan game was a revelation, but his performance in the Chicago game went even further when by his play—running and passing—he accounted for some 450 yards of territory. He is elusive, has a baffling change of pace, a good straight-arm, and, finally, seems in some way to get a map of the field at starting and then threads his way through his opponents."

But the Chicago game exacted a toll on Grange. He was a walking bruise, which diminished his ability to run in the final two games of the season. Against Minnesota in Minneapolis, Grange scored on a 10-yard sprint early in the first quarter, his only memorable play. He had rushed for 56 yards when, late in the third quarter, a Minnesota defender tackled him hard, and he landed squarely on his shoulder. He didn't return, and Illinois lost, 20–7. An X-ray taken the following day revealed that Grange had suffered a dislocated shoulder, ending his season. The next week, the orange-and-blue beat Ohio State, 7–0, in their season finale. Illinois finished the 1924 season in second place in the Big Ten behind Stagg's Chicago squad.

Illinois *didn't earn* an invitation to a postseason bowl game, but Grange's play still cast a shadow that stretched over the entire landscape of college football in the final months of 1924, spreading as far as the East Coast. In December the *New York Times* wrote, "It is seldom that a player's fame spreads so rapidly and definitely throughout the country. Grange is known and his deeds are followed from coast to coast with almost the same interest as in his own section of the country."

Grange completed his spring semester and returned home in the summer of 1925. He enjoyed slipping back into the familiar rhythms of Wheaton and its slow-paced lifestyle. But he was famous now, which meant that Wheaton was no longer the retreat it once was. Reporters followed him as he resumed his job delivering ice. One *New York Times* writer, who traveled to Wheaton, noted that Grange made only $30 a week but that he "likes his job because, he says, it's real work and keeps him fit." But Grange didn't enjoy the attention. Still shy and introverted, he couldn't understand why people became tongue tied around him and why, even at his neighborhood diner, people would point and stare. When he made his rounds on his ice route, he frequently posed for pictures with his customers. And several women, to whom Grange had been delivering for years, suddenly started appearing in their most expensive Sunday dresses when he knocked on their door. Even his boss, Luke Thompson, began acting differently around Red, using Grange's name to promote his company and its recent relocation.

Red was uncomfortable with it all. He tried to maintain as low a profile as possible wherever he went, but it was impossible for him to avoid detection because nearly everyone in town wanted to be close to him, wanted to bask in the glow of his fame. But Grange just wanted to get on with the business of playing football in his senior year; then, perhaps, he would become a sportswriter or pursue a career in movies. All summer, rumors flew in Wheaton and in Champaign that Grange had already received several contracts ranging from $25,000 to $300,000 to act in movies. He did take a screen test in Milwaukee with producers from Universal Pictures Company, but never signed a contract. He was waiting for the right offer.

Early in the summer Grange received a note from Zuppke, who wrote letters to all of his players about an upcoming game that fall against the University of Pennsylvania. Illinois had lost several important players to graduation—end Frank Rokusek, tackle Dick Hall, guards Lou Slimmer and Roy Miller, center Gil Roberts, and backs Wally McIlwain and Heinie Schultz—and the coach knew that his team wasn't going to be as strong as it had been in 1924. He didn't admit it to reporters, but the Illini were essentially going to be a one-man team in '25.

Zuppke's letters stirred his boys' passions. He wrote that no one on the East Coast—not the sportswriters from the highbrow eastern newspapers, not the fans, and certainly not the Penn coaches and players—believed Illinois could stay close to the Quakers in a game, much less beat them. This was the same motivational card that Zuppke had pulled from his deck a year earlier for the Illinis' game against Michigan. It worked so well then that he decided to try it again.

Zuppke viewed a match-up against Penn as a measuring stick for his program. The Quakers, a longtime powerhouse in college football, were members of the sport's ruling class, along with Harvard, Princeton, and Yale. Between 1900 and 1925, Penn won nearly 90 percent of its games. Zuppke had been firing up his boys for the contest since late in the '24 season. One day at practice in November, Zuppke asked the players who would be returning for the '25 season to gather around him. He hadn't yet told them that he'd already added Penn to next year's schedule. He yelled, "You boys who will be back next year, how would you like to play the University of Pennsylvania on their home grounds in Philadelphia?"

The players hollered their approval.

"All right then," Zuppke said, "I'll see what I can do."

Zuppke had planted a seed. More than anything, he wanted to prove against Penn that a Midwest team could travel across the country and topple an established eastern power on its home turf. Even before the '24 season was over, Zuppke pored over scouting reports that detailed all of Penn's tendencies on offense and defense. He was looking for any weakness he could find—and looking for a way to introduce Grange with a bang to everyone in the East.

The most important sportswriter in America, a writer who could sway public opinion like no other, still had not seen Grange play. Grantland Rice had been fascinated with Grange ever since his performance against Michigan in the fall of 1924. Rice had been referring to him as the Galloping Ghost for months. (Warren Brown, a sports reporter for the *Chicago American,* actually coined the nickname, but Rice popularized it.) In early October 1925, Rice, who worked for the *New York Herald Tribune,* rode a train to Champaign to watch Grange play against the University of Nebraska Cornhuskers in Illinois's first game of the season.

Illinois had been beset by injuries before even taking the field.

Garland, Grange's little brother, emerged as a standout speedy half-back on the freshman team in '24. Expected to be a running threat on the varsity team, he suffered an injury in preseason practice and dropped out of school to return to Wheaton. Starting quarterback Harry Hall wasn't ready to play, still suffering from a weak collarbone he'd broken against Minnesota in the 1924 season finale. Because of the injuries, Rice didn't believe that the Illini had much of a chance to defeat the heavily favored Cornhuskers, who were led by an All-America tackle named Ed Weir.

On the eve of the game, Rice wrote: "[It would take] great football to beat this Nebraska team, and Illinois will run into heavy trouble, even with Grange, unless the somewhat green Zuppke forwards [linemen] can face the pressure without caving in . . . Grange will be tested tomorrow up to any human limit, and if he can make any notable headway against this rival in his first contest, he will add another fresh supply of laurel branches to his college collection of the same."

Playing in front of nearly thirty thousand fans at Memorial Stadium on a crisp autumn day, Grange was bottled up all afternoon. From the opening whistle, Grange had no room to run; his offensive line was no match for the big boys from Nebraska. Ed Weir, not Grange, dominated. The strapping Cornhusker tackle was virtually unblockable, taking Grange down for several losses. Grange gained only 57 yards rushing and failed to make even one first down. Nebraska won, 13–0, and Illinois suffered its first loss at Memorial Stadium since the dedication. Afterward many East Coast sportswriters who had made the long journey to Champaign to get a glimpse of Grange suggested that Red wasn't as good as he'd been portrayed; that he certainly wasn't a larger-than-life football hero. On this day, he was just an ordinary football player on an ordinary team. Rice, wearing his standard gray fedora, wasn't impressed as he left the press box and walked into the cool prairie night to begin his long trip home to New York.

But over the next two weeks, Grange started hitting his rhythm with his young offensive line. On October 10, he dashed for a 70-yard touchdown run against Butler in Illinois's 16–13 win. The following week, against Iowa, he ran back the opening kickoff 85 yards for a touchdown and accounted for more than 250 yards of offense in the Illinis' 12–10 loss to the Hawkeyes. Although the orange-and-blue weren't as talented as they had been the previous season, Grange was coming on. Writers on the East Coast may have written Grange off, but two men in Chicago were convinced that his best days were yet to come. As Grange prepared for Illinois's next two opponents— Michigan and Penn—the two men held a clandestine meeting that would have a bigger impact on the future of pro football in America than either could have ever imagined.

8

CASH AND CARRY

I*t was a regular workday* for George Halas. Sitting behind his desk in his office at the team's new headquarters at 111 West Washington Street, he toiled over the same things he always did in October of each football season: writing press releases, diagramming new plays, studying scouting reports and searching for weaknesses in his upcoming opponents, dreaming up fresh promotions to lure fans to Cubs Park, and examining his ever-shrinking budget. In the autumn of 1925, Halas was as concerned as he'd ever been about his franchise. His team was losing money—nearly every franchise in the newly minted NFL was in the red—and he didn't know how long his Bears could survive. Maybe his mother was right; working for the railroad *would* have been a lot safer.

As Halas prepared for his team's next game on this afternoon, a visitor came through the door, stepped rapidly across the office and sat down in a chair in front of Halas. After a quick hello, he asked, *Would you like Red Grange to play for your team?*

The visitor announced himself as Frank Zambreno. He explained that he was a native of Chicago and an associate of a man named Charles C. Pyle, a movie theater owner who lived in Champaign. Zambreno confided to Halas that Pyle had a plan. He was going to convince Red Grange to allow him to hire him as his business manager and agent. Once Grange had agreed to this, Pyle would direct him to immediately sign a contract with the Bears. Zambreno now wanted to know whether Halas was interested.

"I am," said Halas, who considered Grange to be as perfect a player as God had ever created. He had even planned to pursue Grange once his college career at the University of Illinois was over, but now here was this man, materializing out of nowhere, saying he could hand deliver the Galloping Ghost to the Bears. Halas never dreamed it would be this easy to sign Grange, because he anticipated having to fight off every other NFL team and engaging in some high bidding for Grange's services. Maybe, Halas thought, his luck was starting to turn.

About the same time as the conversation between Halas and Zambreno, Grange strolled into the Virginia Theatre in Champaign to see the movie *The Freshman,* a new burlesque comedy starring Harold Lloyd as a bespectacled, naïve college football player named Harold Lamb who rises from obscurity to become a star player. It wasn't lost on audiences that, in many ways, the character of Harold Lamb imitated the life of Harold Grange, which only heightened Grange's growing fame. Hearing rave reviews about the movie, Grange paid 50 cents for a ticket and ambled into the 1,525-seat movie house with a ceiling dome finished in silver leaf. Before Grange could find a seat, an usher approached him. After quickly scribbling a note on a piece of paper, the usher handed it to Grange along with a free pass to the Virginia and Park theaters. The note read: "Mr. Pyle who runs this theatre wants you to have this. It's a pass that'll get you in the Virginia Theatre as often as you want for the rest of the year. And you can use it for the Park Theater, too, since Mr. Pyle operates both places." Grange happily accepted the pass, his first free gift for playing football at Illinois.

A couple evenings later, after a long day of practice, Grange returned to the Virginia. After showing the usher his get-in-free card, Grange sauntered into the lobby, adorned in a Spanish Renaissance design with busts of Spanish adventurers such as Hernán Cortés and Francisco Hernández de Córdoba. Pyle was an American adventurer, and as soon as he spotted Grange, he rushed toward him with a beaming smile on his face. Extending his hand, he introduced himself and invited Grange up to his second-floor office to chat for a few minutes.

They climbed a staircase and entered Pyle's spacious office. As the six-foot-one, 195-pound Pyle took a seat behind his desk, Grange closely studied the forty-five-year-old theater owner. His most striking facial feature was his thin, neatly trimmed mustache. His graying, dark hair was slicked back with pomade. Dressed impeccably, he wore a well-tailored suit accompanied by distinguishing accoutrements: spats, a silk tie with a diamond stickpin, a fine derby hat, and a polished walking stick. This man was class personified, Grange thought. In the past, Red had always felt shy when meeting people for the first time, but he was slowly shedding that protective cocoon. He was now a confident young man—his success on the football field bolstered his self-esteem.

The two exchanged pleasantries and briefly shot the bull. Then Pyle asked with the slyest of smiles, "How would you like to make one hundred thousand dollars, or maybe even a million?"

Grange's body stiffened. This sounded too good to be true, and he suspected that Pyle was offering a bribe.

"You'll have to get someone else," Grange replied.

Pyle explained that everything he had in mind for Grange was on the up-and-up, perfectly legal, but that he couldn't provide the details right now. The time wasn't right. But he had a plan, Pyle said, and if everything worked out the way he believed it would, then both he and Grange would soon have more money in their bank accounts than even the fat cats on Wall Street, where the market was booming. Give me a few weeks, Pyle said, and let me line things up. He shook Grange's hand and explained that he'd be in touch as soon as his plan was ready.

Grange left the office, wondering two things: Was this suave-looking man full of hot air, or was he a man of his word? And, more important, who the heck was this Charles Pyle anyway?

On March 25, 1882, Charles Cassius Pile was born in Van Wert, Ohio. Seven years later, his father, William, who had been a farmer, moved his family to Delaware, Ohio, where he planned to become a minister. But before the family hitched up a wagon and made the 115-mile trek, William changed the spelling of the family surname from Pile to Pyle. The jokes about his name—pile was slang for hemorrhoids—made it an easy decision. He feared that his congregation would snicker under their breaths every time he rose to speak. He also didn't want his young son to be the target of abuse in the schoolyard because of the jokes their last name spawned.

William suffered from tuberculosis, which slowly ate away at him. He coughed incessantly, often spitting up blood, and endured frequent high fevers. But when he stepped into the pulpit, his tongue turned silver as he spoke of the kingdom and glory of God. Little Charles, watching his dad closely from the pew, learned at a young age that a person could use his mind and his mouth rather than his muscles to make a living. After his father died in 1890, his mother told him he should become a man of the cloth, because already, at age eight, Charles Pyle had that magical gift of persuasion. His words were like fairy dust; once he sprinkled them over someone, it was as if the person were under his control.

With bright gray eyes and a warm, calm demeanor, Charles was the kind of child people immediately trusted and wanted to please. And Pyle played on this. He was sixteen years old when he promoted his first sporting event, a bicycle race between Barney Oldfield and a local kid named Holden. Oldfield was a famous race-car driver. In 1903 he would become the first driver ever to complete a lap on a one-mile track in a minute or less. When Henry Ford built two cars specifically for racing, he would ask Oldfield to drive one of his vehicles. He also raced bicycles. Pyle lured him to Delaware by dangling the juiciest of carrots: cash.

Pyle promised $25 to the winner, while he would keep $7 for organizing and promoting the race. In front of a small paying crowd, Oldfield crossed the finish line first and pocketed the victor's purse. But the real winner was Pyle, who felt a rush of excitement like no other when he counted his take. It was as if he'd found his true calling.

When he wasn't promoting small events like the bicycle race, the teenage Pyle worked as a grocery store clerk and as a train butcher. Smiling brightly, he'd walk through the passenger cars and sell items such as cigarettes, fruit, and candy. Though he wasn't even old enough to shave, he relished the interaction with the public and the chance to see the world outside of Delaware.

At the age of sixteen, Pyle developed pleurisy, an inflammation of the membrane surrounding the lungs that causes chronic coughing and shortness of breath. Later in his life, Pyle told reporters he contracted it from a basketball injury, though this was likely a white lie to conceal his often frail health, like his father's condition. The family doctor suggested that he move to a dry, arid environment to ease his condition.

This was the opportunity he had been waiting for. His mother wanted Pyle to enroll at Ohio Wesleyan University and pursue the clergy, but Pyle had bigger dreams. His work as a train butcher had given him a glimpse of the world, and now he wanted to explore it, to make his own way and forge his own identity. Not only that, but Pyle believed he needed to leave his small town to make his fortune. He was determined to earn enough money to lift his mother, who made and sold dresses, out of her working-class existence. So in 1900, at the age of eighteen, Pyle kissed his mother on the cheek and stepped onto a train that would take him to California, traveling west in search of riches like the gold miners of the mid-1800s.

Pyle quickly talked his way into a job selling time-service clocks for Western Union. He tried to convince passengers at every depot and others on station platforms on his way west to buy one of his clocks. Though Pyle had a way with words and evinced the trusting quality of a reverend, few bought his clocks. After several weeks, he was out of money. He ditched the clock business and began selling the extra railroad passes that he'd acquired in his weeks on the rails. Pyle made a few dollars, but he still wasn't content operating this one-man travel agency. He wanted to do something bigger, something grander, something that would make him so much money that he could buy whatever he wanted whenever he ventured into department stores.

Pyle eventually settled in the mountains of northwestern California in the small town of Trinity, where the Trinity Gold Mining Company was flourishing. What little money he had to his name vanished one night during a card game. In just a few hands, he'd gone broke. Pyle was stuck in a foreign place with few friends and even fewer opportunities to find employment. Life looked bleak.

He spent days scheming and dreaming of ways he could fill his pockets with cash. His thoughts kept drifting back to the bicycle race that he had organized in Delaware. That $7 profit he'd made was so effortless, so quick. He made a decision: He needed to find another sporting event to promote. He didn't know anyone famous in Trinity, so he decided that the event, not the personalities of the participants, had to be the prime draw. He needed a sport with wide appeal, one that could attract a crush of spectators. He opted for the bloodiest sport he knew: boxing.

Pyle didn't look like an athlete; certainly not a boxer. He was tall and rail thin, and his pleurisy often caused him to wheeze when he breathed. But he needed money, and he figured the quickest way to earn cash was to be both an actor on the stage and a promoter behind the scenes. So Pyle would fight. But first he needed a hook to entice spectators to a boxing match. He eventually found it when he learned that a local miner had injured his thumb. To help the miner and his family, Pyle promised to donate half the proceeds to them.

Pyle then found an elderly man who agreed to fight him. A former miner and amateur boxer, Pyle's opponent weighed only 112 pounds and couldn't even stand straight, the result of having spent his life in the mines. Neither combatant was distinguished, but this didn't stop Pyle from promoting the coming bout as if the two were the most feared prizefighters alive. Pyle put up posters all around town and told all the people he came across that they would witness one of the great events in sports history when he walked into the ring to challenge the aging miner.

On the day of the event, some 210 miners paid $1 each to watch Pyle go to battle. The turnout raised the prize stakes; Pyle knew he could make over $100 with a knockout punch. But as soon as the opening bell rang, Pyle went on the defensive. He had trouble landing blows to his opponent's hunched body. And the former miner showed surprising spunk and strength as he attacked Pyle, displaying the toughness forged from a lifetime spent working a drill. After several minutes of fighting, Pyle's face was cut and splattered with his own blood. To the howling and hooting crowd, it looked like another punch or two would put Pyle on the ground.

But Pyle, realizing his financial health was on the line, stormed back. He landed several hard punches late in the fight. When the fight was declared over, both men were standing. The judges, after a brief discussion, declared the bout a draw. Each fighter received $52.50, a lifetime of earnings to Pyle. For a few cuts, bumps, and bruises, he had a measure of financial freedom.

With a renewed determination to make his mark on the world, Pyle moved from California to Silverton, Oregon, landing a job with an acting troupe that performed plays at venues throughout the Northwest. Pyle received $10 a week to be the Margarita Fischer Company's advance man. A few days before the traveling act moved to its next destination, Pyle would place placards all around the next town, promoting its upcoming show. He would do anything and everything to get the word out about the Fischer troupe of twelve actors, including talking a blue streak to bartenders, mayors, and shopkeepers. He could flatter people like few could—the quickest way for him to earn trust and get what he wanted.

He was a natural. With his father's flair for words, he could smooth-talk anyone who would listen into attending a show. He had memorized a convincing pitch that could sell Brooklyn Bridges and was delivered with great speed and gusto—just like the elixir salesmen of years past. Pyle also began to assume more responsibility with the company. He painted scenery, worked the ticket booth, and booked travel arrangements for the company. He even wrote puffy, superlative-laced reviews of the shows, which he then sent to newspapers in California and Oregon, where the articles frequently appeared. And whenever he talked to reporters, he always had an arsenal of ready quips and quotable lines to deliver.

For several months, Pyle learned the craft of promotion. More important, he learned what made people tick, what they desired, what they were willing to spend their hard-earned money on. He didn't know it at the time, but he was learning how to become a sports agent and world-class promoter.

Following his Illinois teammate Earl Britton, Grange charges up the field against Michigan on October 18, 1924, in what was hyped by sportswriters as the original "Game of the Century." By the end of the afternoon, Grange would become a national sensation after he ran for five touchdowns—four in the first 12 minutes—and rushed for 402 yards against a team that hadn't lost in two years. GETTY IMAGES

Grange first flashed his once-in-a-generation talent at Wheaton High School in Wheaton, Illinois. Here in the fall of 1920 the seventeen-year-old Grange is seated third from the left, front row.

Beginning at the age of sixteen, Grange worked as an iceman every summer for seven years. The hard labor was the perfect workout regimen for a budding football star. It also added another layer of mystique to the legend of the Galloping Ghost— and made him an icon for the working class.

The one moment that had a bigger impact on the future of the NFL than any other: the signing of Red Grange to a professional contract. With his agent, C. C. Pyle, on his left and Bear co-owners George Halas (seated next to Grange) and Dutch Sternaman on his right, Grange puts his name on the piece of a paper that would make him a wealthy man—and the NFL's first star.

WHEATON COLLEGE (ILL.) SPECIAL COLLECTIONS

Soon after signing his contract with the Bears, Grange splurged and purchased a fashionable raccoon coat—the ultimate sign in 1925 of a man who had made a mint. Here he's shaking the hand of his stoic yet proud father, Lyle, the police chief of Wheaton.

WHEATON COLLEGE (ILL.) SPECIAL COLLECTIONS

On the verge of bankruptcy, Halas staked his professional career on Grange, signing him to the richest contract in NFL history in the fall of 1925. After welcoming him to the Bears, Halas would have plenty to smile about. GETTY IMAGES

Minutes before his professional debut against the Chicago Cardinals on November 26, 1925, Grange stands on the sideline at Cubs Park with all eyes on him. It was estimated that more than 200,000 fans were turned away at the gate because the game was sold out. A week earlier the Bears couldn't even draw 10,000.
GETTY IMAGES

What made Grange so special when he had the ball in his hands? No one in the history of the game before him could cut, twist, stiff-arm, and sprint away from defenders with such ease and grace. With Grange, football was as much ballet as brute force, as he shows here in what was the most important game of the barnstorming tour and in NFL history: Chicago versus New York on December 6, 1925, in the Polo Grounds.
WHEATON COLLEGE (ILL.) SPECIAL COLLECTIONS

Reticent as a child and teenager, Grange was forced out of his shell because of the public's insatiable desire to hear him speak. At every depot the Bears pulled into during their barnstorming tour, Grange would stand on an elevated platform and utter remarks to packed crowds that sometimes reached as many as ten thousand. WHEATON COLLEGE (ILL.) SPECIAL COLLECTIONS

As his celebrity grew, so too did Grange's appeal to women. Everywhere he went during the barnstorming tour, women asked the Galloping Ghost for photographs—and much more.
WHEATON COLLEGE (ILL.) SPECIAL COLLECTIONS

When the Bears stopped in Washington, D.C., during the barnstorming tour, Grange met with Illinois senator William McKinley (right of Grange). The senator then chaperoned Grange and Halas to the White House for a meet and greet with President Calvin Coolidge. When told that Grange played for the Bears, the confused president, who thought Grange was a bear keeper, responded, "I always did love animal acts." LIBRARY OF CONGRESS

No athlete in America in the mid-1920s— not Babe Ruth, not Jack Dempsey, not Bill Tilden—received more fan mail than Red Grange. WHEATON COLLEGE (ILL.) SPECIAL COLLECTIONS

As stipulated in his contract with the Bears, Grange sat out two quarters of every game during the barnstorming tour to preserve his health. Whenever he was on the bench, Halas (left of Grange) was close by. No coach and player in NFL history would have a bigger influence on the growth of the professional game than this duo. GETTY IMAGES

Pyle was never far from Grange's side during the barnstorming days. Not only was Pyle his agent, but he also served at different times as Grange's PR man, bodyguard, secretary, and dinner companion.

Even in the winters of their lives, Halas (seated left) and Grange remained close friends. They were both members of the charter class that was inducted into the NFL Hall of Fame in 1963.

• • •

Pyle's mother sent her son several telegrams asking him to come home to Ohio and study to become a minister. Pyle agreed to pay her a visit, but he wanted to show her that he was already a smashing success. So using the money that he'd made with the Margarita Fischer Company, he bought the finest outfit of his life at a department store. When he arrived home, he told everyone—including his mother—that he was a lumber executive in the Pacific Northwest and was making more money than he knew what to do with.

Appearance was everything to Pyle, and he conned everyone in his hometown. Yet when it was time for him to travel by rail back to Portland, Oregon, where he would meet up with the acting company, Pyle didn't have enough money to pay for the entire trip. When his locomotive pulled into Great Falls, Montana, in the dead of night, Pyle was nearly penniless.

As always, Pyle had a plan. While he had been sitting in his Pullman car, Pyle wondered how many miles Great Falls was from other cities around the globe; places like New York, London, Paris, and Tokyo. Pyle believed that residents of Great Falls would be interested in this information and would be willing to pay for it, so Pyle spent his last remaining coins on an atlas and carefully calculated the distances. He then designed a poster of Great Falls that included all of the geographical information as well as the state's game laws. Taking the poster from shop to shop around the city, he asked store owners to buy advertisements that could be placed into a four-page leaflet that would feature all of the information on the poster. Nearly a dozen merchants bit, buying more than ten thousand copies. With $60 of profit in his pocket, Pyle left Great Falls and traveled to Portland, where he rejoined the acting troupe.

He fell in love. Pyle was smitten the first time he laid eyes on Dorothy Fischer, whose father owned the theater company. They married in September 1905 and had a baby girl, Katherine, two years later. But the childbirth was hard on Dorothy, and after the pregnancy she fell chronically ill, which stressed the marriage. Dot, as everyone called her, was eventually hospitalized with a malady that no doctors could identify. Three years later, Pyle walked away from the marriage without even filing for divorce, leaving his wife and child to fend for themselves.

He started his own acting company and became the star of several traveling shows, including *The Tennessee Partner* and *The Golden Giant Mine*. He staged *Uncle Tom's Cabin* with a four-person cast and *The Three Musketeers* with only one musketeer. He was so creative—and stingy with his pocketbook—that he sometimes had one actor play two roles in the same scene and have a dialogue with himself or herself. Pyle's love of the theater and staging allowed him to cultivate a keen sense of timing; an awareness of the precise moment when something needed to be said. He also developed a sharpened sense of the actor's touch—his voice inflections, his facial expressions, and his body gestures. He could deliver a line with the best of them, a skill that would serve him well for the rest of his life.

Pyle continued to figure out ingenious ways to make money. He organized a big tent show, which he called C. C. Pyle's Greater Lewis & Clark International Exposition. Opening in Moscow, Idaho, it grossed only $7 the first night. The show was a bust—one of many in Pyle's career—and closed almost as soon as it opened.

He then tried his hand in movie houses, which attracted large crowds in the early 1900s. He went into partnership with a California businessman named F. W. Parker, and the two purchased a theater in Eureka, California. Pyle named it Theatre Margarita. Pyle had come up with a unique concept to entice the public: Instead of charging customers for admission up front, he would allow them to pay later—a kind of movie credit card. But the payment system backfired when people failed to pay their overdue bills. Once again, Pyle lost nearly all of his money.

Pyle later bought a projection machine and some films and then hit the road. He earned good money for two years showing the movies in theaters around the Midwest, but because of a few poor investments, he lost everything and was forced to sell his equipment. Before he was even thirty, Pyle had lost more money than most people made in a lifetime.

His next stop was Boise, Idaho, where he found an empty store on Main Street. Though his bank account was drained, he charmed a banker into giving him enough cash so he could sign a two-year lease on the store at $100 a month. Envisioning a movie theater in the space, he instructed a carpenter to build seats inside and a ticket booth outside. The carpenter asked for money so he could buy all the materials he needed.

"Come with me," Pyle said, leading him to the local lumberyard. Pyle told the head of the lumberyard to bill his new movie theater for all of the carpenter's expenses. "Give this man everything he wants," Pyle said, and the deal was done.

Soon after construction was under way, a local businessman approached Pyle about his project. Pyle saw this as an opportunity. He put the hard sell on the businessman, telling him how moving picture houses were the wave of the future, how a pot of gold awaited anyone willing to take a risk. The businessman soon signed on to be Pyle's fifty-fifty partner and paid him $2,500, giving Pyle more cash flow than he had ever had.

He had achieved his ultimate dream: the freedom to do whatever he pleased. Born with a chronic case of wanderlust, Pyle always looked for the next big gig, the big score, the big talent. He felt compelled to be constantly on the move to explore the country, to find where he could make the next big deal. When another businessman approached him to buy his share of the theater, Pyle quickly negotiated a deal. He took the money that he made in his partnership deal and paid off his debts to the carpenter and the lumberyard. Then he sold his 50 percent share in the movie house for another $2,500. Construction wasn't even finished yet, but Pyle had already made around $4,500 on the theater. Before the first show opened, he was on a train out of town in search of his next moneymaking endeavor.

He moved on to Pocatello, Idaho. Never one to play it safe, Pyle threw all of his money into an amusement park and vaudeville theater. The investment backfired. Local politicians soon passed a law that forbade amusement parks to operate on Sundays, a devastating blow. He lost money by the day, prompting him to abandon the business. In 1910 he moved to Chicago to see if he could find his fortune in the Windy City.

Pyle had $1,900 to his name when he arrived in the upper Midwest. But his bank account was threatened when Dorothy filed for divorce, demanding financial support for herself and their child. Pyle was able to talk his way out of it; he convinced the judge to rule in his favor and not grant her any alimony. Once again his silver tongue had saved him. Now unattached, he was looking forward to the second act in his life. He was hoping to come across the opportunity of a lifetime.

For the next fifteen years, Pyle led a relatively quiet life, content to stay in one place for the first time in his adulthood. He stuck with the movie business in Chicago and built a small film empire. He owned a chain of six theaters in Illinois, including one in Champaign, and when he learned that a young man named Red Grange frequented his theater, the wheels in Pyle's mind began to turn. Back in 1912, Pyle had offered Jim Thorpe, who won two gold medals in the 1912 Summer Olympics in Stockholm, Sweden, $10,000 to go on a baseball exhibition tour across the United States. Thorpe, on the advice of his football coach at the Carlisle Industrial Indian School, Glenn "Pop" Warner, turned Pyle down. Thorpe was the big one that got away. Pyle didn't plan on letting it happen again.

So Pyle wondered, *What if I promoted Grange and I could get him to play for the Chicago Bears?* Pyle considered all of the promotional possibilities that he could generate for this kid from Wheaton who, in the fall of 1925, had become a public fascination. Pyle envisioned every sort of business opportunity: There could be Red Grange dolls, Red Grange T-shirts, Red Grange candy bars, even movies starring Red Grange. The opportunities were almost limitless, given the sporting public's infatuation with the Galloping Ghost. Now Pyle just had to meet him. He had to get Grange in his theater and talk him into doing business, just as he had done with so many others his entire life.

After *his meeting* with Pyle at the Virginia Theatre, Grange continued his regular routine, staying as invisible as possible. In the morning and early afternoon, he attended classes, then returned to his fraternity house for a brief rest before heading to the football field, where he was Illinois's lone bright spot in its 1-2 start to the 1925 season.

To kick-start his sputtering offense, Zuppke approached Grange at practice one day. "Red, I think you should move to quarterback," the coach said. "If you call the signals, I think the boys will have confidence in you."

Grange liked the idea of handling the ball on every offensive play, of being able to control the ebb and flow of the game. But the switch wasn't easy. Zuppke personally tutored him for two weeks, spending time on the field and in the classroom, teaching him the art of quarterbacking. Instead of just running and letting his natural instincts take over, Grange now had to call the plays, organize his teammates, and make sure they were lined up in the proper positions. To succeed, Red had to know as much as his coach did, so Grange essentially lived by Zuppke's side in the days leading up to the Illinis' fourth game of the season, the contest against their most hated rival, Michigan.

It was Illinois's homecoming. A year had passed since Grange scored six touchdowns against the Wolverines in what was now widely considered the greatest single game performance in the history of American football, and on the morning of this game, ribbons and banners hung in front of every sorority and fraternity house. More orange-and-blue banners were draped on many of the brick buildings on Main Street. Back in Wheaton, Mayor Marion Pittsford signed a proclamation declaring October 24 a holiday in honor of Grange. On game day, Wheaton became a ghost town, as all major businesses along Main Street shuttered their doors so that their employees could attend the contest.

Michigan was determined to stop Grange, no matter the consequences. Before the game, Wolverines coach Fielding Yost had anticipated that Grange would quarterback the Illini. He instructed his defenders not to bite on any fake handoffs; they were to focus their attention on Grange. He ordered his star player, Bennie Friedman, who played quarterback on offense and linebacker on defense, to shadow Grange on every offensive play that Illinois ran; to stick to him so closely that he could smell his breath.

A cold rain fell on Champaign the morning of the game, a miserable autumn day. But the contest had been sold out for weeks, and thirty minutes before kickoff, the stands were full. More than twenty thousand people were turned away at the gate; many milled around the perimeter of Memorial Stadium for a few hours, monitoring the action by the rise and fall of the crowd noise.

When he jogged from the locker room and onto the field, wearing his number 77 jersey, the crowd lifted a roar that could be heard on the other side of campus. The Michigan team seemed energized by the surge. Before kickoff, Yost yelled above the din to his players that they needed to follow Grange on every play as if their lives depended on it, that they couldn't let him run loose like last time. Yost had decided to fire coach George Little midway through last season's game and insert himself back on the sideline. Since Grange had torn through the Wolverines defense, not a day had gone by that Yost didn't think about him. It was now time for vengeance; to restore Michigan's rightful place in the Big Ten.

For the next two hours, the Wolverine defense punished Grange. Though the rain stopped an hour before the opening kickoff, the field was soaked, which hampered footing. Grange, at quarterback, didn't break free for any long runs. When he did scamper into the open field, his lack of footing prevented him from dashing into the end zone.

Just before halftime, Grange handed the ball to Earl Britton, who then flung a pass deep down the field. But a Michigan defender stepped in front of the Illinois receiver to intercept the ball at midfield. Several plays later, Michigan kicked a 24-yard field goal, which proved to be the only points in the game. The Wolverines spoiled Illinois's homecoming, 3–0.

No one was more disappointed than Grange. Though he gained 147 yards on the ground, he felt he'd let down his team, his school, his town, and his fans. But there was simply nowhere for him to run. In the locker room, Zuppke reminded Grange that he could still author a spectacular senior season, starting with the next game against the University of Pennsylvania on its home field. Zuppke had been talking to his players about Penn since the summer, believing that the game—and the outcome—would define the season.

Many sportswriters had declared Penn the national champions a year earlier, and now the Quakers had opened the 1925 season 5-0.

The eastern press, eager for its first up-close look at Grange, pegged Penn as a four-touchdown favorite. Grantland Rice predicted that Grange "may have no chance against Penn, for the Penn line will outplay Illinois unless the Brown, Yale, and Chicago battles have worn away its zest and impending weariness slows up its charges."

George Halas couldn't catch a break. At Stagg Field, which was ten miles south of Cubs Park, over fifty thousand fans regularly poured through the turnstiles on Saturday afternoons to watch the University of Chicago play football. But Halas's Bears still struggled at the gate early in the 1925 season. In good weather, some ten thousand might show, but attendance usually hovered around five thousand. To make matters worse, the Bears struggled early on, playing boring and hapless football. Two of their first three contests ended in scoreless ties, as Chicago opened the season 0-1-2.

With each poor showing, the crowds continued to shrink, and Halas continued to lose money. This made him more determined than ever to sign an A-list college player. He wanted Grange. And if he didn't lure number 77 from Illinois, Halas didn't know how much longer he could stay in the game.

High above Philadelphia's Franklin Field in the press box, every prominent sportswriter on the East Coast sat poised in front of his typewriter, including Grantland Rice, Paul Gallico, Damon Runyon, and Ford Frick. The most media representatives ever to cover a college football game—more than one hundred writers and radio broadcasters—were on hand to see Grange. Rice had been unimpressed with his play earlier in the season against Nebraska, and now he wondered the same things that all the writers did: Could Grange possibly live up to his legend? Could he cast a spell over this crowd the way he had over others?

Many fans and sportswriters were skeptical of his ability. They argued that all of his yards had been gained against lesser competition. To them, Midwest football was no match for East Coast football. "Grange has been advertised as the greatest back of his age," wrote one East Coast reporter. "Skeptical Pennsylvania consequently sits back with an expression that says plain as words, 'Well, big boy, strut your stuff. We're watching.' "

A Philadelphia reporter captured the mood of the city two days before the game, which would take place on Halloween afternoon. "Not in years, recent or otherwise, has the town been steamed to such high white heat of expectation. Red Grange is coming to town. On Broad, on Market, or on Chestnut Street, or wherever you would linger this morning, you would hear only one topic: Red Grange was coming out of the West . . . As far as only Philly knew, Grange was coming alone."

On the morning of the game, despite a chilling rain, a capacity crowd of sixty-four thousand awaited the opening whistle. Another twenty-four thousand fans without tickets were unable to squeeze in, an unofficial record for the number of fans turned away at Franklin Field. By noon, the rain had passed. Just after one o'clock, Grange trotted onto the soggy field, every set of eyes latched onto him. Bundled in heavy winter coats, fans pointed excitedly at number 77, telling their friends that there he was, the Galloping Ghost, running around in the stadium that was suddenly awash in sunshine.

Minutes before kickoff, the Illinois 150-piece marching band entered through the main gate. The Illinois Central and Pennsylvania Railroad had offered a special student fare of $31.14 round-trip, but a snowstorm delayed the band's train. The players didn't expect their band to appear. When they saw them march onto the field, it stirred the entire team, filling them with a spine-tingling surge of school spirit. They watched as the band belted out the Illinois fight song, "Oskee Wow-Wow." As kickoff approached, every Illini player wanted to prove a point, not just to Penn but also to every football fan in America who believed that East Coast football was superior to Midwest football.

The home team kicked off. Standing near his own goal line, Grange pulled the ball into his arms and blasted up the field until he was tackled at the Illinois 36-yard line. Zuppke had devised a unique game plan for Penn. The Illini normally used an unbalanced line, with four linemen to the right of the center and two to the left, and Grange usually ran to the strong side of the field. But in reading the scouting reports on the Quakers, Zuppke discovered that Penn typically overshifted, putting nearly all of its defenders on the strong side. This left the weak side vulnerable. Zuppke planned to attack it, even though Illinois had rarely done that in the past.

Before the opening whistle, Zuppke spoke with Grange. "In the first two plays of the game, run Britton through the strong side," the coach said. "On the third play, line up strong on the short side of the field, and you take the ball around the weak side."

Grange followed orders. On the first two snaps, he handed the ball to Britton, who was hit hard by the Penn defense and lost yardage on each carry. But Zuppke, looking on intently from the sideline, wasn't worried; he was setting a trap. On third down, Britton punted the ball because the coach didn't want to risk losing any more yards.

The Quakers failed to pick up a first down, then kicked the ball back. Facing first-and-10 from his own 44-yard line, Grange huddled with his teammates and told them he would fake a run to the strong side of the field and then head to the weak side. Grange called the snap count, then was hiked the ball. He took two steps to his right, then sharply reversed course. Running left around the weak side, he broke into the Penn defensive backfield. Across the 50-yard line, a defender lunged at him, but Grange cut and spun away untouched in a move that was ballerina-smooth. A second Penn player charged at Grange, but he smashed the headgear of the player with a pulverizing stiff-arm, dropping the defender to the ground. Grange then shifted into high gear and sprinted down the left side of the field. When he crossed the goal line to score a 56-yard touchdown, no defender was within 25 yards of Grange.

For a split second, the crowd didn't react; everyone was frozen by what had just transpired. The majority of the fans were Penn backers, but it was Grange they had come to see, and now, in one single play, he had exceeded everyone's expectation. This run was Grange displaying all of his powers—the speed, the stiff-arm, the quick-as-a-wink cuts, the twisting—and soon after the referee signaled touchdown, the crowd finally sizzled in appreciation and affection. The gallop was a thing of beauty, and these sophisticated football fans knew they had witnessed something as rare as a blue moon, something special. It took all of one play for Grange to prove to the East Coast fans and writers that he was deserving of his glowing reputation.

Grange wasn't done. In the second quarter, he returned a kickoff 55 yards to set up Illinois's second touchdown. Then, with a few minutes left before halftime, he bolted around the left end to score from 12 yards out to give Illinois an 18–2 lead over heavily favored Penn. The sportswriters in the press box were stunned—not one of them had forecasted this.

With just over a minute before halftime, Zuppke waved Grange to the sideline. He wanted to give his star a little rest before the start of the second half. As Grange made his way to Zuppke, his jersey was completely caked with mud; fans in the stands couldn't even make out his number. When he reached his coach, Grange took off his golden leather helmet, and for the first time, the crowd could see his red locks. A few trainers huddled around Grange, wrapping blankets around his shoulder pads, then Grange slowly began to jog toward the locker room. With white puffs of breath coming out of his mouth, Grange gazed up into the grandstands, and he could see everyone in the stadium staring at him. Women put their hands over their mouths, as if they were seeing someone famous, like a Hollywood star such as Charlie Chaplin. The men in the crowd doffed their hats. Before Grange reached the portal to the locker room, they began clapping politely. Quickly, the clapping grew louder, then louder still. Grange had never seen anything like this, how these fans of an opposing team were showing their appreciation for what he'd just done on the football field.

John O'Hara, a reporter for a paper in Pottsville, Pennsylvania, noted the scene: "There wasn't a man or woman not standing in the whole stadium. There he was, the boy who had come through when the chips really were down, dragging his blanket behind him, and it was wonderful . . . Somehow or other I felt that the eyes of the whole East were on that solitary figure, and for some reason or other I was proud of him."

• • •

*P*enn *coach Louis A. Young* was in a mild state of shock. During half-time he told his players that Grange wouldn't run free in the last thirty minutes of the game like he did in the first thirty. He commanded his defenders not to overshift to the strong side and to watch for weak-side runs, where Grange had made most of his yards.

The change in strategy was successful—somewhat. Grange didn't gain as many yards in the second half, but midway through the third quarter, with the ball on Penn's 20-yard line, he gathered his teammates in the huddle and told them that they were going to run their flea-flicker play, which Zuppke had invented fifteen seasons earlier.

Illinois lined up to kick a field goal. Intuitively, Zuppke knew what Grange was up to and leapt off the bench, frantically waving his arms to signal to him to change the play. But Grange pretended that he didn't see his coach and ignored his unspoken directive. Zuppke then tried to send in a substitute with the order, but Grange pushed him back to the bench. He had a hunch and overruled his coach—something only he could get away with.

Grange, the holder on field goal attempts, knelt 8 yards behind the center with one knee on the ground to receive the snap. When Grange yelled "Hike!" the ball sailed over his head into the arms of Britton, the kicker, who quickly lobbed the ball to Chuck Kassell, the team's right end. He then turned around and pitched the ball to Grange, who ran untouched 20 yards around the right end and sprinted into the end zone to score the final points of the game. Illinois won, 24–2.

A few minutes before the game-ending whistle blew, as the fading light of the cool afternoon gave way to the encroaching dusk, Zuppke pulled Grange out of the game. Once on the sideline, Grange snapped off his helmet and lifted a blanket across his shoulders. He slowly walked toward the locker room. For the day, he had gained 363 yards on 36 carries and scored three touchdowns. The fans again rose to their feet.

Grange offered a tentative, barely noticeable wave to the crowd, then kept walking with his head bowed and his face as expressionless as a mannequin. Yet fans in the first rows could see there was a tinge

of sadness in his eyes, as if this moment marked the end of something. And it did, because after triumphing on college football's
grandest stage, it was now going to be harder than ever for Grange to
guard his precious sense of privacy. There was a price to be paid for
this memorable performance.

The sportswriters in the press box struggled to find the adjectives,
similes, and metaphors that would adequately describe what they
had witnessed. One writer, after pacing back and forth in the press
box for several minutes, simply threw up his hands and cried, "I can't
write it. The story's too big for me."

Damon Runyon coolly assessed, "Grange of Illinois is three or
four men and horse rolled into one for football purposes. He is Jack
Dempsey, Babe Ruth, Al Jolson, Paavo Nurmi, and Man o' War. Put
them all together and they spell Grange."

Harry Cross of the *New York Times* wrote, "The east has heard of
the great achievements of [Grange] and has taken them with a grain
of salt. It did not believe that he could be as great as the middle west
said he was. But he is. He is not a myth. He dashes and dodges over
the gridiron with a speed and an alertness which sets him high up on
a pedestal among this generation of football players . . . An artful
dodger he is, as artful as anything one will see on a football field in
many, many moons."

Paul Gallico noted years later, "This chips-down performance
must rank with the called home run of Babe Ruth, the tipped off
steals of Ty Cobb, Tilden's danger-line tennis and Jones's pursuit of
four major titles in one year. This was delivering the goods."

After steaming through the hills of western Pennsylvania, through
the Ohio Valley, and across the flatlands of eastern Illinois for nearly
twenty hours, the train carrying Grange and his teammates pulled
into Champaign late on Sunday night, the quietest time of the week
at the depot. But hours after the game, the mayors of Champaign
and Urbana had issued proclamations asking citizens to give a resounding welcome home to Grange and the team. Over twenty

thousand fans showed up—more people than had attended a single NFL game so far in 1925. By the time the locomotive screeched to a stop, the fans were screaming, "We want Red and Zuppke! We want Red and Zuppke! We want . . ."

When Grange peered out his window at the excitement in the station, he wished he could magically disappear. Wanting to avoid the circus, he walked to the end of the train and tried to quietly slip out of the last railcar. A fan spotted him and yelled, "There's Grange!"

Within moments, Grange was lifted onto the shoulders of his most fervent believers and paraded around the station like Caesar in Rome. And it didn't stop there. The fans carried him for two miles, through the business district and all the way to his fraternity house. Without more than a pause and a wave, Grange walked through the front door and climbed the stairs to his second-floor room. But the fans wouldn't go away. He had seduced them by almost single-handedly bringing legitimacy to Midwest football, and now they showed their love for their local boy by serenading him with cheers and chants, wanting him to come out of the house. Eventually Grange walked to his bedroom window and saw a jostling crowd looking skyward—as if the messiah had come. Hesitantly, he lifted the window open, raised his hands—hushing the noise—and then loudly said a few words.

"We, er, had a fine visit down East," Grange stammered. "I don't know how to thank you fellows for everything, but the team deserves the credit. And we're certainly going to do everything in our power to lick Chicago next Saturday."

Never comfortable with the adulation that people heaped upon him, Grange was touched by this show of support. It was one of the finest hours of his young life.

Five days later, Grange ran onto the field at Memorial Stadium to face Chicago. Several sportswriters from the East Coast, including one from the New York Times, traveled to Champaign, but there was little exciting news to report. Grange had one of the least memorable performances of his college career, gaining only 64 yards of total offense and failing to score a touchdown on a wet, muddy field. The Illini prevailed, 13–7, but something was bothering Grange. It showed in his body language and in his demeanor.

Soon after his headline-making performance against Penn, rumors began circulating that Grange had already signed a contract to play professional football. This was front-page news in sports sections not only in Champaign and Chicago, but also in New York and Philadelphia. No college player had ever dropped out of school before graduation to pursue a career in the NFL, and most of the power brokers at Illinois—especially Zuppke—were fundamentally opposed to Grange turning pro. Like most college coaches, Zuppke considered the NFL to be a cesspool of corruption. In his view, it was a league of cheating players, incompetent referees, unruly and sometimes out-of-control crowds, ever-changing rosters and schedules, pervasive gambling, and, if rumors were true, of fixed games. Zuppke believed that the NFL was no place for a player like Grange to make his career. Rather, he wanted Grange to become a motion picture actor or a sportswriter—two careers in which he could use his Illinois education. Anything, Zuppke believed, was more noble than becoming a pro football player.

Several reporters also decried the idea. One local sportswriter, W. V. Morgenstern, wrote, "Red Grange is likely to find the path to glory a lot rougher than it ever was in Conference with Illinois. The Wheaton iceman's biggest foe is more likely to be his own team than the opposition . . . The enormous salary that Grange probably would get would be a big cause of jealousy among his own teammates. That's the reason most of them are playing the game—the salary . . . The pros 'broke' the great Chick Harley after he had left Ohio and tried to play with them. They even went so far in one game as to walk off the field when he came on. Grange's brothers among the pros might not go that far, but they certainly would not extend themselves giving him any assistance."

Pyle wasn't the only one whispering promises of NFL riches into Grange's ear. Tim Mara, the owner of the New York Giants, made a special cross-country train trip from the Big Apple to Champaign to meet with Grange late in the 1925 college season—even though the

Giants were in the middle of their maiden season. Mara wanted to sign Grange to a contract, offering him a chance to play in the nation's biggest city under the brightest lights. Though Grange refused to sign anything, rumors ignited that he had been offered $40,000 to play three games for the Giants once his college career was over.

Reporters followed Grange around campus and hung around his fraternity house, asking his friends and classmates if he was turning pro. They also traveled to Wheaton to speak with Grange's father, Lyle. When asked what he'd tell his son to do, Lyle responded, "I think he's entitled to cash in on the long runs his gridiron fame has brought him. It has been expensive for me to send Harold and his brother Garland through the university. We are not rolling in wealth, and I think the public would approve of anything Harold does."

NFL owners salivated over the prospect of Grange turning pro. He was the one college player who could become the face of the struggling league. The owners understood that in the eyes of the public, Grange could do no wrong. He could be the NFL's white knight, riding in from the heartland to give the struggling league widespread and near-instant credibility. The NFL needed that. More than anything, though, it needed fans.

C. C. *Pyle had a secret* meeting to attend. The theater owner went to Chicago by train on November 9, two days after the Illinois-Chicago game. Neither he nor George Halas wanted to be seen together in public, so the Bears owner rented a room at the Morrison Hotel, a recently opened downtown high-rise.

Late in the afternoon, Pyle pounded on the door of Halas's room. When Halas pulled it open, he closely inspected Pyle. His thin, carefully trimmed mustache, his walking cane, his immaculate suit, and his shiny shoes conveyed elegance and dignity. Halas, having never met the man, was inclined to like him and invited him inside.

Pyle had earlier sent a message to Halas through his friend Frank Zambreno: Pyle had a verbal agreement with Grange about playing professional football and was now ready to speak on his behalf. Halas was thrilled, and his first words tumbled out: He wanted

Grange to join the Bears immediately following his final game at Illinois. Pyle replied that this sounded like a good idea but added that he had a bigger and far more lucrative plan.

Pyle laid out the details: After the Bears' final two games on their 1925 schedule—Grange would play in both—the team would head east on a barnstorming tour, traveling to such metropolises as Washington, DC, Philadelphia, and New York. Then, after returning to Chicago for a brief Christmas break, Pyle proposed that the Bears and Grange then set out on a second tour, first going south to Florida and then west to California and Washington State, where the final game would be played.

Halas asked who would make the arrangements.

"I'll make them," replied Pyle, adding that he would travel east immediately to begin setting up a schedule if Halas agreed to the plan.

Halas liked what he heard. This vision of Pyle's was grand and sweeping. Halas could not have conjured it up himself, but now that he was presented with it, he believed it could be wildly successful because of one person: Grange. Halas, like Pyle, understood that the sporting public was as intoxicated with Grange as any athlete in the country. He had just proven a week and a half earlier against Penn that he wasn't a fluke, that he could flourish against the stiffest competition. This only increased the public's infatuation with Grange, and Halas firmly believed that a barnstorming tour featuring the Galloping Ghost would attract new fans to the NFL. Pyle's idea made perfect sense.

But Halas was a financial novice with no clue about the cost of such an endeavor. His coffers were virtually empty, so he couldn't make Pyle a cash offer or pay him an advance. Halas then said that they should split whatever money they made 2 to 1. Pyle nodded. Halas then said that the Bears would pay for all the tour's costs, including transportation and hotels.

"Of course," Pyle replied.

Halas asked if Grange would agree to these conditions.

"He will," Pyle said.

"All right," replied Halas. "It is agreed the Bears will get two-thirds and—"

Pyle interrupted. "Oh no, George," he said. "Grange and I will get two-thirds. The Bears will get one-third."

In a heartbeat, the air in the room grew thick with tension. These terms were not acceptable to Halas. He argued that if he received only a third of the profits, he stood to actually lose money on the tour because he had to pay his players and cover the team's travel costs. The two men passionately argued their respective cases throughout the remainder of the afternoon and deep into the evening. Pyle kept reminding Halas that he could take Grange to another team; Halas responded that his biggest fans were in Chicago, the logical home for Grange. They tossed and parried their positions back and forth for hours until both were exhausted and agreed to resume their talks early the next morning.

Finally, after twenty-six hours of negotiating, the two struck a deal: They agreed to split the earnings fifty-fifty. Halas would cover the travel budget and the salaries; Pyle would guarantee that Grange would play for the Bears in every game for at least two quarters. The two put the pact into writing. They then agreed that if anyone asked them, they would say that no contract existed between Red Grange and the Chicago Bears—a statement that was neither completely false nor totally true.

The next day, Pyle lit out for the East Coast to start setting up the tour. The Red Grange experiment was on.

Grange's final game at Memorial Stadium was little more than a practice session. Only twenty thousand watched the Illini play Wabash College, a third-rate team. Zuppke had said early in the week that Grange would only play a couple of winters, causing many of the loyal orange-and-blue fans to stay away. In the final quarter, Grange galloped onto the field for three plays, but he never touched the ball in Illinois's 21–0 victory. After the game was over, the crowd rose to its feet and clapped as Grange slowly walked across the field toward the locker room for the final time in his college career. Grange lingered on the field for a few moments—uncommon for him—and waved his golden helmet high into the air. Then he disappeared into the concrete catacomb of the stadium.

. . .

As *Grange was finishing* his football career in Champaign, Pyle was meeting with owners of several NFL teams back East, pitching to them the idea of playing the Bears in postseason exhibition games. He revealed that Grange would be playing but asked that this tidbit of information be kept confidential.

Yet word soon leaked out to reporters that Grange had already signed a contract with the Bears, despite having one game left to play for Illinois. Several newspapermen called Halas asking for confirmation; he insisted that Grange hadn't signed anything with his organization. But Halas was a shrewd promoter like Pyle, and he soon told one of his close friends, Don Maxwell, the sports editor of the *Chicago Tribune,* that Grange would in fact join the Bears the moment his college season ended. Three days before Illinois's final game, against Ohio State, the *Tribune* ran a story under the headline "Rumor That Grange Will Sign with Chicago Bears Persists," detailing the arrangement among Pyle, Halas, and Grange. Halas wasn't quoted as a source in the article, but he was behind it, pulling the strings to his benefit. He wanted the news out there as soon as possible to spike ticket sales.

In the days before the Illinois team departed for Columbus, Ohio, reporters and photographers hounded Grange more than ever. Zuppke gave him a day off from practice, allowing Grange to stay in his bedroom at the fraternity house and avoid the media scrutiny. His fraternity brothers didn't answer the door or the telephone, but the reporters entrenched outside made his room feel like a jail cell.

But Grange had to leave his room. He was summoned to the office of Illinois president David Kinley, who asked Grange point-blank if he had signed a contract to become a professional football player. Grange flatly denied it, prompting Kinley to tell reporters, "Red Grange says that he has not signed a contract, and this is good enough for me. He will play [against Ohio State]."

Grange needed to get away for a day, so he took the train to Wheaton to seek the advice of his father. Lyle Grange wasn't a fan of the pro game—he detested the lack of sportsmanship in the NFL—but he wanted Red to do what made him happy. And if he could get rich by playing pro ball, Lyle told his boy over dinner at a small diner in town, there was no shame in that. Before the Granges finished eating, a reporter for the *Chicago Tribune* approached and asked Red what he was going to do. "I'm all mixed up," Red told the reporter. "And I'm worried. But you can tell everybody that I'm not going to sign up for anything—pro football, selling real estate, movie contracts, anything—until I play my last football for Illinois next Saturday."

The pressure continued to mount. Before his final practice at Illinois, Grange was striding toward the locker room when an Associated Press reporter approached him. The reporter claimed to have evidence that Grange had signed a contract with C. C. Pyle and was already a professional, which would make him ineligible to play against Ohio State. "They have nothing on me," Grange told the writer. "I have not received a penny. I have not signed a contract. If Pyle were asked the same question, he would give the same answer."

Grange stormed away, frustrated that questions about his future plans were dogging him and overshadowing his final college game. A few hours after his last practice, Grange and the rest of the team piled onto a train early in the evening for the three-hundred-mile ride to Columbus. As the locomotive rolled east, Zuppke sat down next to Grange. Outside, the sky turned darker and clouds rolled in from the west in advance of a storm. The weather suited Grange's mood. He felt like he had been in the eye of a storm during the past few weeks, and although he knew it would soon be over, Grange was worn down by the constant hounding and the intensity of the media glare. Sensing Grange's state of mind, Zuppke—Grange's coach, mentor, sounding board, and friend—leaned over and asked a simple, familiar question: What did he intend to do after the Ohio State game?

Grange didn't know what to say. He knew Zuppke wouldn't approve of his turning pro and playing for the Chicago Bears, but he couldn't lie to this man. So Grange said that he planned to make an announcement following the game, then everyone would know what he was going to do. Zuppke was looking for more concrete information, but he accepted that answer and eventually rose and left Grange alone. The emotionally drained Grange closed his eyes and drifted to sleep.

Near noon the next day, the train pulled into the depot at Columbus, completing the sixteen-hour trip. The team's arrival time had been published in a local paper days earlier, alerting fans that the great Red Grange would be stepping off the train from Champaign at a few minutes after noon on November 21. And now, as Grange's gray eyes peered through the train's windows, he was flabbergasted at what he saw: Thousands of football fans, maybe as many as ten thousand, had gathered at the station to catch a glimpse of him. When Grange emerged at the door of his railcar and stood on the steps, the crowd went wild and surged toward him. A reporter from the *New York Times* wrote that if the train carrying Grange "had been bearing the president, Jack Dempsey, and Douglas Fairbanks, it is doubtful if the awaiting crowd would have been any larger."

With a few of his teammates positioned as lead blockers, Grange stepped onto the platform and slowly inched his way through the tightly packed, screaming, jumping-up-and-down mass of humanity. With every step he took, people pushed at him, trying to pat Grange on the back or shake his hand. Finally the phalanx of teammates escorted him to a waiting car, which zoomed away. But there was no escape for Grange. More admirers, as many as five thousand, lined the streets that led to the Great Southern Hotel, where the Illini were to stay. No athlete in the history of American sports—not Ruth, not Dempsey, not Thorpe, not Tilden, not Man o' War—had ever received such a welcome in a city that wasn't his hometown.

The attention shook Grange. Another crush of fans waited for him at the hotel entrance. Earl Britton rode with Grange in the back of the taxi. As soon as Britton opened the door, the crowd erupted with glee. Britton told Grange to follow close behind him, and the two bulled their way into the lobby. Grange quickly retreated to his room, where he remained for the rest of the day. He truly didn't understand the visceral reaction that he incited in people. But the people knew: They were drawn—like bees to a flower—by his football skill, his modesty, his innocence, his good looks. These were the ingredients, the magnetic mosaic, of the myth of the Galloping Ghost.

Over the previous two years, Grange's character and talents had come to represent many things to many people. To Illinois students and alumni, he was an athletic hero, a player with more innate football skill than perhaps anyone who had ever donned a leather helmet. To fans in the lower and middle classes, Grange was hope for a better future. He had risen from their ranks to be the most talked-about athlete in America yet remained one of them, a working-class guy with a stout work ethic. And to casual followers of the game, he was a representative of all that was good in America in 1925. When he played, anything seemed possible, any dream could come true; Grange exemplified the defining characteristics of the Roaring Twenties.

The public demand for news about Grange was insatiable, but for twelve hours he didn't venture from his hotel room, not wanting to be photographed or asked any more probing questions from reporters. On the morning of the game, Grange finally emerged from seclusion. With every step he took from the hotel to the football stadium, it seemed there was a pop and a flash burst in his tired, worn-out face.

Newspapers from Los Angeles and New York dispatched reporters to cover Grange's final collegiate game. One hundred papers were represented in the press box, which was about ninety-five more than had sent reporters to cover the Chicago Bears' game against the Detroit Panthers six days earlier. The stands were nearly full an hour before kickoff, everyone wanting to watch Grange warm up. Ohio State's towering stadium held sixty-three thousand, but for this "Grange game," another five thousand temporary bleachers were added and over fifteen thousand standing-room-only tickets were sold, which brought the total to eighty-three thousand—the largest crowd at that time to attend a football game in the Midwest.

The stadium had been built three years earlier and, like Illinois's Memorial Stadium, it was one of the dozens of monstrous football cathedrals that were popping up on college campuses in the early 1920s. These great arenas were constructed to accommodate the growing interest in the sport, and no one benefited more from this stadium-building trend than Grange, the first person in the history of college football who by merely showing up could fill these massive venues.

Now thousands looked down at the grassy field at Ohio State, squinting in the bright autumn sun, trying to see when number 77 would come out of the Illini locker room. And then, there he was, jogging onto the field for his final hours as a college player. Everyone in the stadium stood as a rolling thunder of noise rose from the sprawling concrete stadium.

Grange didn't play with the kind of flair that fans had come to expect. The rampant speculation about his future and what he should or should not do had sapped his energy. Still, he was steady, ripping off a few long runs in which he broke tackles and bulldozed defenders. He failed to score, but he did make the play of the game. Late in the fourth quarter, Grange intercepted his second pass of the day, deep in Illinois territory, to thwart a Buckeyes scoring attempt and preserve a 14–9 victory for the orange-and-blue. In his final college game, Grange rushed for 113 yards on 29 carries and completed 9 passes for 42 yards, including a 17-yard touchdown strike in the second quarter.

After the final whistle blew, Grange rushed to the locker room, pushing past fans and opposing players who wanted to shake his hand. As soon as Grange entered the locker room, more than fifty reporters encircled him. He escaped by jumping onto a bench. The reporters all shouted the same question: *What are you going to do now, Red?*

Grange reached into his locker, pulling out a written statement. The real reason why all of the reporters had been assigned to cover the game was about to be revealed. Clutching their notebooks and gripping their pencils, the reporters—many with burning cigarettes hanging from their lips—leaned in closely on all sides of Grange, listening intently as he began to utter the words they were sent to collect and record.

"I intend to organize my own team," Grange said. "I will try to round up the Four Horsemen of Notre Dame. Britton will join me, but we will not make an attempt to obtain any players now in college. Both Britton and myself are leaving the University of Illinois now. I do not know whether I will return to school. I am out to collect all the money I can in the next four years. Maybe after that, marriage will come in for some consideration."

Grange explained that he wasn't going back to Champaign with his teammates but home to Wheaton to begin building his own team.

That, however, was a categorical lie. Instead he planned to go directly to Chicago to sign a contract with the Bears, the one Pyle had already brokered. But Grange didn't want to reveal his true intentions to reporters. He wanted to push the bloodhounds off his scent, so he created a fake trail for them to follow.

"I know this can't last forever," Grange told the reporters. "But I've got everything I've ever wanted. And I'm going to make the best of what's at hand while it's here. My dad and brother, Garland, mean everything to me. I'm going to see the kid through school, and I'm going to make Dad take it easy if I can. But I doubt that. He just insists on working at something. If anybody thinks I'm going to settle down to a life of playboy ease, they'd just better come out and talk to my dad. He's the boss."

Zuppke stood close to Grange as he spoke to the newspapermen. When he heard his star player say that he was quitting school, Zuppke grew so upset that he visibly shook. Once the reporters left Grange's locker, he slipped off his uniform, showered, and dressed. Zuppke then walked with his star player to a taxi, which ferried them to the team hotel. Zuppke had a last chance to try to convince Grange that he was making the mistake of his life. As the cab sped close to the hotel, Zuppke told Grange, "Keep away from professionalism . . . Football isn't a game to play for money."

Nearing the hotel, Zuppke ordered the cab driver to keep circling the city. He needed more time to present his case to Grange. For over an hour, the two argued their points in the backseat. Grange noted that Zuppke earned an income from football, and that it was hypocritical for him to say that he couldn't do likewise. "What's the difference [with what you do] if I make a living playing football?" Grange asked.

Zuppke retorted that the college game was different from the pro game, that college football was pure, that it was a sport that young men played simply for the love of the game. But pro football, argued Zuppke, had been corrupted by money and gambling, that men played it only to earn a paycheck. Plus, Zuppke said, if Grange turned pro, it would hasten the demise of college football. He said that if professional football ever became popular, it would transform college football into a mere training ground for the NFL. As an iconic figure, Grange could start a trend—one that Zuppke believed would ultimately be the undoing of college football. Grange disagreed vehemently with each of his coach's points. When the cab finally pulled up to the hotel, the coach and player were so frustrated with each other that they wouldn't talk again for over a month.

The press was waiting for Grange in the lobby, but he had anticipated them. He donned a black wig and stuck a cigar in his mouth, both given to him by a friend. He walked past the horde of newspapermen without detection and rode the elevator to his room. After waiting a few hours, he stuffed his clothes into a suitcase and discreetly slipped out the door, pulling the brim of a fedora low over his eyes and turning up his coat collar high. He made his way to a fire escape, climbed down, walked a few blocks to the train station, and boarded a midnight train to Chicago.

Grange checked into the Morrison Hotel under a fake name. His final day as a college football player had been as long as it had been stressful, but finally, just before sunrise, Grange shut his eyes and fell asleep. In a few hours, everything would change for Grange—and for the NFL.

9

A PLUNGE INTO THE PRO POOL

They had come for Red Grange. Tim Mara, the owner of the New York Giants, staked out the lobby of Chicago's Morrison Hotel, clutching a contract. Leo Lyons, the owner of the NFL team based in Rochester, New York, also wandered around the hotel. In his pocket he had a $5,000 check made out to Grange. He was ready to dole out that amount for every game he played for Rochester.

But they were too late. Just hours after Grange's final college game, Halas and Pyle met in room 1739 in the newly opened Morrison, which stretched up into the Chicago skyline more than five hundred feet, higher than any other building in America outside of New York City. Along with Bears co-owner Ed Sternaman, the three negotiated through the night in the room that Halas had reserved. They had agreed a month earlier on the outline of a contract, but they had to sort through the details, the mounds of minutiae. For several hours, as a wintry darkness fell outside the hotel windows, the three men floated offers and counteroffers. After a marathon session of negotiating, they reached a final agreement: The Bears would pay Grange $100,000 to play thirteen games: the final two regular season games and the eleven-game tour across the United States organized by Pyle. Plus, Grange and Pyle would receive 60 percent of the profits at the gate, while the Bears would take in the remaining 40 percent.

The quick-thinking, quick-talking Pyle had bested his counterpart, winding up with the better end of the deal for himself and his client. Pyle operated from a position of power. He continually reminded Halas that he wasn't the only NFL owner willing to pay a fortune for Grange's services. In the end, Halas had to cave in to Pyle's demand or risk losing Grange to another NFL team.

Later that morning, Pyle, dressed in his signature double-breasted charcoal-gray suit, escorted Grange into Halas's room, where Halas and Sternaman were waiting. From a nearby radio, the faint sounds of a church choir could be heard in the background, softly filling the air. Grange first signed a contract with Pyle, officially making him his manager. Then, seated between Halas and Pyle at a small table, Grange grabbed a pen and put his name on a contract with the Bears. It was official: Red Grange, age twenty-two, was a Chicago Bear.

Pyle opened the door to let in a few dozen sportswriters, tipped off earlier by Halas. He had just paid an unprecedented price to sign the most electrifying college player of his time, and now Halas wanted to start getting his money's worth of media attention. And looking up, he saw more reporters hustling into the room to attend this makeshift press conference than had covered his Bears all season. With flashbulbs popping and puffing small clouds of white gas with every exposure, a reporter asked Grange, outfitted in a gray jacket and tie, about his views on professional football.

"Why, I cannot see that there is any difference between the game as it is played on college gridirons or on the fields used by men who turn their attention to the sport for financial reward," Grange replied. "I am at a loss to comprehend all the fuss that has been made in my case simply because I propose to capitalize on such success as I have attained while playing at the University of Illinois. There are scores of baseball players who were mighty good men on college diamonds who upon leaving their universities have entered professional baseball and are now earning comfortable livelihoods through their skill at pitching, fielding, or batting. No one ever criticized those fellows for signing pro baseball contracts.

"I have always loved football, and when I play the game, I want to play with and against the best teams possible. The closer the battle, the better. There isn't any particular thrill in taking part in a one-sided contest. I have associated with the best men in the Western Conference for three years and learned much about football. In the professional circuit, I expect to be pitted against seasoned players— the best men the various clubs have to offer. Here the competition should be of a keen order."

After Grange finished speaking, Pyle took over, addressing the cluster of reporters in the hazy, smoke-filled room. "Mr. Grange has at no time sullied his pure amateur standing by any act of professionalism," Pyle said. "He waited until his last game was played, and today the contracts for his future were drafted and entered into. I believe Harold Grange has made a wise decision in following up his splendid, spectacular college career by engaging in professional football while his popularity is at its zenith.

"There is a large body of the public clamoring for the opportunity to see him play, who never had a chance during his college days. Joining the Chicago Bears, Mr. Grange will be continuing to play under the same teaching he received at the University of Illinois. He will give the lovers of the professional football game the same sterling effort he gave the followers of the college game. He is destined to be as great a success in his newly chosen field as he was in the one just brought to a very successful conclusion."

Soon after the press conference ended, Grange meandered into a downtown department store. He was newly rich, and he wanted to splurge. He paid $500 for a raccoon coat, a trendy piece of wardrobe. It was the ultimate display of a man who had just made a mint.

Wearing *his fluffy*, furry new coat that fell to his shins, Grange walked through the bitterly cold Chicago afternoon and onto the field at Cubs Park, where just a few hours after signing his contract the Bears were hosting the Green Bay Packers. As spectators spotted Grange strolling toward the bench with Pyle at his side, a murmur moved through the crowd of seven thousand. The news of Grange's joining the Bears had yet to leak out, but now, seeing Grange on the sideline, the fans stood on their feet and cheered. Even without his familiar number 77 uniform, they recognized the red hair of the Galloping Ghost and emitted a roar uncommon at Bears games.

Shivering on the bench in the fifteen-degree weather, Grange surveyed his new teammates. They were bigger and quicker than anyone he had played with at Illinois. The hits on the field were more violent and more explosive than in the college game. Grange also noticed that there was an excessive amount of dirty play: punching after the whistle, kicking in pileups, even jabbing at players' groins. This was win-at-all-costs football.

During halftime, several hundred fans jumped over the retaining wall in the stands and onto the field, rushing at the man in the raccoon coat. But before they reached Grange, who was still sitting on the bench, dozens of police officers formed a ring around him and restored order. The mayhem delayed the game for several minutes. With several police officers standing close to the bench, Grange took in the second half, watching the Bears defeat the Packers, 21–0, raising their season record to 7-1-2.

In the locker room after the game, Halas announced that Grange was now a member of the squad and that he'd make his professional debut in four days—on Thanksgiving afternoon—against the Chicago Cardinals, a crosstown rival on the city's South Side. When Halas finished telling reporters that Grange was a Bear, the news became the lead story in the sports sections of newspapers across the country the next day.

Nearly every major news outlet weighed in with an opinion, most decidedly negative. The *Cleveland Plain Dealer,* in an editorial, wrote that Grange had "undoubtedly harmed college football, and has done a disservice to the institution which he has represented on the athletic field."

The Associated Press reported, "Harold 'Red' Grange today plunged into the business of capitalizing on his gridiron fame by signing to play professional football, against the wishes of his father as well as George Huff, director of athletics of the University of Illinois, Coach Robert Zuppke, and others who had hoped he would accept other offers held out to him."

And Sid Mercer, a reporter for the *New York Evening Globe,* wrote, "Academic prestige at the University of Illinois receives a severe setback in Grange's defection. He could have availed himself of some good offers, remaining in college and graduating next spring, but he prefers to set out at once on his shekel-gaining expedition down the gridiron of life . . . The noble act of ice peddling will no longer be uplifted by Grange. He has hung up his tongs along with his familiar No. 77 jersey and is leaving the dear old campus flat on its back to take a quick plunge into the pro pool. He has quit school to prevent the possibility of studies interfering with his close application to pursuit of the dollar."

Despite the tenor of the news, the public was unfazed. Tickets for the Bears-Cardinals game on Thanksgiving Day couldn't be printed fast enough. On the day after Grange's signing, more than twenty thousand were sold. Determined to make a windfall from the spectacle of the Galloping Ghost's first pro game, Halas printed up extra standing-room-only tickets, which he sold out of a Spalding sporting goods store on State Street in downtown Chicago. On the final morning of the SRO ticket sales, more than five hundred people stood in line outside the box office, waiting for it to open.

A local newspaper estimated that two hundred thousand people wanted to see the game, to see what Red Grange would do now that he was officially a professional football player. Grange, dressed in a necktie, had appeared on the cover of *Time* magazine a few weeks earlier—he was only the third athlete to whom editors at the two-and-a-half-year-old publication had given top billing—and that exposure heightened the public's curiosity about the tailback. "Folks who were razzing the daylights out of pro football, those thousands who told their office mates that they wouldn't give a dime to see one of those commercial games, are turning hand springs through the loop," wrote one Chicago newspaperman. "They are begging for someone to sell them a ticket at five times the regular price."

Realizing the intense interest in the game, WGN radio hastily scheduled a live broadcast. On the morning of the game, the radio station issued a press release:

Red Grange and football hold the Thanksgiving Day stage at W-G-N on the Drake Hotel. A twist of the dials to 370 meters at

10:45 a.m. today will carry listeners to the roof of the Cubs Park, where Jim Jennings is to begin the broadcasting of the game between the Chicago Bears and Chicago Cardinals. Grange is making his professional debut today as a member of the former aggregation. The customary W-G-N method is to be followed in miking the game—the announcer's story will have for a background the cheers and shouts of the spectators, brought in by other microphones situated at various points of the field and in the stands.

On game day, a crowd of thirty-six thousand filled the single-tiered Cubs Park, a baseball stadium with a football field marked out within it. Another twenty thousand fans were turned away at the gate, but many of them stood outside in the cold wind that blew off Lake Michigan, waiting to hear the crowd detonate when Grange trotted onto the field for the first time. One desperate group of fans bowled over a gate in left field, hoping to get within eyeshot of Grange. But police were quickly called in, and they drove back the unruly fans.

On the streets surrounding the stadium, Model Ts and roadsters and Marmon Opera Coupes were lined up bumper to bumper for ten blocks in every direction. Neighborhood kids charged a few coins for parking in driveways and yards. And scalpers who had made up thousands of bogus tickets stuffed wads of cash in their pockets, even though most of their tickets were printed in the wrong color. On this cold Thanksgiving morning, for the first time in the history of professional football in Chicago, the wheels of profit and greed were turning as quickly in the surrounding neighborhood as if a World Series game between the Cubs and the Yankees were about to take place. Anticipation, like the winter chill, hung in the air.

When Halas walked out of the locker room before the game, his eyes grew large and twinkled as he scanned the overflowing crowd up and down, up and down. Never before had there been such a massive gathering to watch his Bears, and now, for the first time—as he marveled at all of these women dressed in long-flowing winter coats and men in their bowler hats and topcoats—Halas knew that professional football had a chance to make it in Chicago. He was very much in the game.

Up in the press box, dozens of reporters from Chicago and across the Midwest filled every seat. Many of them had never attended a professional game before, and in the hours before kickoff, they frantically tried to learn as much as they could about the NFL—its franchises, its rules, its key players, its coaches. The press box was so full that many of the reporters had to stand for the entire contest, unable to find an empty seat.

Before kickoff, Grange sat alone in the locker room and read some of the thousands of well-wishing telegrams addressed to him care of the Bears' front office. One came from a group of icemen in Milwaukee, which stated that they were "glad to see one of our boys get in on the big money." The outpouring reinforced what Grange was beginning to understand: He wasn't just another football player, he was more—a symbol of success, and of hope, to America's working class everywhere.

When Grange finally appeared at the steps of the dugout and trotted onto the field, the shivering, bundled-up crowd rose to its feet and loudly welcomed him to the world of the NFL. Through the drizzle, the fans could see that Grange, his breath rising like steam from his mouth, was wearing the number 77 jersey he'd made famous at Illinois—even though, up until then, no Bear had a uniform number higher than 29. Grange didn't acknowledge the greeting— he rarely did—because he was concerned about one thing: giving the fans the show they had paid to see. He passed by the live bear cub mascot that was tethered to a peg in front of Chicago's dugout. Unlike the boisterous crowd, the Bears' mascot remained placid when Grange appeared.

The slick field mitigated Grange's superior quickness and cutting ability. And from the start, it became clear that the Cardinals weren't going to let Grange run wild anyway. When Paddy Driscoll, the Cardinals' punter, unleashed his first kick, the fans booed loudly, because Driscoll kicked the ball away from Grange, who was the Bears' deep back. Throughout the game, Driscoll punted away from Chicago's newest player. Grange did manage to catch three of Driscoll's punts, but he failed to break loose on any long runs and totaled only 56 return yards. And, from his position at right halfback,

Grange carried the ball 16 times for just 36 yards. The game ended, 0–0, a classic defensive battle. The Cardinal defenders had zeroed in on Grange on every single play—whether he had the ball or not. No opposing NFL players wanted Grange to make fools of them. Players had already heard too much about the Galloping Ghost—the most hyped football player in history—and teams game-planned to stop him. Some opposing players even brazenly boasted about wanting to hurt Grange and create a name for themselves by knocking out the mighty rookie.

After the final whistle blew, hundreds of fans rushed the field to try to touch Grange. But he was barricaded by a large group of baton-wielding, blue-coated police officers who escorted him through the dugout and into the locker room. Once inside, reporters immediately surrounded Grange, who sat on a wooden chair. A large red welt was visible under his left eye, an injury he'd suffered when he rammed into one of his teammates on a running play. "They are two great teams, the Bears and the Cardinals," Grange said. "They are better than any of the college teams I ever played with or against. The lines are wonderful; it is almost impossible to gain through them. I don't think that a college team would have a chance to beat either one of those two out there today . . . The men out there today not only knew what they had been taught in college, but they have added a lot of experience. That's why they are so much better; they know so much more. This was the hardest game that I was ever in, but it was very clean. It was much cleaner than most college games."

When Halas read Grange's remarks in the newspapers the following day, he was delighted. Not only had Grange delivered the biggest crowd in the history of professional football to date, he had also become an ambassador and promoter of the game. His was a voice that would reach even non-football fans. Halas knew that promoting the NFL was as much about public relations as it was about the quality of play on the field, and he was pleased that Grange understood that as well. Just three days after landing Grange, Halas sat in his small office, counting the gate receipts from Grange's first game. As he crunched the numbers, Halas did something he hadn't done in years: He cried in happiness.

The night after the game, Paddy Driscoll was having dinner with his wife when he began recounting the action on the field for her. He told his wife that he thought the crowd had been too rough on Grange, that it should have cut the rookie some slack and not booed him when he punted the ball away from him. "Paddy, they weren't booing Red," she said. "They were booing you for not giving Red a chance!"

Driscoll had no idea that he was the villain, but that was made clear to him the next day when he picked up a copy of the *Chicago American* and read:

> Paddy Driscoll—shame on you! Forty thousand folks, including street car conductors, white wings, bootleggers, sailors, saxophone players and night watchmen went up to the Cubs Park yesterday to see "Redheaded" Grange pull off eight or ten 70-yard runs. No one doubts that Red could have staged some of his pinwheeling on the chalk lines if he had the chance. But Mr. Driscoll saw to it that he had very little opportunity to get away with any of his dazzlers.

Zuppke was furious. A few days after Grange's signing, he spoke at a Rotary club dinner in Champaign, a function that served as the team's end-of-the-season banquet. Zuppke felt betrayed by Grange. From the dais, the coach unleashed a verbal pummeling on his one-time close friend and player, who sat in silence in the audience.

"I have no fight with professional football," Zuppke said. "But Grange is green—greener than when he first came here to Illinois. He must watch out for persons who will try to make their own fortunes out of his tact and his talent. Suppose he does get sixty thousand dollars for his professional football services? Will he be able to guard that from those who will seek to take it away from him? Wouldn't he be better off in the long run if he took up some substantial business and profited by it? He must remember the old saying of 'Easy come, easy go' . . . Grange has been an asset to the University of

Illinois, but the University of Illinois has been a greater asset to him. And the saddest thought that I have in this whole business is that Grange will no more return to the University of Illinois and graduate than the kaiser will return to power. The Grange we know, and the Grange we have seen for three years, is a myth . . . I tell you that no other one-hundred-thousand-dollar player is going to be on one of my teams."

These words hurt Grange. But instead of saying anything to his former coach, he simply rose from his chair at the end of the banquet, put on his hat and coat, and left the building, not even grabbing the letterman's sweater he had been presented earlier in the evening.

Pyle was so busy working out the final details of the upcoming barnstorming tour that he hired a personal assistant. It was clear that Pyle himself had never played football, because this tour was going to be as physically challenging to the players as anything they had ever done in their lives. He arranged two tours. During the first, before Christmas, the Bears would play ten games in seven eastern cities over an eighteen-day span, including the final two games of the previously scheduled regular season. (The first game of the tour was actually against the Cardinals.) After a brief break over the Christmas holidays in Chicago, the Bears would embark on the second tour. It would feature nine games in five weeks, and take Grange and the Bears to Florida, California, and Washington State.

It was the first leg of the tour that troubled the players. Playing ten games in eighteen days had never been done before in American football history, and many of the Bears feared that their bodies couldn't endure the physical toll the tour would demand. With only eighteen players on the team, most played both offense and defense, rarely resting. Even so, the players also knew the tour could very well be the spark that would light the fire of pro football's popularity in America.

A heavy snow fell on the Windy City three days after Grange's debut. But another sellout crowd filled Cubs Park to see the game against the Columbus Tigers, which was strictly a traveling team. In the locker room before kickoff, Halas taped ankles and asked if the players supported the tour. Each one responded with a resounding yes. Not only did they love the game, but they also knew they could make some money. Even the last player on the roster stood to earn more than $1,000 from the tour.

After dressing, Grange and the rest of the Bears ran onto the snow-covered field and were loudly greeted by thirty-five thousand— while across town only five thousand fans watched the Chicago Cardinals beat Rock Island, 7–0. Grange, expressionless and serious, once again seemed oblivious to the noise and the attention. Although he never confessed to being burdened by his fans' expectations, he didn't radiate a sense of joy. Still, he found a way to wow the crowd. In the first two quarters, Grange ran the ball several times for long gains, slithering through the line and twisting and breaking one tackle after the next. He sat out the third quarter. Halas ignored the frequent chants from the stands: "We want Grange! We want Grange! We want Grange!"

He reentered the game when the fourth quarter began. Though he fumbled after a jarring hit, he accounted for nearly 140 yards of offense as the Bears won, 14–13. After two games, he was still unbeaten as a pro. More important, his teammates were beginning to accept Grange as one of them. For the first time in his pro career, he had proved that he could be an elite player in the NFL.

Halas gingerly walked into the locker room. He had started the game at right end. Playing a little more than two quarters, Halas now had cuts and cleat marks up and down his body. After the coach and owner took off his pads, he announced to reporters that he had signed Earl Britton, Grange's teammate from Illinois, to a professional contract. Halas knew he needed fresh bodies for the crosscountry tour that awaited the team, and Britton had proven in college that he had the talent to be a fine pro. Plus, his presence could make life easier for Grange, who would need a friend to lean on in the coming weeks. After all, no athlete in America was under more pressure to perform.

10

THE BARNSTORMERS

O*ne by one,* the players strolled with suitcases in hand into the newly opened Union Station in downtown Chicago and entered the Great Hall, one of the biggest public waiting areas in America. Dressed sharply in bowler hats and topcoats, they took seats on the long wooden benches that were awash in beams of bright winter sunlight, which filtered through the one-hundred-foot-tall barrel-vaulted atrium ceiling. Beneath them lay Tennessee pink marble floors, and around them stood eighteen Corinthian columns that were offset by terra-cotta walls. In the golden age of rail travel, this was a traveler's paradise.

Redcaps flitted about the concourse, hauling bags for weary travelers. Scores of businessmen rushed through the terminal, toting their briefcases and their worries as they headed off for another day of work. And newsboys hawked copies of the *Chicago Tribune,* the *Chicago American,* the *Chicago Daily News,* and the *Chicago Herald-Examiner.* Holding the papers above their heads, they yelled, *Read all about it, read all about it! Red Grange and the Chicago Bears beat the Columbus Tigers!*

As their Pullman train eased into the station, players kissed their wives good-bye and hugged their mothers and shook hands with their fathers. During the next two weeks, the team would travel more than three thousand miles and play eight games in eight different cities. The players would eat most of their meals on the train and would sleep many of their nights in the train's small bunks. They would even do some training on board, as Halas planned to have his boys do push-ups and sit-ups to keep them in shape over the coming days.

When the moment finally arrived and the conductor yelled "All aboard!" for the eleven-thirty departure to St. Louis, Grange and his teammates sauntered into their private railcar and sank into their leather seats. The train's whistle then pierced the air, steam hissed and spewed from the engine in a white plume of vapor, and the large metal wheels clanged and ground forward. This was the beginning; the Chicago Bears were off on the first-ever multicity tour by an NFL team.

Grange sat next to Pyle and stared out the window—as was his custom—as the train pushed southward toward St. Louis. As he gazed at the stubs of cornstalks poking through snow that had been dumped on the Midwest, Grange didn't know what the next two weeks would bring. Would fans show up in the same numbers as they had in Chicago? Would the competition be as vicious as the first two games? Would he be able to give the fans the show they expected? As the train glided over the twin slender rails, these questions hammered his mind.

Grange stayed to himself. He was the new kid and the youngest on the team. The other Bears were mostly close friends and drinking buddies. Puffing on cigars, they swapped tales—some a little taller than others—and plotted how they were going to spend their free time in the towns and cities where they would play. They talked of hitting jazz clubs, visiting big-city speakeasies, meeting different ladies, maybe even stopping at a brothel or two. They knew this trip was going to test their physical and mental mettle, but they also planned to have fun, and lots of it. They were young and carefree and in the prime of their lives, and now the country was laid out before them, full of delicious possibilities.

It didn't take long for the players to give their private railcar a nickname: the Doghouse. Once these men were turned loose on these unsuspecting cities, there was no telling what kind of trouble they would stir up.

The team went directly to a hotel in St. Louis for the night. The next afternoon, the Bears arrived at Sportsman's Park two hours before the one-thirty kickoff against a team called the Donnelly All-Stars. Francis Donnelly, a St. Louis mortician, had hastily assembled the All-Stars in less than a week. Pyle and Donnelly had a previous relationship, and when Pyle spelled out his plan to take Grange on a cross-country promotional tour, Donnelly excitedly told Pyle that he'd like to be a part of it. Donnelly worked the phone and recruited more than a dozen local players with college or pro pedigrees. They had practiced together less than a week. Halas was confident that this would be an easy victory for his Bears.

On the day of the game—December 2, 1925—the temperature dropped rapidly. At kickoff it was twelve degrees above zero, with a windchill factor of nearly twenty below. The frigid weather—combined with the fact that this was a Wednesday game—compelled many ticket holders to stay at home or at work. But the freezing cold didn't slow down the Galloping Ghost, who played the finest game of his young pro career.

Playing in front of eight thousand fans wearing heavy coats, Grange was virtually unstoppable, scoring four touchdowns and gaining a total of 190 yards in Chicago's 39–6 victory. But the fans wanted more. Halas knew his star player would not survive the tour if he played every quarter of every game—Grange's contract stipulated that he had to play only two quarters each game—so Halas benched him for the second and third quarters. When Grange took a seat, angry fans cursed loudly at Halas, demanding that he insert Grange back into the game. But Halas ignored the cussing fans.

Grange would frequently find himself stuck in this pattern. Even when he performed at his peak, fans wanted more out of him. Expectations were so high—the fans had read the hyperbole-filled newspaper accounts of his performances and heard exaggerated radio reports—that it was virtually impossible for him to live up to his advance billing. The Bears certainly tried to make Grange look the part; Halas directed his quarterback to hand the ball to Grange whenever the team was close to scoring a touchdown, to inflate Grange's statistics.

But Grange didn't care about his numbers. To him, this tour was about one thing: money. He was a sober-eyed realist, not a dreamer, and he knew the most effective way to capitalize on his fame at Illinois was to turn professional immediately. But just one game into the barnstorming tour, he saw the fickleness of fandom. After the St. Louis game ended, Grange walked off the field, his head down. He had nothing to be ashamed of, but for the first time, he began to realize that winning wasn't everything. Not anymore. Grange was now a showman, not just a football player, and the only way he could sate the appetite of his adoring fans was to give them a performance they would remember long after the clock ran out.

After the victory over the All-Stars, the Bears showered in the locker room, gathered their equipment, and hustled to the train station. They boarded a locomotive bound for Philadelphia, site of their next game in three days. This would be the team's longest break of the tour's first leg, but Halas and Pyle didn't give Grange much downtime. At nearly every depot where their train stopped, they would escort Grange off the train and the trio would speak to reporters, contacted ahead of time by Halas, who promoted Grange as if he were running for president. Grange smiled for the cameras and patiently answered reporters' questions. The twenty-two-year-old understood that he was the star of this traveling show, the singular attraction who could sell tickets and make money, and so he obliged every demand made by Pyle and Halas.

The team checked into a downtown Philadelphia hotel, where Halas let them rest for twenty-four hours. Grange was already battered and bruised. His head throbbed—possibly the result of a mild concussion—and his legs and arms were so sore that just climbing out of bed pained him. As the target of opposing defenses, his body was paying a high price.

Yet Grange enjoyed being back in Philadelphia, where just two months earlier he had bedazzled the crowd at Franklin Field as a collegian. In 57 minutes in ankle-deep mud against Penn, Grange had totaled 363 yards and scored three touchdowns to give Illinois a 24–2 victory over the heavily favored Quakers. The memories of that game came rushing back when he walked around the field at Philadelphia's Shibe Park before Chicago's matchup with the Frankford Yellow Jackets. Just like his previous visit to Philadelphia, the weather was miserable, with mist falling from the blue-gray sky and the temperature hovering at twenty degrees. This was the kind of raw weather that many football players loved, but not Grange, who preferred sunny skies and a dry field for better footing. The field on this day was a giant vat of mud; the traction would be treacherous.

When Grange and the rest of the Bears emerged from the locker room for their fourth game in ten days, a crowd of twenty-three thousand greeted them, including most of the members of the New York Giants, the team that the Bears would play in less than twenty-four hours. Most of the fans wore red or yellow rain slickers, and many huddled under umbrellas. Right away, it was clear that Grange would not have the same impact on this game that he'd had against Penn. He seemed a step slower and a little less nimble. He carried the ball seven times in the first quarter for just 15 yards. But he did score on a short touchdown run late in the quarter to tie the game, 7–7.

He sat out most of the second quarter and all of the third. The fans once again expressed their dismay that Grange wasn't in the game, which also disappointed the horde of reporters assigned to the game. For the first time, the best-known sportswriters in America—including Grantland Rice, Damon Runyon, Ford Frick, and Westbrook Pegler, the titans of 1920s sports mythologizing—covered a professional game. Halas and Pyle invited the writers to travel with the team for the rest of the tour's first leg, and many accepted their offer.

This one act—convincing the most prominent sportswriters of the day to cover Grange and the Bears—was nearly as important to the growth of the NFL as Grange himself. Halas and Pyle knew that without press coverage, their tour would be a financial failure. They needed exposure to get the word out about Grange, and this meant they needed the press to write stories about the Bears. To entice the newspapermen to join the team on the road, Pyle paid for all the booze and food aboard the train. He knew the quickest way to win over sportswriters was through their livers and their stomachs. Pyle's marketing savvy came through again.

Grange trotted back onto the waterlogged field at the start of the fourth quarter. Midway through the period, he took a handoff and bulled from the 1-yard line into the end zone. With just a few minutes left in the game, the Bears held a 14–7 lead.

Chicago stopped the Frankford offense, forcing a punt. Grange dropped back to field the kick. The ball was booted high, and Grange ran to catch it. The crowd rose, as if sensing that this was the moment that Grange would finally break loose and give them a memory worth savoring. But instead Grange let the ball hit on the ground and bounce out of bounds. In an instant, the fans turned on Grange, booing him as if he'd just committed an unforgivable sin. One reporter noted, "The fickle football public is not unlike the jams that crowd Shibe Park and other ball fields in the summer and hoot when Babe Ruth strikes out and then jump out of their seats when he hits a home run."

The comparison to Ruth was apt, and it was made by many of the sportswriters who covered this game. Like Ruth, Grange had swelled into a larger-than-life figure. He wasn't as affable or as charismatic as the Bambino, but his personal biography had captivated the public in a way that no other American athlete ever had. He was Paul Bunyan in a jersey, a man who rose from common folk in the middle of the nation to become a giant blessed with almost supernatural powers—at least this was how sportswriters across the country portrayed him. This fed the public's desire to see Grange for itself, to get close to him. Not even Ruth possessed such a magnetic pull over his legion of admirers.

A few plays after Grange let the ball roll out of bounds, the referee blew his whistle, signaling the early end of the game due to darkness. Chicago won, 14–7. The players' uniforms were so caked with mud that their numbers were hidden, a relief to Grange. He rushed off the field in relative anonymity and disappeared into the locker room. Once inside, Halas announced that they didn't have time to shower; they needed to quickly gather their belongings and hurry to the train station. The team was running late and in danger of missing its train to New York, where the next day the Bears would play the Giants. Before he left, Grange was one of the few players who quickly changed clothes. He tossed his soaking uniform, shoes, and pads onto a scale in the clubhouse; they weighed forty-five pounds.

Muddy, tired, and cold, the Bears hustled to Broad Street Station in downtown Philly. As they boarded the train that would carry them into the heart of Manhattan, one of the players reminded Halas and Pyle that the team would have to wear its dirty uniforms for the Giants game, because there wouldn't be time to get them washed and dried before kickoff. Pyle grinned and told Halas, "This tour will make you so wealthy, Halas, that next year you'll be able to afford two sets of uniforms!"

Even before the train pulled out of the station, Grange sat off to the side, alone. A few hours earlier, a fan had given him a portable phonograph, and now, as the metal wheels of the locomotive turned atop the tracks, he listened to a jazz record. The music soothed him. "Gosh, I'm tired," Grange told a reporter as the music played. "I wish I could get away somewhere. Why can't people just leave me alone?"

Grange then turned and looked out the window, staring out into the darkness. The burden of celebrity was growing heavier by the hour.

11

MY WORRIES ARE OVER

The locomotive steamed through the winter night, heading north at forty miles per hour toward New York City's Penn Station. Inside the Pullman railcars, several players ducked into the men's and women's washrooms, which served as their makeshift locker rooms, and pulled off their mud-stained black-and-orange jerseys, their black high-top football boots with wooden cleats, their still-frozen black socks, and their snow-soaked gold knickers. After showering in tiny stalls and struggling to keep their balance as the train swayed back and forth over the rough roadbed, they donned black and gray double-breasted suit jackets with high-buttoned lapels. Many of the men planned to hit the underground speakeasies in the big city, and now they looked their Saturday-night best, hoping in a few hours to dance the Charleston with any red-lipsticked beauty that might sashay their way.

The Pullman cars clickety-clacked closer to the Big Apple. In the distance, a faint halo of light glowed over the city, home to several of the most prominent sportswriters in America, who were now aboard with the team. For the first time, Grantland Rice, Paul Gallico, Westbrook Pegler, and Allison Danzig were all getting an up-close look at Grange and the Bears. "[Grange is a] youth who has risen from the obscurity of a Middle Western village to the position of the most advertised athlete the world probably has ever known," Danzig wrote in the *New York Times*. "[People are] attracted to Red Grange because he is the living symbol of the power and the glory that all aspire to and dream of and which only the chosen few can attain."

Pyle, always the center of attention, regaled the reporters with stories from his itinerant life. Dressed impeccably in a $200 tailor-made suit and his derby and spats, Pyle would put his hand on the shoulder of a reporter and say, "My dear boy," then launch into soliloquies about his days as a showman, about the greatness of Grange, and about how he was going to make professional football as popular as professional baseball. Pyle would then supply the reporters with nips of alcohol from the flask he carried in his breast pocket—always a coveted treat during Prohibition.

The train's wheels screeched to a stop in Penn Station. Lugging duffel bags, the Chicago players followed Halas on foot to Times Square and the Hotel Astor. Located at Broadway and West Forty-fifth Street, the Renaissance-style hotel was the most ostentatious structure on the Great White Way, which Times Square was now called because of the new electric lights on the streets. The Astor's lobby featured a twenty-one-foot-high colonnade of marble and gold, and in the back of the lobby was the Orangerie, a blossom-filled Italian tropical garden that fragranced the air. Grange and the other players strolled wide-eyed into this immaculate lobby. They had stepped into the big time.

But the hotel's real draw was the circular Astor Bar, located in the basement. In the Roaring Twenties, this was the epicenter of social life in New York. The alcohol-free establishment—Prohibition was in its heyday—attracted show business stars, political heavyweights, writers, and the business elite. As jazz notes filled the smoky air, patrons drank glasses of different kinds of fruit juice served by waiters wearing spotless bolero jackets. Once the waiters were out of sight, the more adventurous in the crowd would pull flasks of hard alcohol from their pockets or socks and spike their drinks. The new mayor of New York City, James J. Walker, liked to spend his evenings at the Astor, as did Babe Ruth.

After he checked in to the hotel, Grange headed to his plush suite located on one of the upper floors. Unlike many of his teammates, he had no interest in prowling the New York nightlife. Tomorrow was going to be a seminal moment in Grange's life. Tomorrow everything would change.

The game between the Bears and the Giants had been announced two weeks prior to Grange's arrival in the city, and ticket sales were brisk in the days leading up to kickoff. Months earlier, New York Giants owner Tim Mara, realizing Grange's potential star power—and his ability to lure fans to the stands—had traveled by rail to Champaign to meet with Grange, then a halfback for the Fighting Illini. Mara offered Grange a contract to play for the Giants. Grange turned him down because Pyle had already secured a secret deal for him with Halas and the Bears. But the trip wasn't a total washout for Mara. Before he arrived back home in New York, he sent a telegram to his family, cryptically writing that the visit with Grange was "partially successful."

Mara was in dire straits—his first-year NFL team was hemorrhaging money. Working as a legal bookmaker, Mara had paid $500 to purchase the one-year-old New York franchise. Most of the other nineteen teams in the NFL were located in or around the Ohio Valley, and East Coast fans were slow to embrace the professional game. Already about $45,000 in debt, Mara was in a financial sinkhole. And with every passing day, he began to believe that pro football wasn't economically sustainable, even in the nation's biggest city. The proof was his ledger sheet.

When the Giants played a home game, most of the 55,987 bleacher seats at the Polo Grounds sat empty. The top crowds reached about 20,000, but many didn't pay admission. The Giants frequently gave away free tickets; Tim Mara's son Wellington often stuffed his pockets full of tickets to hand out to his friends in grammar school.

The sporting public in New York simply wasn't drawn to professional football like it was to Major League Baseball. Even though the New York Yankees had just finished almost thirty games behind the pennant-winning Washington Senators—the Bronx Bombers' 1925 season had been lost because a "stomachache" kept Babe Ruth out of the lineup for two months (the real cause of Ruth's absence: an STD)—baseball fans still filled up Yankee Stadium, the sparkling cathedral in the South Bronx that had opened in 1923. The baseball Giants and Dodgers also drew well. But attendance at the football Giants games was discouraging, so much so that New York governor Al Smith told Mara to cut his losses. During one Sunday supper earlier that fall, Smith bluntly told Mara, "This pro football will never amount to anything. Get rid of that team."

Mara knew he had to do something drastic, something unprecedented, to save pro football in New York. That was why he went to Illinois to see Grange. When he returned to New York, he told his family that while he didn't sign Grange to a contract, he did the next best thing: He convinced Pyle and Halas to bring Grange to New York for an exhibition game on December 6. Mara hoped that fifty thousand curious people would flood into the Polo Grounds to see what this Red Grange lad was all about.

On the eve of the game that Mara hoped would save him, a driving rainstorm lashed at Manhattan. The storm had followed the Bears up the East Coast from Philadelphia. Lightning crackled in the sky and thunder rumbled over the midtown skyscrapers. Though all sixty thousand tickets were sold, at prices ranging from $2.50 for a seat at midfield to 50 cents for a spot in the bleachers, Mara fretted that the poor weather would keep fans at home and prompt an outcry for refunds. On Saturday night, he shut his eyes, expecting the worst.

At three in the morning, Mara's phone rang. It was one of his closest friends. "Look out the window," the friend told Mara, "the moon is out."

The weather had broken. Hours later, the sun dawned gold over Manhattan; a glorious winter morning. Grange rose from his bed at the Hotel Astor. After eating a breakfast of eggs, sausage, toast, and orange juice with his teammates—their normal morning fare on the tour—Grange and the Bears rode the subway uptown to 155th Street and Eighth Avenue, home of the Polo Grounds.

Grange ambled out of the subway station with his easy, graceful gait just before noon. Within minutes, fans quickly recognized the Galloping Ghost, whose picture had appeared almost daily in the

New York papers during the past week. Now here he was, finally, in living color, and the mere sight of the Ghost strolling toward the stadium caused women to shriek and grown men to charge at him with a pen and paper, hoping for an autograph.

Surrounded by a special detail of fifty police officers, Grange entered the stadium and ducked into the locker room. Mayor Walker had assigned the extra police to Grange because he feared for the red-head's safety. In the days before the game, sportswriters in New York had written heroic biographical pieces about how he'd risen from the wheat fields of Middle America to become the finest football player in the nation's history, and the last thing Mayor Walker wanted was a mob of fans to encircle the fresh-faced running back or cause him injury in any way. To prevent this, the mayor beefed up security for Grange, giving him more protection than even President Calvin Coolidge enjoyed when he visited New York.

The request for tickets was unlike any in the NFL's brief history. As soon as Pyle had scheduled the game two weeks earlier, he wired all of the New York newspapers, informing editors that Red Grange would be playing at the Polo Grounds against the New York Giants. The following day, the news appeared in all of the major New York City dailies with accompanying photographs of Grange and stories of his feats, causing an immediate surge in ticket sales, just as Pyle had hoped.

Long lines stretched around the stadium as the gates opened at eleven-thirty. The sky had now turned overcast, and a gentle mist fell. Fans in rain slickers excitedly pushed through the turnstiles, and the stadium was more than three-quarters full by noon, two hours before kickoff. Hundreds of kids sneaked through a hole in the wooden fence that encircled the Polo Grounds; scores of adults simply climbed over it. Hundreds of fans, without seats, loitered in the aisles; perhaps a thousand more stood on the rafters. And nearly five thousand people who couldn't get tickets gathered on the jagged cliff of Coogan's Bluff, which overlooked the bathtub-shaped stadium. Gene Tunney, the heavyweight boxer, stood among them. By one o'clock an estimated seventy thousand people had a view of the grassy field.

Up in the wooden press box, more than one hundred reporters, the most ever to cover an NFL game, hunched over their typewriters. Dozens of radio reporters clenched their microphones. Grantland Rice and Damon Runyon eagerly awaited Grange's arrival. Neither believed that the NFL would ever succeed in New York, but with each passing moment, with every seat being filled, with the feeling of a fresh chance now in the air, their opinions were being altered. An hour before kickoff, the crowd was larger than any other in professional football history. Even before Grange appeared on the grass, a steady rumble of excitement arose throughout the entire stadium and drifted up into the mottled sky.

Babe Ruth took his seat at midfield. Then, at one-fifteen, the Chicago Bears dashed out of the locker room and onto the slick playing surface. Suddenly there was number 77, his red hair blowing in the December breeze, his orange leather helmet tucked under his arm. Every set of eyes at the Polo Grounds followed Grange, carefully watching him, studying him as if he were the latest version of the Model T. More than a dozen photographers rushed at Grange, capturing his every move, his every flick of the wrist as he tossed a football to a teammate. Ruth was flabbergasted at the star treatment the photographers gave Grange—and miffed that the glow of celebrity was being redirected from him onto the Galloping Ghost. "I'll have to sue that bum," Ruth joked to one of his friends sitting nearby. "They're my photographers!"

Grange's jersey, like those of his teammates, was still unwashed, muddy, and damp from the previous day's game in Philadelphia. And even though cuts and bruises dotted Grange's body like some sort of skin disease, he moved effortlessly through the team's orchestrated exercise routine as the fans looked on. At every game on the tour, thousands had arrived early simply to see Grange warm up, just as fans would gather to watch Babe Ruth take batting practice. This was part of Grange's powerful allure, making the ordinary—simply running down the field and faking out an imaginary defender—look extraordinary. He didn't awe crowds with his raw power or brute force like Ruth did whenever he blasted a moon shot over the outfield fence during batting practice. Rather, it was Grange's fluidity, his ability to almost dance on the field, that captivated all those who watched him go through his pregame routine of running, passing, and catching the ball.

When Grange peered up into the stands at the admiring fans, he noticed something unusual about this New York crowd. Besides working-class men, he saw scores of high-society women decked out in long-flowing dresses, fur coats, and white gloves, sitting next to their husbands in three-piece suits, dark overcoats, and bowler hats. They were the kind of highbrow crowd that attended Saturday night Broadway shows: doctors, lawyers, even Wall Street businessmen, all settled into their seats to take in the spectacle.

From the time he broke on the national scene at Illinois, Grange had appealed to a vast audience. But never before had so many from the upper crust gathered to see him play. This added to the already high stakes of the game: If Grange could dazzle them, he could extend the appeal of the NFL to an audience the league had never reached before. The well-heeled were giving the NFL a chance because the coming of Harold Red Grange to New York was the showcase sporting event of the season, the hottest ticket in town. Wrote Allison Danzig in the *New York Times*:

> From every station in life they came. . . . To one and all there was the same appeal. All of them were victims in common of that fetish for hero worship which is inspired by the man of might on the baseball diamond, in the boxing ring, or on the football gridiron.

His pregame warm-ups complete, Grange retreated to the locker room along with his teammates to receive final instructions from Halas. Dozens of photographers trailed behind Grange as he loped across the field. Even though he'd yet to run a single play, the crowd gave him a small ovation.

Following Grange into the bowels of the Polo Grounds, Halas and Pyle were already feeling a sense of relief, of triumph. Their dream of conquering New York was unfolding before their eyes. Weeks of planning and arm-twisting and deal making had made this

event possible, and now Halas and Pyle experienced a sense of vindi-
cation and accomplishment. Each had his own reasons for wanting
to make it in New York—Halas knew it was the key to gaining nationwide credibility; Pyle knew it was the key to unlocking a vault of
cash—and both viewed this game as the most important of the tour.
Now that it was here, they were as excited as everyone in the crowd.
Their New York moment had arrived.

When the Giants ran onto the field minutes before the opening kickoff, a second roar thundered from the crowd, causing the creaky stadium to shake. Mara followed his team out of the locker room and let
his eyes fall over the overflowing crowd, a mass of humanity that, to
Mara, seemed to flow up to the clouds. Tears welled. He had hoped
that this Grange game would generate interest, but he never thought
that the city would embrace the game like this; his wildest dreams
just didn't stretch that far. He was overcome by the moment. "My
worries," the joyous Mara told a friend, "are over."

Mara made sure that the Polo Grounds went all out for the
arrival of Grange. Orange-and-blue bunting, in honor of the Bears,
adorned the boxes along one side of the field, and red-and-blue
bunting, the Giants' team colors, was draped on the boxes on the opposite side. Team pennants decorated the goalposts and fluttered in
the wind. Basile's Regimental Band, seated in the bleachers, played a
variety of rousing tunes throughout the afternoon. Though there
weren't any cheerleaders on either of the sidelines, the Polo Grounds
had the festive feel of a college game, a deliberate and pioneering
strategy orchestrated by Pyle and Mara. They knew that the total fan,
experience of NFL contests had to be as exciting and entertaining as
the college game, and so on this afternoon, for the first time in pro
football history, they tried to replicate the aura of college football.

Just after two o'clock, under a still-falling mist, the two teams lined
up for the kickoff. The crowd rose to its feet when Grange took his
position as Chicago's deep man at the Bears' 5-yard line, ready to receive the kick. Grange and his teammates had played four games al-

ready on this cross-country tour, but they'd never seen a stadium so crammed full of onlookers, a stadium so full of exhilaration, a crowd so full throated with exuberance. The biggest crowd they had played in front of was thirty-six thousand at Cubs Park for Grange's first game as a Bear, but that was nothing like this. The Bears were only eleven days into their barnstorming trip across the United States, but now, here in gray New York, the players and Halas and Pyle were quickly realizing that this tour could turn out to be the sixty-six days that might just save pro football in America.

The Giants' Babe Parnell, using a straight-on approach, booted the ball high into the wintry sky. It traveled through the soft mist and landed in Grange's outstretched arms at the 20-yard line. He darted up the field. In just four steps, he reached full speed—another of his athletic gifts. Making one cut, then two, he sidestepped a defender. The crowd boomed as Grange blazed across the field. But just as he was about to break away for a long run, he was tackled at the 32-yard line by a Giants defender.

The Bears failed to make a first down on their opening possession and punted. After three runs into the line netted only a few yards, New York's Parnell punted back to the Bears. Starting at their own 35-yard line, Chicago quarterback Joseph Sternaman, the brother of team co-owner Ed, handed the ball to Grange for his first carry of the game. He was hit as soon as he grasped the ball, but fell forward for 3 yards, causing a moan to reverberate throughout the stadium. The fans had read so many superlative-laced stories about Grange that there was an expectation that he could score at will; that every time his fingers touched the ball, he would slice through the defense like a bolt of lightning, like he was playing kids in a pickup game in Central Park.

But Chicago continued to march down the field. On the next play, Laurie Walquist, the right halfback, burst through the line for a 20-yard gain. Grange was then held to 2 yards on another carry up the middle. From the sideline, Halas could see that every Giants defender was zeroing in on Grange, so the coach decided to use his star runner as a decoy. Sternaman faked a handoff to Grange and cut up the field for 12 yards. After a few more plays that didn't feature Grange, the Bears moved the ball to New York's 1-yard line. Sternaman again faked to Grange, then barreled into the end zone. Sterna-man missed the extra point, but the Bears led, 6–0.

The Giants elected to kick off back to Chicago. Now Grange came alive. On their third play of the drive, Walquist took a pitch from the quarterback. Just before a New York defender slammed into him, Walquist flung the ball down the field into the arms of Grange, who then broke a tackle and skirted for 30 yards before being brought down. A few plays later, Grange took a handoff and stormed to his right. Suddenly he stopped, cocked his arm, and rifled a pass to Walquist, who caught it in stride for a 23-yard gain. Minutes later Sternaman, behind a devastating block by Grange, bulldozed across the goal line. After another missed extra point, the Bears held a 12–0 lead.

This time the Giants opted to receive the kickoff. As New York drove up the field, Grange played defensive back, covering Giants end Joe Williams. With the ball near midfield, New York quarter-back Hinkey Haines received the snap and hurled a pass in the di-rection of Williams. Grange and Williams soared into the air, and Grange knocked it down. The two players fell to the ground in a heap. Williams rose first. But before Grange could lift himself from the muddy field, Williams, in full view of the referee and everyone else in attendance, threw a powerful punch at Grange. His fist con-nected to the back of Grange's headgear, slamming Grange's head to the ground. No penalty was called. Grange struggled to his feet, then staggered like someone who had downed one belt of whiskey too many. A few plays later, he wobbled to the sideline and took a seat next to Halas and Pyle. Grange remained on the bench for the rest of the first half. When the whistle blew, signaling the end of the second quarter, the Bears led, 12–7.

In the locker room, Halas and Pyle were generally pleased but also slightly panicked. A record crowd had turned out to see Grange, but their star had done precious little to excite the fans. This was bad for business. Halas was intent on doing whatever it took to win the game—winning, above all else, still mattered more to him than showcasing Grange, even if this was an exhibition game—and he recognized that this was a coming-of-age moment not just for his team but for the entire NFL. This was the biggest game in the history of the league, and if the NFL's marquee player could give the fans a signature memory to hold on to and tell their friends about, Halas and Pyle believed it could do more for the growth of the sport than any shrewd public relations campaign. In this most important hour, they needed Grange to deliver.

Halas and Pyle huddled around Grange. He was still woozy from the vicious hit, but he proclaimed he was fit to play and could go back into the game. Halas and Pyle and Mara—the three men who were benefiting most from Grange's fame—were all exploiting and taking advantage of the young back, but Grange didn't care. He knew the tour would be borderline suicidal, but he wanted to play as many games as possible in as few days as possible because that was the best way to make the most money. Though far from a savvy businessman, Grange did understand one thing: This tour was making him very wealthy. That was why he was determined to get back into the game.

Grange tentatively ambled out of the locker room and cautiously lowered himself onto Chicago's bench. When the teams ran out onto the field for the second-half kickoff, Grange stayed on the sideline. Though Pyle had told reporters before the game that Grange would play the entire game, his and Halas's plan all along was to sit him on the bench for at least a quarter. Grange was their commodity, their path to riches, and they weren't going to risk their investment by subjecting him to more hits—both legal and illegal—than they had to. Now Halas and Pyle instructed him to take a seat on the bench and rest. His time would come, but not yet.

This didn't sit well with the crowd. Seeing that number 77 wasn't on the field, the fans started chanting, "We want Grange! We want Grange! We want Grange!" Even as the two teams traded punts and the game turned into a defensive struggle during the third period, the chant continued, growing louder with each minute that Grange sat hunched over on the sideline with a large dark coat draped over his shoulder pads. No two people were more attuned to the chants than Halas and Pyle, but they stood their ground. They were banking that the rest would make Grange fresher than any other player on the field once he was sent in, and then Grange would finally be able to flash his once-in-a-generation skills, his magic.

At the start of the fourth quarter, Grange was still on the sideline with the score Chicago 12, New York 7. It was now late afternoon. Though the skies were overcast, the sinking sun floated on the horizon, bathing the Manhattan skyline in a pinkish glow. The shadows of the Polo Grounds stretched across the field, and the temperature dropped into the twenties, as fans huddled tighter in their raccoon coats and topcoats and workaday jackets. Everyone in the stadium was restless. They had come to see Grange play, not to see him sit on the bench, and they wanted to experience with their own eyes the athletic splendor they knew he was capable of producing.

Then, at just past four-thirty in the afternoon, Grange rose from the bench. His simple act of standing seemed to send an electric jolt crackling throughout the stands, as nearly everyone in the stadium jumped to his or her feet. When Grange cantered onto the field, the crowd came to a fever. But Grange was oblivious to it all. He didn't look up into the stands or raise a hand to his fans; he just jogged into the huddle, joining his Bears teammates, who were now on defense.

After the teams exchanged punts, Grange lined up in his defensive back position. Only a few minutes remained in the game, but the stands were still packed with people hoping to see Grange do something unforgettable. On second down deep in their own territory, the Giants called a pass play. The teams lined up, facing each other across the line of scrimmage. Quarterback Hinkey Haines, a former Penn State player, yelled "Hike!" and was snapped the ball. He dropped back several steps, giving his ends time to run down the field. As several Bears defenders charged at him, Haines heaved a pass toward the south sideline in the direction of a New York end—and of Grange.

The ball hissed through the twilight. Grange anticipated the throw. The moment the football left Haines's hand, the Ghost cut in front of the Giants end. Grange then leapt in the air and snatched the ball cleanly out of the air at New York's 30-yard line and tucked the ball under his arm. The crowd rose.

He sprinted down the sideline, running past his teammates, who leapt off their bench as he approached, and past the photographers that lined the field. Grange dodged one tackler, stiff-armed another.

Then he busted into the open field. Nothing between him and the goal line.

This was the moment everyone at the Polo Grounds had talked about for days, had anticipated and imagined, the moment they had been waiting for since the opening kickoff. Grange crossed the 10-yard line, the 5. It looked so natural, the way he ran, like a bounding deer. If Grange was born to do one thing, it was this: to run with a football in his arms.

He single-handedly was changing the way football was played. With Grange, the game was no longer a plodding, straight-ahead battle of brute strength; no longer a game that resembled rugby-style scrums where men pushed and shoved one another backward and forward. With Grange, the game gained a second dimension, one that was orchestral, lyrical, elegant. He was helping to make football truly appeal to the masses. And this unexpected play from Grange illustrated why the NFL could matter, why there could be a place for the professional game on America's sporting landscape.

Grange galloped across the goal line, scoring his first touchdown of the game. He simply dropped the ball to the ground and trotted back to his position along the line for the extra point try. Sternaman's boot put the ball through the uprights. Minutes later the final whistle blew. The scoreboard read Chicago 19, New York 7.

Grange was surrounded. Moments after the game was over, Giants players and photographers alike rushed at him. He shook every hand that was thrust at him, and then, cordoned by a dozen police officers, walked off the field and into the locker room.

Football in America changed that afternoon. New York Giants owner Tim Mara was now financially secure. Halas reaped a windfall—as did Pyle and Grange, who together earned an estimated $50,000 for this one game. More significant, the game proved that the NFL could thrive in the nation's most influential city. Up to this point, professional football had been mostly played in the Midwest in cities that had populations of five hundred thousand or fewer. But now Grange, Pyle, and Halas had demonstrated that the sport could make it in East Coast metropolises, drawing crowds that could rival those of any Major League Baseball game.

Grange also showed that football was no longer a sport to be dominated only by rich boys at Harvard, Penn, and Yale. This working-class midwestern kid had more star power than any player in the history of the game, and soon young boys from the streets of Brooklyn to the cornfields of Nebraska to the sandlots of California would begin playing the game so they could be like Red.

When they finally left the Polo Grounds an hour after the game, Grange and Pyle boarded a subway and rode it back to their midtown hotel. Grange was feeling ill, but Pyle didn't let him rest. After briefly stopping in their rooms at the Hotel Astor, Grange and Pyle visited radio station WEAF just after ten o'clock for a talk show that would be heard in more than a dozen cities around the country.

"Hello, folks," Grange said into the studio microphone. "I caught a little cold up at the Polo Grounds this afternoon, so if I'm not quite as clear as you would like, I'll have to ask you to pardon me . . . They tell me that I am playing to a larger audience this evening than ever before in my life—perhaps two or three or four million people. Well, it seems like a big honor. And it certainly is a big responsibility. Football is like life. One fellow carries the ball and gets most of the credit. Yet ten men have helped to push him through, and without them he could not have gained an inch."

Though reporters guessed that Grange had earned around $30,000 on this day, he insisted that he didn't play the game for money. He emphatically said that the rewards in football are "spiritual rather than material, but they are certain."

After the radio chat was over, Grange returned to his suite at the Astor, aching and tired. He'd played five games in nine days in front of more than 181,000 people. He limped. His left arm hurt so much that he couldn't lift it above his head. And both of his eyes were black. The barnstorming was far from over and there would be more pain to endure, but the tour was achieving exactly what Pyle and Halas had hoped it would: It was making pro football in America.

12

THE MOST HARASSED YOUNG MAN
IN AMERICA

They came with their wallets open, dangling breathtaking sums of money in front of Grange and Pyle in a suite at the Hotel Astor. The morning after the Giants game, Halas and the Bears players traveled to Washington, DC, for the next stop on the tour, but Grange and his agent stayed behind. Shortly after rising out of bed, Grange stopped by Pyle's room, where Pyle was shaving. Holding his razor out before him, he said with a sparkling, thousand-dollar smile, "Son, this is the blade that knows no brother. We are going to take a deep cut at the dough on Old Broadway, let the chips fall where they may."

Indeed, if there were any questions about Grange's status as an American icon, they were answered on this chilly New York winter morning. After the game, Pyle had announced in the locker room that he and Grange would be entertaining anyone who wanted to talk business and endorsement deals in Grange's suite the following morning. Now a long line of men in finely pressed business suits stood outside the door, wanting to be associated with America's newest boy wonder.

A company that produced sweaters agreed to pay Pyle and Grange $12,000 in order to use Grange's name on its product. Grange also signed endorsement deals for a football doll for a fee of $10,000, a line of shoes for $5,000, a line of ginger ale for $5,000, a baseball hat for $2,500, and several other smaller items, including a type of meat loaf. A cigarette company offered him $10,000 to say that he smoked its brand, but Grange refused because he didn't smoke. He did, however, accept $1,000 from the company, allowing it to use his name and likeness in its advertisements as long as it didn't imply that Grange puffed on its product.

This was a historic day. Grange was now officially the first football player ever to put his name on endorsement contracts, the NFL's first pitchman. Babe Ruth, Ty Cobb, and a handful of other baseball players had cashed in on endorsements, but no NFL player had ever had the popularity to bite such lucrative fruit. As he signed each business deal, Pyle sat close by, grinning like a man who was holding a royal flush in a game of stud poker. Pyle received a cut of every transaction, and his mind raced as he calculated all the money that he was making.

Late in the evening, after the contracts had been consummated, Grange retreated to his room. As he relaxed, he heard heavy pounding on the door of his suite. Grange turned the knob, and there he was, the Babe, looking even bigger in person than in all those movie clips that Grange had seen over the years. The two pressed the flesh and then Grange invited Ruth inside.

What a pair they were, these two towering American folk heroes, talking in the heart of the big city. Ruth, now thirty years old with five years in Yankees pinstripes, took command of the conversation. He was an old pro at being famous and dealing with all of the attendant pressures, and he dispensed a few pearls of fatherly wisdom to Grange. "Kid," Ruth said, "I want to give you a little bit of advice. Don't believe anything they write about you, good or bad. And further, get the dough while the getting is good, but don't break your heart trying to get it. And don't pick up many checks. Don't let them [boo]birds get you down, kid. You've got to expect that in this business. All you gotta do is run for another touchdown, and they'll yell their brains out for you."

The two stars shared some laughs and continued chatting into the night. Ruth was the shining example of what it meant to be a star in the golden age of sports: Not merely an athlete, he was also a promoter, an endorser, an actor, a speaker, a personality of mass appeal.

Grange was becoming more Ruthian by the day, and now Grange detailed for Babe what the first games of the tour had been like, how even grown men and women cried when he was in their presence. Then Ruth entertained his new friend with anecdotes from his wild past. Grange eventually shook Ruth's hand and invited him to the Bears' game in Boston, where they would be playing in just two days.

When Ruth finally left, Grange turned off the lights in the suite. He and Pyle had made more than $40,000 in the span of twelve hours. The business of being Red Grange, professional football player, was good.

The tour continued the next afternoon. The Bears were scheduled to play three games in the next three days, and Grange met his teammates in the nation's capital for a contest in DC's Griffith Stadium against an all-star team. Grange was now so worn down that he had trouble simply running. The crowd of seven thousand was invigorated at the sight of Grange coming onto the field for the opening kickoff. But number 77 played like he'd been up all night. He gained only 16 total yards in two quarters of action and threw two incomplete passes. On defense he made only a few tackles, acting as though he had no interest in delivering any punishing hits. Several writers in the press box noted Grange's listless play and how that had disappointed the fans. Hoping to avoid bad press, Halas inserted Grange late in the game and ordered him to kick an extra point, which he booted through the uprights. The Bears won, 19–0, but the outcome almost seemed like a loss to Halas and Pyle. The only way for the tour to continue to flourish—and for the money to keep flowing in—was to have their marquee attraction, Grange, be the hero of every game. Grange's spirit was willing, but his body was giving out. Worse, he was still a marked man on the field. The DC players, like those on other teams, frequently punched and kicked him long after the whistle had blown. Grange was now beginning to dread playing football.

Grange, Halas, and Pyle were invited to meet with Illinois senator William B. McKinley (no relation to William McKinley the twenty-fifth U.S. president) after the game. McKinley was a great admirer of Grange; he had often attended practices at the University of Illinois for the simple pleasure of watching him run. The senator escorted the group to 1600 Pennsylvania Avenue. Sports celebrities didn't make frequent visits to the White House, but President Calvin Coolidge's aides were quick to capitalize on this potential PR boon. This was in keeping with the president's open-door style. Coolidge met more often with the press than any president other than Theodore Roosevelt, and because of his accessibility, the public felt as if it knew Coolidge.

But Coolidge was not a big talker. One time at a dinner party, a woman sitting close to the president told him that she had bet that she could coax at least three words out of him during their conversation. Without even looking at the woman or offering the slightest trace of a smile, the president replied flatly, "You lose."

Coolidge was in the Oval Office when Grange, Halas, and Pyle—all dressed in tailored dark suits—entered for their meeting. Coolidge rose from behind his desk. Senator McKinley made the introductions.

"Mr. President, this is Red Grange and George Halas with the Chicago Bears."

"I'm glad to know you," replied Coolidge as he shook Grange's hand. Then, believing that Grange and Halas were bear keepers, the president added with a straight face, "I always did like animal acts."

Grange and Halas were speechless. Coolidge, who didn't follow sports and wasn't adequately prepped for the meeting by his staff, was one of the few people in the United States who didn't know who Red Grange was. But instead of explaining that he was a professional football player and that the Bears were currently on a cross-country tour, Grange merely smiled and said to the president, "Thank you very much."

Minutes later, as they were ushered out of the Oval Office and beyond Coolidge's hearing, Grange and Halas laughed uncontrollably—even though Grange sometimes felt as if he were living in a zoo as the fans pointed and gawked at him.

The show rolled on. After meeting the president, Grange, Halas, and Pyle boarded a train at DC's Union Station, joining the rest of the team. Soon after the locomotive steamed out of the station, a reporter for the *New-York Evening Post* cornered Grange. He asked the young player how he was feeling. Grange sighed deeply and replied, "Gee, I'm tired. I'm played out, pipped." Grange then added that the tour, which featured another game the next afternoon in Boston, was more taxing—both mentally and physically—than he anticipated. "It's not all as easy as I thought. And the criticism—whew! I went into this for all I could get . . . I'm getting it—in the neck!"

Soon after the reporter left, Grange slumped in his seat and shut his eyes, wanting to sleep off his fatigue. Pyle sat nearby, going over Grange's fan letters, his interview requests from reporters, and the propositions he'd received from businessmen, including one from a boxing promoter who offered him $1,000 to step into the ring. Pyle acted as Grange's traveling secretary, his public relations coordinator, and, at times, his bodyguard. When reporters approached Grange on the train, Pyle would often intervene, telling the reporter, "Red is not in a position to give an opinion on that," or he'd just shoo the reporter away.

Grange still kept to himself on the Pullman. Instead of playing cards or chitchatting with his teammates about girls or games—the two most discussed topics among the players—he just stayed in his seat and quietly looked out the window when he wasn't sleeping. One of his close childhood friends, Beans DeWolf, had joined the tour in Washington, DC, at the request of Red's father, who was concerned that his son was lonely. But even Grange's buddy from Wheaton had trouble goading Grange into a smile. Why was he so withdrawn? Red never said, but it was clear that the pressures of fame and the brutality of the tour had siphoned his energy. His muscles hurt and the reporters and photographers seemed to be lurking everywhere, chronicling his every move. He just wanted to be left alone, but that was never going to happen as long as Pyle was in his life.

Pyle often tried to entertain Grange by sharing some of his outrageous, grandiose ideas. One time he laid out a bold vision to Grange for a new kind of stadium, one with a dome over it. He even showed Red the blueprint that he had drawn up for this ahead-of-its-time plan. "Each seat has glass in the back with a crank, so people can crank a piece of glass in front of 'em, see?" Pyle said. "And the further back you are, the higher the magnification. It's like looking through binoculars. And the roof opens and closes. There's only one problem: It would cost about three million dollars to build."

Grange was in awe of Pyle's agile, creative mind. Though there was an element of over-the-top showmanship to Pyle—he managed to find time to visit a barber for a daily trim while on the road—he had an uncanny ability to dream up unique concepts and projects. He was a natural-born entertainer, one reason why Grange was so drawn to him, even though Grange was aware that Pyle, like a wild animal, was driven purely by self-interest.

As the train rolled on toward Boston, Ford C. Frick, a reporter for the Hearst newspaper chain, who in 1951 would become the commissioner of baseball, sat close to Grange and pecked away at his typewriter. Frick had been following the tour for days. After closely studying number 77, he now wrote that Grange was slowly falling apart and that his psyche was becoming as fragile as a child's. He noted that Grange was "the most famous, and by the same token, the most harassed young man in America. Red Grange can't eat, he can't talk, he can't go out for a stroll down the street without being, at once, the center of all eyes . . . Youngsters, their eyes bright with adoration and hero worship, rush to touch his clothing; adults, still youthful at heart, come in to pat his back, to shake his hand and engage him in conversation . . . Perhaps somewhere there is an end to human endurance, and unless this writer is sadly mistaken, Harold 'Red' Grange, the wonder man of the gridiron, is nearing the end of that marvelous nervous energy which has carried him thus far in a campaign which is unparalleled in athletic history."

The train neared Boston. Grange rose at six in the morning from his sleeper bed. When he trudged to the bathroom to wash his face, a photographer sneaked in and popped a few photographs. Grange had no sanctuary. No matter where he was or what he was doing—even something as mundane as scrubbing his ears—someone would be watching. The young man from Wheaton craved a break from the tour, from the penetrating eyes, from the finger-pointing fans, but Pyle wouldn't let that happen, not with contracts to honor—and bushels of cash to be made.

Soon after arriving in Boston, Pyle and Grange visited the downtown office of Joseph P. Kennedy Sr., who owned a small production studio named FBO (Film Booking Offices of America). A few days earlier, Kennedy had signed Grange to a $50,000 contract to star in a film to be shot over the summer. The thirty-seven-year-old Kennedy had yet to enter the field of politics, but he already possessed the gift of small talk. As soon as Grange entered his office, Kennedy chatted on and on about his young boys, especially eight-year-old John Fitzgerald. The elder Kennedy often watched young John play touch football with his brothers on the lawn of their Cape Cod summer home, and he believed that John—whom the family called Jack—would one day be an outstanding professional football player, maybe even as talented as Grange. He showed Grange and Pyle photographs of his children, including tiny Robert, who had been born three weeks earlier. As usual, Grange didn't say much during the visit, preferring to listen and let Kennedy talk the afternoon away.

A few hours after leaving Kennedy's office, Grange and the Bears walked into Boston's Braves Field, a concrete-and-steel stadium that could seat thirty thousand, where they were scheduled to play the Providence Steam Roller, an NFL team. It was another bitterly cold day. The temperature was six below zero and the field was frozen solid. But in spite of the frigid conditions and the fact that the game was played on a Wednesday early evening, they came for Grange.

An hour before kickoff, more than three thousand fans were already sitting in the stands, entranced, watching him go through his pregame warm-up routine. But something was wrong with number 77. He was limping. He appeared slow, lethargic. And when he tried to reach up and catch a ball, he had trouble lifting his left arm. Muscle by muscle, bone by bone, he was breaking down. A swarm of photographers hounded Grange on the field, forcing him to confine his warm-up to a tiny corner on the sideline so the commotion and puffs of white smoke coming from the cameras wouldn't disrupt the other players.

A few minutes before kickoff, a broad-shouldered man waddled up to Grange as he stood near the wooden bench. Babe Ruth was all smiles as he put his arm around him. "Hiya, kid. How you doing?" Ruth asked. "Sit down. Maybe you'd better lie down."

The presence of Ruth—a familiar figure in Boston, having played for the Red Sox for six years beginning at age nineteen—comforted Grange. Many reporters speculated that Grange was now a bigger figure on the American sports scene than Ruth, who told Grange to hang in there, to keep trying to do his best, to ignore the bad press. Though the two had known each other less than a week, they shared a kinship, a bond—the bond of stardom—that only a handful of athletes in America could understand. Other than Pyle, Grange didn't have anyone to tell him how to deal with the unrelenting demands of the media and the fans.

The two talked for several minutes. Grange soaked in all of Ruth's words, as if they were sustenance, as if he were learning from a teacher. Before Ruth took his seat in the stands, the two posed for photographers. Grange smiled widely for the cameras, his eyes squinting in the bright winter sunshine, his face aglow with genuine happiness. Ruth had done something for Grange that few had accomplished on the tour: He had lifted his spirits.

By *kickoff*, fifteen thousand fans were huddled in Braves Field, now a virtual refrigerator. To heighten interest in the game, Providence's general manager, Charles Coppen, had signed several former college stars to a one-game contract. Notre Dame's Don Miller and Jim Crowley, who formed half of the Irish's famed Four Horsemen backfield, were in Steam Roller uniforms. Unlike Grange, Miller and Crowley felt fresh, rested, ready to unleash holy hell on Grange. But number 77 hadn't had a break from football in five months, dating back to preseason practice with Illinois. As Halas and Pyle watched him limp onto the frozen field for the opening kickoff, they were most concerned about one thing: keeping their star healthy.

As stipulated in his contract, Grange played his mandatory two quarters, but he failed to show any of the flair that he had displayed just days ago in New York. He rushed the ball five times for 18 yards. He threw three passes: Two were incomplete, one was intercepted.

Late in the third period, Providence lined up in punt formation. Grange drifted back to be the return man. The Steam Roller punter then booted the ball directly at Grange. He may have been directed to do so at the orders of Coppen, who surely wanted to see Grange electrify the crowd. But instead of catching the punt, Grange let it bounce out of bounds. Even before the ball came to a rest, the crowd turned on him, booing loudly and shouting profanities and phrases like "Get the ice tongs!" The reaction startled Grange and left him shaken.

Chicago lost, 9–6, its first defeat since Grange joined the team. Moments after the game ended, a horde of angry fans spilled onto the field and charged at Grange, screaming that he was a fraud, a quitter, and they demanded a refund for their tickets. A man who got too close to the team's star player received a punch in the face from one of Grange's friends—most likely his childhood buddy Beans—sparking a small riot that required dozens of police officers to quell. When Grange finally squeezed his way through the jeering crowd and into the safety of the locker room, he confessed that he'd just learned a hard lesson: If a professional athlete doesn't perform to the best of his ability, he'll be subjected to boos.

A few hours after the loss, Grange and the Bears were back on the wooden platform at South Station, waiting for their train. They had played two games in two days and now—beaten, bruised, and battered—they were embarking on an all-night trip to Pittsburgh, where they had another game the following day. Contracts had already been signed so the traveling football show had to go on, even if it ravaged Grange and shortened the life span of his promising professional career.

At this point in the tour, there were few good vibes aboard the train. Players were hurt and tired and even angry; many felt that Pyle, who seemed to always have a snake oil salesman's smile on his face, was taking advantage of them. While Grange and Pyle had already pocketed more than a combined $200,000 through seven games in salary and endorsement deals, the other players were earning about $60 a game. This payout system struck most of the players as unfair, especially now that several of Grange's teammates had succumbed to injury.

The Doghouse resembled a mobile triage unit. Players had white bandages wrapped around their arms, their knees, even their heads. Nearly everyone had a limp. Black eyes were as common as bathtub gin, and bruises dotted the body of every player. The women's washroom was transformed into a sick ward, which now, as the locomotive rumbled through the night toward the Steel City, was crowded with injured players. Laurie Walquist, a right halfback, was being treated for a fractured toe on his left foot, an injury that would sideline him for the rest of the tour. The Bears were so short of able bodies that Halas asked team trainer Andy Lotshaw, who had never played organized football, to suit up for the Pittsburgh game. Lotshaw reluctantly agreed, although he believed he was volunteering for a suicide mission. He'd had a front-row seat to the savagery of the tour, and he knew that the chances of surviving without an injury were slim.

The cheap shots aimed at Grange and his teammates had grown in frequency and ferociousness with every game. Nearly every opposing player seemingly wanted to prove that he deserved the attention and acclaim from fans and reporters, not Grange. They kicked, stomped, punched, elbowed, gouged eyes, bit, spit, and even pulled hair at every opportunity. The games were turning more barbaric by the play. Grange, peering out the train window into the cold dark winter night, silently wondered just how much more he could take.

Pittsburgh was just as raw and gray and icy as Boston had been. The Bears were in no mood for another game, especially in the numbing cold at Forbes Field against another team of local all-stars. When Grange went through his usual pregame warm-up, he looked stiff, as if he were forty-two, not twenty-two. He was a picture of an athlete falling apart.

Chicago received the opening kickoff. Once on offense, Grange was handed the ball, causing a wave of excitement to pulse through the crowd of only 4,111. But Grange couldn't break through the line of scrimmage and was quickly tackled. A few minutes later, he caught a punt and ran up the field, trying his hardest to summon all of his skills. But his energy and his talent had literally been beaten out of him. Grange couldn't cut the way he once did, couldn't accelerate the way he once did, and a Pittsburgh defender rammed into him, lifting Grange backward and into the air, then slamming him onto the ice-hard ground—a devastating hit. Grange landed square on his left arm, the same arm that he'd injured against the Giants. Slowly lifting himself from the frozen turf, he immediately knew something was very wrong with his arm, which throbbed in pain with every movement, every heartbeat.

Grange cradled his limp left limb in his right arm and struggled to the sideline. The crowd hollered in displeasure, booing loudly as he slowly walked to the locker room. Grange didn't understand. *Can't they tell I'm hurt? That I can't play?*

Halas was even more upset than the freezing fans at Forbes Field. Grange possessed a talent that was as rare as capturing lightning in a photograph, and the coach-owner-player immediately feared that the final days of the tour would be a financial bust if number 77 couldn't play. Grange had seduced so many with the beauty he could create on the field—over the last three years he had played before more than one million fans—but now it looked like Grange wouldn't be returning to the field anytime soon. With one hard tackle, everything suddenly changed.

Inside the locker room, Marion Leonard, another friend from Wheaton who had recently joined the tour, wrapped a bandage around Grange's arm. The pain was torturous. Leonard helped Grange take off his blue jersey, his shoulder pads, his cleats, and his knickers. A few minutes later, Grange emerged from the locker room wearing his flamboyant raccoon coat and took a seat on the strip of plywood that was used as the bench a few feet from the grandstand. Many in the crowd spent the next three quarters hurling verbal stones at Grange, using foul language, calling him washed up, a bum, a has-been. He watched his team lose, 24–0. It wasn't just the low point of the tour for Grange, it was the nadir of his athletic career.

After lighting into his men in the locker room for their indifferent play, Halas asked Dr. Gustav Berg, the team doctor for both the Pittsburgh All-Stars and the Pittsburgh Pirates baseball team, to examine Grange's arm. Halas would have liked his own trainer to inspect Grange, but Lotshaw had been knocked silly during the game and was in no condition to evaluate the Bears' most precious player. Berg issued a grave diagnosis: Grange had suffered a torn ligament and a broken blood vessel in his arm. The doctor recommended at least two weeks of rest.

Yet later that night, as Grange sat on his bed in the Schenley Hotel, surrounded by a group of reporters, he said that he had simply bruised his arm and planned to be on the field for the tour's final two games in Detroit and Chicago. Grange felt a responsibility to honor his contract, even if playing caused a crippling pain in his arm.

After the reporters left his room, Grange struggled to fall asleep. His left upper arm was now almost twice the size of his right arm. Red splotches covered the skin. A large lump nearly the size of a tennis ball had formed on his shoulder. The debilitating pain gnawed at Grange, keeping him from drifting into dreamland. He simply stared at his hotel room ceiling, dozing fitfully. He was wide awake when the sun rose over the Steel City. He eventually swung his feet to the floor, sat on the edge of his bed, and asked himself: *Is all of this really worth it?*

Pyle *was gone*. He'd left Grange and Halas and the Bears before the Pittsburgh game, traveling to the West Coast to organize the second leg of the barnstorming tour. It would begin in Florida, stop in New Orleans, proceed to Los Angeles, and then go through Portland before ending in Seattle. Pyle believed that a second tour would cement Grange's status as the most famous athlete of his time, and that would translate into one thing: big money. So while Grange couldn't even sleep because he was in so much agony, Pyle was plotting to keep the cash train moving along the tracks.

After the Bears arrived in Detroit the following morning, another doctor examined Grange. He confirmed the original diagnosis and added even worse news: He had discovered a blood clot in Grange's injured arm. The doctor then told Grange that he had to rest for the next two weeks—or risk death, because if the clot broke off and traveled to his heart, it could trigger a fatal heart attack. The best way to dissolve the clot and heal the injuries would be to keep his arm as still as possible. The doctor swaddled Grange's arm, which was one elongated bruise, in a thick white bandage and placed it in a sling.

To Halas's despair, the injury kept Grange from playing the next day at Detroit's Navin Field against the Panthers, an NFL team. Halas knew ticket sales would plummet once the news leaked out, but he felt obligated to phone Panthers owner and coach Jimmy Conzelman to tell him that Grange wouldn't be suiting up for the game. Conzelman then called the local newspapers and informed them that Grange wasn't going to play. The following morning, the news was splashed across the sports pages of several Detroit newspapers.

Conzelman, who had hoped to net more than $20,000 from the Grange game, didn't know what to expect. Several hours before kickoff, as he sat in his office at Navin Field, he glanced out his window and saw a long line outside the ticket office. *What a great sports town!* Conzelman thought to himself as he inspected the throng. *Grange isn't going to play, but they're still lining up to buy tickets.*

Minutes later his phone rang. The manager of his ticket office quickly brought the owner back to reality: He reported that more than nine thousand fans were lined up demanding their money back. Conzelman instructed his ticket manager to honor these requests, and Detroit ended up refunding more than $18,000 worth of tickets. This demonstrated the power of Grange: The fans didn't come to see a football game, they came to see him. (For the next few years, Conzelman would swear that the reason his team didn't survive in the NFL—the Panthers folded after the 1926 season—was because Grange didn't play in this game. He believed that Grange's injury had turned away potential fans and thus made a thriving franchise in the Motor City virtually impossible. Professional football wouldn't return to Detroit until 1934, when the Lions were born.)

Grange watched from the sidelines as his teammates lost, 21–0. Only a few thousand fans stayed to watch the game. The highlight came during halftime, when one of Grange's friends grabbed a megaphone and, near midfield, yelled, "Laaaa-dies and gentlemen, I take great pleasure in introducing to you our great gridiron hero, pride of the United States—Harold E. Red Grange!"

Grange stepped forward in his raccoon coat and winter cap, waving to the crowd with his good arm. A crush of photographers rushed at him, their cameras popping and flashing. He tried to smile—he was getting better at manufacturing forced grins for the cameras—but now he just couldn't. His arm hurt too much.

"Don't frown like that—smile!" yelled one photographer.

"Aw," Grange grumbled.

"Take your hat off!" yelled another photographer.

"Aw, it's too cold," Grange replied. But, seconds later, he took off his hat—accommodating as always.

On *their way back* to Chicago for the final game of the tour against the Giants, the Bears' Pullman stopped briefly at the station in Elkhart, Indiana. Most of the players stayed on the train, but Edward Healy and George Trafton walked across the street to a lunch counter. As they were eating sandwiches and chatting with locals, the train began pulling out of the station. The players had lost track of time. In a panic they bolted across the street, but because they were so banged up from the tour, they could only hobble. Healy grabbed the handrail of the rear car and lifted himself aboard, but Trafton, who'd played nearly every minute of every game, couldn't catch up. Standing in the back of the rear car, Healy laughed uncontrollably at the sight of the shrinking Trafton standing on the train tracks in a short-sleeve shirt and shivering against the bitterly cold winter wind with a partially eaten sandwich in his hand. He had to hitchhike 110 miles back to Chicago.

As *soon as the Bears* returned home, another doctor looked at Grange's arm. An X-ray revealed several ruptured muscles in his shoulder and internal bleeding, which had caused the blood clot to form. This doctor, too, warned that if Grange played in the final game of the first tour, the clot might migrate to his heart and kill him. After Halas announced to reporters that Grange wouldn't play against New York, thousands of fans marched to the Bears' ticket office and refunded their tickets. The next day, Grange sat on the bench and watched his exhausted teammates lose, 9–0, to New York.

Not long after the game was over, Damon Runyon banged at his typewriter, writing an assessment of the Bears' East Coast barnstorming tour and the importance of Grange to professional football. "The general public has heard, vaguely, of professional football as played in different cities of the country for years, and with some success, but the game had not made much headway," Runyon wrote in the New York *American*. "It had been slowly gathering momentum, however, and during this past season it began attracting more attention than ever—and more customers. It invaded new territory, including New York City, and it commenced getting valuable word-of-mouth advertising as a thing worth seeing.

"But it needed a Jumbo. Professional football needed a Jumbo, and it got its Jumbo when it landed Harold Red Grange of the University of Illinois. He attracted nationwide attention to the professional game. He put it on the front pages of newspapers . . . Red Grange [has] done more for professional football than Ruth did for baseball, because baseball was an institution when Ruth began, while Grange has probably made professional football an institution."

Outfitted in his raccoon coat and surrounded by a dozen police officers, Grange left Cubs Park about thirty minutes after the Bears' loss to the Giants. The first leg of the tour was over; it was time for Grange and his teammates to recuperate. But the fans still couldn't get enough. As Grange gingerly strolled toward a taxi, admirers mobbed him, yelling his name, patting his back, reaching for a handshake. The fans may have been disgruntled when they were in the stadium and watched Grange do nothing but sit on the bench, but they still were smitten with their home-state star, still in the early days of a love affair. Everywhere he had gone during the eighteen-day tour, even when he didn't play, it was like this for Grange, who was now the most popular man in America.

Grange climbed into the cab, and a hundred of his most devout followers stood on the sidewalk and watched the car disappear into the frigid December evening. Grange and Pyle had made more than a combined quarter of a million dollars over the last two weeks. Though Grange had paid dearly for this money, the tour had been an overwhelming success. In the seven games that Grange had suited up for, he had played before nearly two hundred thousand fans—most of whom had never attended a professional football game. And over the previous three weeks, he had generated more inches of coverage in newspapers across the country than anyone, even more than President Coolidge. For the first time, major American newspapers were covering the NFL, and that was all because of Grange, a player around whom an entire league was being built. But now, as the taxicab carrying the star rolled through gathering darkness, motoring away from his fans and past the row houses that surrounded Cubs Park, there was only one thing he wanted to do: rest.

13

THE LADIES' MAN

Red Grange was home again. The day after Chicago's loss to the Giants, he caught a train to Wheaton. The Bears had nine days of vacation before the second stage of their tour kicked off in Coral Gables, Florida, and so Grange headed home. He was now a man of means, and one of the first things he did when he reached Wheaton was to share his good fortune with the two people who mattered most to him: his father and brother.

For Garland, Grange bought a roadster, a two-seat car that had no roof and no rear or side windows. This was a popular car that implied wealth and accomplishment, which was why he presented it to his kid brother. For his father, Grange wrote a check for $1,000 and told him to spend it however he desired—on a new apartment, a new house, new clothes, a new car, whatever he wanted. This was one of the happiest days of Red's young life, because all of the work he had put in on the gridiron over the last five years had been building to this moment, this crowning hour, when the oldest son could walk through the door of his family's home with a checkbook in one hand and the promise of a brighter future in the other.

When Red visited his old high school friends, they saw how much he had changed since being away. Now, for the first time in his life, Grange could take command of a room full of people. He had given so many interviews over the last three years that he now felt comfortable talking in front of large groups and telling stories from his life and times. He was also more at ease around women. The shyness that he once felt around them had melted away with the passing of time, and when he was at home over these nine days, many of the girls that had attended high school with Red couldn't believe how much he had matured, how much he had opened up. This was the upside of fame for Grange: It forced him out of his shell.

For the second leg of the tour, which would feature nine games over thirty-six days and cover more than seven thousand miles, the newly wealthy Pyle lavished his money on the team, ensuring that the players traveled in comfort and style. Pyle rented the Bears their own first-class Pullman, which the players quickly dubbed, tongue-in-cheek, Bethula, meaning "virgin" in Hebrew. Pyle also hired a personal porter for the team, a black man named Clem, who was charged with transporting the players' luggage and serving as their waiter. By the mid-1920s, the peak of train travel in the United States, more than two hundred thousand black men—including many former slaves—worked as Pullman porters. And now the Chicago Bears, the richest football team in America, had someone at their beck and call to shine shoes, make beds, fluff pillows, and mend clothes.

Pyle couldn't spend his money fast enough. He opened up an office in New York at the ritzy Hotel McAlpin, where he entertained potential endorsers of Grange at the hotel's Marine Grill, one of the most expensive restaurants in the city. He spent $25,000 for one thousand glossy photographs of Grange, which his star player signed and Pyle handed out for free. Though Pyle kept a little red notebook in his breast pocket to record every last cent of his expenditures, careful record keeping didn't stop him from throwing around his cash as if he had an endless supply. If, for example, a waiter on a train remembered his name and called him Mr. Pyle, he would always leave a $10 tip, no matter how inexpensive the meal, simply because Pyle relished the recognition of strangers. For Pyle, this was the ultimate sign of success.

Realizing that he needed additional bodies on his team for this second leg, Halas signed four more players before leaving for Florida, increasing the roster from eighteen to twenty-two. He also bought his players sweaters with the word *Bears* emblazoned across the chest, along with matching knickers and kneesocks—clothes they could wear on the train. Halas also purchased an extra uniform for every player. During their first tour, there often wasn't enough time between games to wash the single uniform each player had, forcing them to play in dirty, wet gear. Now that Halas had money, his team would look professional—both on the train and on the field.

The Bears arrived in Coral Gables three days before Christmas. But when the team walked onto the field where it was to play the Coral Gables Collegians on December 25, Halas was shocked at what he didn't see: stands. There was just a wide-open field with no seating. Expecting a large crowd, Halas verbally lashed out at the game's promoter and then quickly made a few phone calls. The next day, more than two hundred carpenters began constructing a makeshift wooden stadium that could accommodate twenty-five thousand fans.

Pyle stipulated that he be paid up front, even before a single ticket was sold, living up to his nickname Cash and Carry. He made the same demand at every stop of the second tour. His take for the Coral Gables game was $25,000, and he left it up to a local promoter to determine the ticket prices. The promoter, figuring that Grange would attract a larger audience than the president, priced the tickets from $5 for the worst seats in the stadium to $18.50 for the best. Those prices were more than 50 percent higher than the cost of any ticket offered during the earlier tour. Pyle suggested to the promoter that he was making a financial miscalculation, but the man stood his ground. Pyle's instincts were right: The high prices kept fans away— even in the booming economy of South Florida, fueled by a land rush by northeasterners and midwesterners who were flocking to the warmth and sunshine to buy real estate. The promoter sold only eight thousand tickets.

Grange felt better than he had in months. The nine-day break al-lowed his shoulder to partially heal—and it showed on the field. Playing against a team of college players that had practiced together only a few times, Grange dominated the game. Early in the first quarter, he took a handoff and tore off a spectacular 45-yard run that featured all of his resplendent moves: He dodged tacklers, he stiff-armed, he flashed his sprinter's speed. Though Grange didn't score on the run, it left the small crowd satisfied and feeling like it had gotten its money's worth. Grange rushed for 98 yards on nine carries and scored the game's only touchdown, a 2-yard plunge. The Bears won, 7–0. More important to Halas and Pyle, they now had proof that their star was back. After the game, Halas quickly fired off a press release touting the talents of his most important player and how he'd recovered from injury, which newspapers across the country reported to its readers the next day. As Pyle and Halas boarded the Bears' Pullman in Coral Gables, they believed that, as long as Grange stayed healthy, the second leg of the tour would be even more successful—and more lucrative—than the first.

Shortly after the game, a crew of carpenters returned to the field and tore down the wooden stands. Twenty-four hours later, there was no evidence that a professional football game had ever been played there.

The Bears next stopped in Tampa, Florida, where they were scheduled to play a local team called the Cardinals. The night before the game, Grange lit a blue streak through the hottest Tampa nightspots with a few of his new friends: Helen Wainwright, an Olympic diver who had won a silver medal in the 1920 Summer Games in Antwerp, Belgium; Jim Barnes, a professional golfer who had recently won the 1925 British Open; and Johnny Farrell, who had five victories on the Professional Golf Association (PGA) of America Tour and would capture the 1928 U.S. Open. Grange was now a bona fide celebrity, and in his free time he occasionally floated in rarefied circles. The twenty-two-year-old was beginning to relish the opportunities that his fame was affording him. Other well-known athletes were attracted to his magnetic appeal, as they were drawn to Ruth and Dempsey and movie actors like Rudolph Valentino and Mary Pickford. Grange was the definition of 1920s cool: He had looks to make women weak in the knees; he had the hefty bank account; and he had the boy-next-door politeness. Grange was doing something for the NFL that no other player before ever had: He was making the professional football player fashionable.

On this evening, Grange had a little *too* much fun with his new friends. Tampa police issued him a speeding ticket for driving sixty-five miles per hour—one of the few times on this tour that anyone stopped the Ghost.

O*ne of the game's other titans* played for the Tampa Cardinals: Jim Thorpe. He was thirty-seven years old now, and his talents had been eroded by age and alcohol abuse. Thirteen years earlier, Thorpe had won two gold medals in the decathlon and pentathlon at the 1912 Summer Olympics in Stockholm, Sweden. That fall he led the Carlisle Indian School, coached by Pop Warner, to an 8-1-1 record, including a victory over an Army team that featured a linebacker named Dwight Eisenhower. Late in the game at West Point, as Eisenhower tried to tackle Thorpe, the future general and president collided with another Army defender and injured his knee so badly that he would never play another down of football. On that afternoon, Thorpe had been at the height of his athletic powers, rushing for over 200 yards in Carlisle's 27–6 victory. But now Thorpe was a shadow of that player, and as he lumbered around the field during warm-ups in front of a crowd of eight thousand, he appeared so slow and out of shape that Grange, who had never seen Thorpe play before, was amazed at how quickly the legend he had read about as a boy had fallen into decay.

Grange played only two quarters against the Cardinals. Thorpe, lining up at halfback, fumbled several times and failed to break free on any long runs. The game was a defensive struggle until the fourth quarter, when Grange turned it on. With the ball on the Bears' 30-yard line, Grange received a pitch from quarterback Joey Sternaman, then cut up the field. For six seconds, Grange was a sight to behold: He broke tackles, he stiff-armed, he stampeded over Thorpe, then scooted into the open field and across the goal line. It was as if this was the torch-passing moment from the Indian to the Ghost. Grange was now the game's greatest player, replacing Thorpe. As for

Thorpe, he saw only the back of Grange's number 77 jersey dashing away as he lay on the ground, his football career and his life in ruins on this New Year's Day 1926. The Bears won, 17–3.

As soon as they showered, the Bears traveled north to Jacksonville for their game the next day. The local promoter there, John S. O'Brien, wanted to copy the barnstorming model that Pyle and Halas had established, and he put together a team of college all-stars for a five-game tour across Florida. Needing a big name, a star that could command widespread attention like Grange, he contacted Ernie Nevers, a former All-America fullback at Stanford University. In the 1925 Rose Bowl, Stanford played Notre Dame and its Four Horsemen backfield. Nevers outshined them all before a crowd of fifty-three thousand, rushing for 114 yards—more yardage than the Horsemen combined—to lead the Stanford Cardinal to a 27–10 victory. Afterward, Stanford's coach, Pop Warner, told any reporter he could find that Nevers had more talent than even the great Thorpe in his prime. Halas called Nevers "the West Coast's answer to Red Grange."

Nevers hadn't planned on playing professional football; instead he hoped to become a pitcher for the St. Louis Browns. But once he read about the sums of money that Grange was pulling in with the Bears—and the level of fame he was gaining—he gave the NFL a second look. He negotiated a contract with O'Brien in which he would earn $50,000 for the five games. His first game would be against Grange and the Bears. Nevers's decision to play underscored the impact of Grange; suddenly former college players across the country wanted to be a part of the professional game.

Once O'Brien had secured Nevers on his roster, he contacted Pyle. "It should be the battle of the century, Mr. Pyle," O'Brien said of the upcoming contest between his Jacksonville All-Stars and the Bears. "I am to cover the South with announcements that no red-blooded man should miss the titanic struggle between the Galloping Ghost and the Lion of the Sierras—Red and Ernie. It will be a sell-out with lamentable numbers turned away at the gate."

"I'm glad to hear it," Pyle replied, "because you will now read with less pain our contract."

Cash and Carry, as usual, demanded his money beforehand:

$20,000 plus a guaranteed 65 percent of the gate. O'Brien agreed, but then he repeated the mistake of the Coral Gables promoter by ramping up ticket prices, charging from $5.50 to $8.50 for a ticket. This was more than four times what tickets had cost to see Grange play at Cubs Park in Chicago, and on game day, only 6,700 fans pushed through the turnstiles. The paltry turnout meant that O'Brien lost about $12,500, but he learned a costly lesson: Professional football hadn't yet arrived as a marquee sport in America, which meant that potential ticket buyers decided with their heads, not their hearts. Pyle was trying to change this dynamic with his aggressive marketing of Grange, building him into the one player that fans would pay an exorbitant amount to see. In stores across America, fans could now buy Red Grange dolls, Red Grange candy bars, Red Grange yeast foam malted milk, Red Grange fountain pens, Red Grange socks. Pyle continually made calls and fired off letters to different companies, trying to capitalize on the media attention. Because of Pyle, Grange was no longer just a football player. He was a brand.

Grange and Nevers came face to face several times on the field, but it wasn't the "titanic struggle" breathlessly promoted by O'Brien. Nevers, who played linebacker on defense, made several hard, jarring tackles on Grange, and the Jacksonville All-Stars successfully prevented him from breaking any long runs. Grange threw a 26-yard touchdown pass to end Vern Mullen for the Bears' first score; Nevers bowled over a Chicago defender for a 5-yard touchdown run in the fourth quarter. But because the All-Stars had practiced together for only a week, they were no match for the finely tuned— and still relatively fresh—Chicago squad. Late in the game, a few Jacksonville players became so frustrated that they started unleashing late hits and in-the-pile punches. The Bears grew so upset with one Jacksonville cheap-shot artist that they chased him into the stands. Chicago won, 19–6.

The Bears had nearly a week off before their next game, in New Orleans. The players enjoyed a leisurely trip along the Gulf Coast, relaxing on their private train, which had several sleeping cars that featured luxurious beds, upholstered chairs, carpeting, card tables, and a small library. Halas had the train parked in a remote area of the New Orleans railroad yard. While the team stayed in the Pullman during the week, Halas, Pyle, and Grange checked into rooms at the Roosevelt Hotel, a five-star palace in the French Quarter and a hot spot for the rich and famous. It housed the Blue Room, where nearly every night big bands and jazz and blues legends like Louis Armstrong and Blind Lemon Jefferson had patrons tapping their highball glasses to the beat of the music.

Grange was now further enjoying the sweet fruits of fame. He had received nearly two hundred thousand fan letters from women during the previous year, and scores of well-dressed ladies showed up at nearly every hotel lobby where the Bears stayed, hoping for a magical meeting with the Ghost. He was, after all, almost as much a sex symbol as he was a football star. And when he ventured into nightclubs and jazz joints—which he liked to do during downtime on the tour—he was always the center of attention.

But he was nowhere near the charmer that Pyle was. Refined, articulate, a man of letters, and a sweet talker for the ages, Pyle seemed to have a woman in every city the Bears visited—or so it appeared to Grange. When the two went out to places like the Blue Room, the sight of Grange would lure the ladies to their table. Then Pyle would go to work, whispering sweet nothings into the ears of any lovely who would listen. They were a formidable one-two punch—the quiet, famous pretty boy and the dapper, smooth-speaking gentleman—and there was rarely a night out during the tour when they each didn't have an array of offers to be joined in their rooms. Grange rarely indulged, unlike Pyle, whom Grange would come to call "the greatest ladies' man that ever lived."

Grange and Pyle weren't the only Bears having fun in New Orleans. One night a player, full of liquid courage, caused so much of a commotion at a bar that the owner called the police. The player, who was wearing the sweater Halas had given him with the word *Bears* on the front and his uniform number on the back, ran out the door at the sight of the police. They chased him back to the railcar. When the player entered the Pullman, he spotted Clem, the team's porter, who was just heading out for dinner.

"Here, Clem," the player said, taking off his sweater and hand-ing it to him. "It's cold out. Better wear this to keep warm."

The player ran into his berth and slid the door shut. Clem put on the sweater and walked out of the Pullman. But after taking a few steps Clem was detained by the police. They took him to the bar to be identified by the manager, but all the manager could do was shake his head. "That looks like the same sweater, all right," the man told police, "but the fellow was white."

The next day the player shared with his teammates the story of how he got away, of how, for one night, he was as elusive as the Ghost.

When Grange wasn't sampling the sights and sounds of the Cres-cent City, he was promoting the upcoming game at Heinemann Park against the Southern All-Stars. The team featured Lester Lauten-schlager, a former Tulane University quarterback who had been named along with Grange to Walter Camp's 1925 All-America team. Lautenschlager, like so many former college players, now wanted to follow in Grange's path and become a professional football player.

Pyle organized a busy itinerary for Grange. He gave a speech plugging the NFL at the Young Men's Business Club before a record four hundred people. Now comfortable addressing large crowds, Grange was the league's first pitchman, explaining that the pro game was a more exciting, more talent-laden version of the college game, that it was the most compelling theater in all of sports. After shaking nearly every hand at the business club, Grange visited the Fair Grounds Race Course, where he watched the Red Grange Handi-cap. After the race, with Pyle at his side and being trailed by several photographers, he ventured into the winner's circle and presented a floral pink football to the victorious jockey, who had ridden a thor-oughbred named Prickly Heat.

Yet in spite of Pyle's and Grange's best PR efforts, only six thou-sand fans filled Heinemann Park, a baseball stadium at the intersec-tion of Tulane and South Carrollton avenues. The extended time off between games benefited Grange. He rushed for 136 yards and scored one touchdown in Chicago's 14–0 win. His numbers would have been more impressive, but a holding call negated a 51-yard punt return for a touchdown. When Pyle saw the referee wave off the electrifying run, he stormed from the sideline onto the field, yelling at the referee, *Don't you understand, goddamn it, that the people here paid to see Red score? That Red is the show?*

The *Bears boarded* their train and sat back for an 1,800-mile journey to Los Angeles. As the iron-horse engine pushed black smoke into the southern sky and pulled the Pullman cars out of the New Orleans rail yard, everyone on the train felt good. The Bears were 4-0 and had only five games left on their second and final tour. Grange was growing more famous by the moment. Pyle was becoming as wealthy as any man in professional sports. And Halas was overjoyed because the Red Grange tour—as he now referred to it—was achieving the one thing he'd hoped for more than any other: It was starting to legitimize, one city at a time, the game of professional football in America.

14

THE STORMING OF LOS ANGELES

The locomotive strained as it headed westward out of bayou country, iron wheels against iron rails, reaching sixty miles per hour. It rolled across the high plains of Texas, over the deserts of New Mexico and Arizona, slowed to climb the steep lower reaches of California's Sierra Nevada Mountains, and finally glided into the glitz and glamour of Los Angeles.

During their time on the train, the players engaged in their usual games of gin rummy and poker, but Grange still preferred to sit by himself next to the window in his Pullman and simply take in the wide-ranging landscape of the American Southwest. His teammates mostly left him alone. They all knew he was different from them in so many ways, but they didn't mock or belittle him. Some of the Bears were in awe of the Ghost and how he always seemed to deliver at the most important times; others didn't understand his behavior, but now even those players who had been skeptical of Grange at the start of the tour viewed him like a little brother learning his way in the world.

With his phonograph on his lap, Grange listened to jazz tunes, barely audible over the joshing of his teammates and the shuffling of the cards. This was when Grange was happiest on the tour: by himself, out of the glare of attention, slipping into reverie as he peered out the window at 1920s America. But whenever the Bears' train stopped at depots along their route to California, Halas and Pyle would put Grange to work. Because at nearly every depot, a crowd would form. Grange, dressed sharply in a coat and tie and bowler hat, would stand on the platform outside the last car and wave to his fans and utter a few remarks, the way several previous presidents had done during whistle-stop campaign tours. The West Coast fans had been reading newspaper accounts of Grange for more than three years, and now, wherever his Pullman stopped, they gathered in great numbers to greet the Ghost.

Almost as soon as he walked off the train in LA's River Station depot, a throng of fans swarmed Grange, asking for autographs and thrusting their hands at him, hoping for a handshake. Newspaperman Damon Runyon, who was traveling with the team, was astonished. Just a month earlier, Runyon, like most East Coast writers, believed that Grange was little more than a regional curiosity. But Runyon had seen the crowds that welcomed Grange grow progressively larger at every stop on the tour, and now there were at least one thousand anxiously awaiting his arrival at River Station. This confirmed to Runyon that Red Grange, like Babe Ruth, was now a full-blown national phenomenon.

The first night in the City of Angels, millionaire William Wrigley invited Grange and his teammates to his island, Catalina, for dinner. It seemed as if every celebrity in town wanted to rub shoulders with Grange. Pyle was in his element as he strolled the streets of Hollywood, arranging several high-profile get-togethers for his young client. During the course of three days, Grange met and socialized with, among others, silent film stars Mary Pickford, Harold Lloyd, and Charlie Chaplin, and the powerful Hearst family, owners of a chain of newspapers that spread across the nation. Grange was so beloved in California that the city council of nearby Glendale named a street after him.

The game against the Los Angeles Tigers in the Los Angeles Memorial Coliseum had been touted in the local papers for over two weeks. Ticket sales had been stout in anticipation of the January 16 contest, and on the day before the game, Pyle arranged another publicity gambit. Grange and a few of his teammates stood on the roof of the thirteen-story Biltmore Hotel clutching footballs. Pyle announced that he would pay $25 to anyone on the ground who could catch a ball thrown by a Bears player. More than five thousand showed up for the contest. At the appointed time, Grange and his teammates began tossing the balls from the rooftop. They traveled through the air at such a high rate of speed that most of the people ran for cover from the falling fifteen-ounce bombs rather than try to make a pain-inducing catch. But four men each cleanly snagged a pigskin before it thumped to the ground, costing Pyle $100 out of his pocket.

That night Grange attended a dinner at the Windsor Tea Room, where a few hundred Illinois alums welcomed Red with a standing ovation. Looking over the large gathering, Grange spotted the man he considered a second father, although the two hadn't spoken since they had parted on poor terms after Grange's final collegiate game against Ohio State. Grange rushed to his old coach.

"Hello, Red," Bob Zuppke said. "I wish you lots of luck tomorrow."

"Hello, Coach," Grange replied. "Have you got tickets for the game? If not, I want you to sit on our bench."

Though it went unstated, this was Grange's attempt to apologize to Zuppke, who still believed that Grange had sullied the reputation of the University of Illinois—and of all of college football—by dropping out of school and turning professional. Zuppke was still angry, still hurt, by what he perceived to be an act of betrayal by Grange.

"Thanks just the same," Zuppke said, spurning the offer, "but I've sat on enough benches for some time to come."

This was the last time the two men would speak for several months.

While in Los Angeles, Pyle was rarely far from Runyon. The two had grown close over the previous few months, often hanging out together in New York at Lindy's, a Broadway restaurant that Runyon famously referred to as "Mindy's" in his stories. Runyon often spent a few months each winter in the sunshine of Los Angeles, and now he entertained Pyle at a few of his favorite haunts. Theirs was a relationship based on mutual interest. In Pyle, Runyon found a quote machine, a character as colorful as any he had come across in his years as a syndicated sportswriter. In Runyon, Pyle found a writer whose words could reach millions, supplying access to the kind of publicity that no amount of money could buy. Pyle constantly whispered into Runyon's ear that Grange was the greatest football player who ever walked the planet, and by the time the two were having late-night bull sessions in Los Angeles, Runyon was starting to agree with that claim.

"My favorite amusement this past fall was reading statements of football experts and coaches that somebody else was a greater football player than Mr. Red Harold Grange," Runyon wrote. "Twenty years from now when we all have long gray whiskers, we will be harking back to Mr. Red Harold Grange as one of the greatest that ever lived."

On game day, more than seventy-five thousand people crammed into the seats of the Coliseum—the largest crowd ever to witness a professional football game on the West Coast. When the Bears and their coach ran onto the field for their pregame calisthenics and warm-up plays, Halas was amazed. First Chicago, then New York City, now Los Angeles. He felt as though he had conquered the three most influential cities in America, and it was at this moment—here, as he turned full circle on the grassy field on this picture-postcard-perfect Saturday afternoon and looked up into the overflowing stands—that he fully believed the NFL was going to make it.

The Los Angeles Tigers were led by George "Wildcat" Wilson, an All-America tailback at the University of Washington during the '25 season. He had scored 37 touchdowns for the Huskies during his career—a school record—and he'd rushed for 134 yards on 15 carries in Washington's 20–19 loss to the University of Alabama in the 1926 Rose Bowl two and a half weeks earlier. Pyle convinced Wilson that he could be the West Coast version of Grange and offered him $5,000 to play. Wilson accepted. Pyle was already plotting to launch his own professional football league the following season, and he envisioned Wilson being his biggest West Coast star; a player who could rival Grange on the playing field and in his ability to attract large crowds at stadiums up and down the coast.

On this afternoon, the wily Wildcat outshined the Galloping Ghost. He ran for more yards than Grange (118 to 34) and even Grange admired Wilson's ability to evade defenders in the open field. But Grange, as was his custom, came through in money time, when the game was on the line. He completed two long passes that set up his two short touchdown runs. Because of the large crowd, Grange didn't want to sit out his standard two quarters, so he played nearly the entire game, trying to give the fans their money's worth. The Bears won, 17–7. As Grange, escorted by several police officers, walked off the field and into the interior of the stadium, he was the object of another standing ovation. One more city, one more game, one more satisfied audience.

A *few hours after* winning at the Coliseum, the Bears climbed aboard their Pullman, Bethula, and headed south to San Diego, where they would play the next day against the California All-Stars, an outfit of local players. At a high school stadium in front of ten thousand fans, the Bears suffered an emotional letdown from the previous day's game and the passion of the Los Angeles crowd. Grange was not himself. His speed was slipping away—he was even caught from behind a few times when he had the ball in the open field—and he seemed wooden, worn. But Chicago won, 14–0. Three games remained before they would be homeward bound.

Immediately after the victory, the Bears traveled north through farm-to-market country to San Francisco. The team had a week before its game against the San Francisco Tigers at Kezar Stadium, located in the southeastern corner of Golden Gate Park. During practices at the stadium, Halas drilled his boys in the fundamentals of the game. Even now, six weeks after the barnstorming began, Halas still coached with focused, almost brutal intensity, as if his job depended on winning the next game. From the practice field, Halas and his players could see across San Francisco Bay, where construction would begin on the Golden Gate Bridge in two years. During their free time, they rode trolleys down Market Street and they walked through the streets of Chinatown, the largest Chinese community outside of Asia. Always looking to make news, Pyle told a reporter while in Chinatown that he had plans to take Grange on a tour of the Far East, that he and Red would bring this American game to Asia. This was Pyle pouring forth nothing but hot air, but it served its purpose: The next day, a local newspaper carried an article detailing Pyle's grand plan.

The Bears players had gotten along surprisingly well for most of this tour. There were times when arguments flamed up and team-mates would bicker like brothers, but there hadn't been any serious problems—until the night before their contest in San Francisco. At the team hotel, Sternaman, the Bears' quarterback and team captain, told center George Trafton that he wouldn't be starting against the Tigers. An argument erupted. Minutes later Trafton, a mountain of a man who had attended Notre Dame and was credited with being the first center to hike the ball with one hand, unleashed a violent haymaker on Sternaman, hitting him so hard that the quarterback flew through a window and landed on the lawn outside of the hotel. The fight ended abruptly, but this moment of aggression revealed that the strain of the tour—the travel, the rigors of the games, the loneliness of the road—was wearing on the players.

The next day, more than twenty-three thousand fans sat in the stands at Kezar Stadium. As soon as the ball was kicked off, it appeared as if that fight from the previous night had taken the wind out of the Bears. They lost their first game of the tour's second leg, 14–9. Grange was ineffective all afternoon. He was held to 41 yards on seven carries and was outplayed by Wildcat Wilson, who was playing for the Tigers and repeatedly tore through the Chicago defense. In the locker room afterward, every Bear wanted the same thing: to go home.

A few hours later, the team was back on its Pullman, steaming northward. The final two games would be played in the Pacific Northwest, one in Portland and one in Seattle. The most taxing barnstorming tour in the history of sports was almost over.

When their train pulled into the rail yards in Portland, several hundred fans were on hand to greet Grange. Once again, he shook every outstretched hand and signed every piece of paper that was thrust in front of him. As he and his teammates made their way through the station to waiting cabs, fans continued to mob the players, especially Grange, as if he were a visiting dignitary.

Realizing that only two games remained, Grange appeared hyperenergized against the Portland Longshoremen, displaying renewed agility and resurgent speed. In front of six thousand fans at a minor-league baseball stadium in Portland, Grange ran as if a championship were on the line. In two quarters of action, he rushed for more than 100 yards and scored two touchdowns in Chicago's 60–3 win. The small crowd had been a disappointment to Pyle and Halas, but the contest was still a success for the NFL, because the local papers wrote more about professional football in the days before and after the game than they had during the entire preceding year.

The Bears hurried out of Portland and rode to Tacoma, Washington, where they checked into the newly opened Winthrop Hotel, which featured twenty-four "modern shops" and "three hundred telephones," according to the hotel manager. The final game of the tour against the Seattle All-Stars was slated for the next day, and even though the team didn't arrive in Tacoma until late in the evening, most of the players met in the hotel bar for one last night out together.

The bar was packed and the women were everywhere, hovering around the players like mosquitoes around ripe food. Pyle, nattily dressed and drawing on one cigarette after the next, sat protectively next to Grange, who was wearing a light tan tweed suit. Grange signed scores of autographs and posed for several photographs. But the Bears were mostly oblivious to the crowd around them. Tonight they gathered in small groups and reminisced, telling and retelling stories from their one-of-a-kind tour. They joked and laughed and shared many do-you-remember-when moments, but a sense of melancholy also filled the room, because they all knew the end was near.

The next day, a crowd of five thousand gave Grange a standing ovation as he jogged onto the field in Seattle, against a team that was anchored by Wildcat Wilson. He had suffered as many as ten concussions since turning pro, but for this last game, he summoned all of his skills, playing perhaps his best thirty minutes of the entire tour.

Grange ran for two touchdowns—each covering 30 yards—and he threw a perfect strike to a Bears end that resulted in a 60-yard score. All in the first half. He didn't play in the third and fourth quarters, but the Bears didn't need him, winning, 34–0. The tour was complete.

Back on their Pullman in Seattle, the Bears began their final ride. It would take them through the Rockies, across the prairies, and into the stockyards and factories that surrounded Chicago's Union Station. The most excited man aboard was Pyle. He crunched the numbers, estimating that he and Grange had pocketed about $150,000 from the second tour, and when combined with the money that they had made from their East Coast swing, the pair had netted about a half million dollars over the previous sixty-six days—days that had forever changed pro football in America.

The Bears had won twelve games and lost five on their two journeys across the United States. They had traveled more than fifteen thousand miles and had played before more than three hundred thousand fans between Thanksgiving Day 1925 and January 31, 1926. Reports of their feats appeared in nearly every major newspaper in the nation, and they had more of their games broadcast on radio than every other professional team combined in the history of the sport. They were the original America's Team of the NFL—and Grange was the league's original star.

As Grange relaxed in the railcar, he traveled into a future that glowed with promise. The NFL was no longer a backwater league, its games no longer confined to one-paragraph stories on the back pages of the country's newspapers. Now little boys across the nation were playing the game on fields and sandlots and imagining that they were the Galloping Ghost, adorned in that famous number 77 jersey. Now grown men gathered in bars, hotel lobbies, and in train stations just to get a glimpse of Grange. Now women who didn't even know the basic rules of football came to games to see what this heartthrob named Red was all about. Now, in this, the golden age of sports, he was the nation's most golden of athletes. Halas called him "the golden lad."

On this last night of the tour, as the train steamed toward Chicago, Grange finally fell asleep. When he opened his eyes the next morning, professional football in America had changed. It had emerged from the dark ages. Soon there would be opportunities for players, coaches, marketers, and agents that had never existed before in the NFL. Soon new franchises in new cities would be born and new stadiums would be erected. Soon the NFL would set out on the path to becoming what it is today: the most popular professional sports league in America.

But one thing had already been established by this night. As Grange slept in his bunk, he was already a legend—a legend that was put to poetry by Grantland Rice, a legend that would grow with the passing of every autumn.

THE FOUNDING FATHERS

Just *days after the end* of the sixty-six-day, nineteen-game barn-storming tour, George Halas pulled open the heavy entrance door of his bank in Chicago. With a large envelope tucked under one arm, he briskly walked past two uniformed guards toward a teller behind the wooden counter. These were dangerous days in Chicago—months earlier, a security guard at Franklin Trust and Savings Bank had been murdered during a robbery—and the bank tellers all stood behind protective thick glass. Halas slid the envelope through a narrow slit in the glass. This was the crowning act, the ultimate moment that Halas had been waiting for ever since Day One of the tour: He was finally cashing in on Red Grange.

On the train ride from the West Coast, Halas had sat alone in his Pullman and, with a pen, calculated how much money his Chicago Bears had earned on the tour, adding and subtracting numbers on the back of an envelope. The total costs of the tour—including players' salaries, transportation, lodging, food, and advertising—were $282,226.67. Halas awarded himself and co-owner Ed Sternaman salaries of $12,000 and bonuses of $23,000. And he set aside $1,685.45 for taxes to the U.S. government. When his computations were complete, Halas determined that he had netted his first substantial profit as owner of the Bears: $14,675.01—which today is the equivalent of nearly one million dollars.

After Halas deposited the money in the bank, he went back to his office and began plotting for the 1926 season. He hoped that Grange would return for the coming campaign, but he also perused the rosters of college football squads across the country, trying to pinpoint another college star that he could sign as soon as the college season was over. The Grange experiment had been so wildly successful that Halas wanted to showcase another young player on a barnstorming tour at the end of the 1926 NFL season. Halas believed that another nation-wide tour would not only be a moneymaker, it would also continue to spread the gospel of professional football across the United States.

But a few days after Halas had put his Grange tour money in the bank, two old friends from the University of Illinois knocked on his office door. Bob Zuppke, the Illinis' head football coach, and George Huff, the school's athletic director, sat down to discuss a subject that they believed had the potential to destroy college football. They wanted to talk about Red Grange.

Zuppke cushioned Halas's surprise by assuring him that Halas hadn't violated any rules when he signed Grange to a professional contract after he completed his senior season at Illinois. But Zuppke then emphatically told Halas that Grange's move to pro ball before he had earned his diploma had outraged college officials in schools across America. It sent the message, Zuppke argued, that college athletics were merely training grounds for professional leagues, which thereby devalued the overall experience of college football—for the players, the coaches, even for the fans. Zuppke concluded forcibly, telling Halas that this should never be allowed to happen again and that the NFL should institute a formal rule forbidding teams from signing college players until they had graduated.

Halas didn't believe that the problem was as deep seated or as widespread as Zuppke contended, but Halas feared that this was a public relations battle he couldn't win, so he reluctantly agreed to support Zuppke's request. The next week at the annual NFL owners' meeting at Detroit's Statler Hotel, Halas conveyed Zuppke's proposal to Joe Carr, the league's president. After a brief discussion, the owners agreed to a resolution that would ensure there would never be another Red Grange tour—or another Red Grange.

James Dooley, the owner of the NFL team in Providence, Rhode Island, read the resolution:

> The National Football League . . . hereby places itself on record as unalterably opposed to any encroachment upon college football and hereby pledges its hearty support to college authorities in maintaining and advancing the interest in college football and preserving the amateur standing of all college athletes . . . It is the unanimous decision of this meeting that every member of the National Football League be positively prohibited from inducing or attempting to induce any college player to engage in professional football until his class at college shall have graduated, and any member violating this rule shall be fined not less than one thousand dollars, or loss of its franchise, or both.

When league president Carr rose to speak at the Statler Hotel, he brimmed with optimism as he gazed at the owners seated in the smoke-filled conference room and delivered a state-of-the-sport address. "This past season has been the most remarkable in many ways of any year in the history of the organization," Carr said. "Attendance at most cities increased many times, and the feeling of the press and public was better than ever before . . . Attendance and publicity were augmented when Mr. Grange elected to become a professional. Much discussion followed the entry of this most talked-of athlete of modern times into our league. I am firmly convinced that the net result has been all in favor of our organization. Thousands upon thousands of people were attracted to their first game of professional football through a curiosity to see Grange in action, and many became profound advocates."

Halas left the meeting in high spirits. He had money in the bank, the league was growing, and even though he couldn't sign another college player who was still in school due to the new Red Grange rule, he believed that Grange would return to his team for the 1926 season. For Halas, life was wonderful.

• • •

Life was good for Grange as well. As soon as he returned to Chicago from the barnstorming tour, he started throwing his money around as if he had been challenged as to how fast he could spend it. He bought several cars, including a shiny Packard Cabriolet with white velvet upholstery. He drank Dom Pérignon champagne whenever he visited a speakeasy. And when he took a date to one of Chicago's finest restaurants, he abided by a simple rule: If an item on the menu didn't cost at least $20, he wouldn't order it.

Grange indulged in all the sweets that came with being young, good-looking, rich, and famous. He attracted attention everywhere he went—at the grocery store, at the movies, even in the restroom at restaurants. He had so much star power that Hollywood beckoned. In May 1926, he played the lead role in the feature film *One Minute to Play,* a comedy about a young man in college who goes against his father's wishes and tries out for the football team. The movie was such a success that Joe Kennedy, the head of film company FBO, asked Grange to give up football in favor of being a full-time actor. Grange declined.

After the filming was complete, Grange returned to Wheaton for the summer, where he resumed his duties as an ice man. He relished the hard labor the job demanded, and it brought a sense of normalcy and routine back to his life. When August rolled around, he felt as rested as he had in over a year. He was ready to play football again.

As Halas assembled his roster for the 1926 season, he telephoned Pyle to work out another contract for Grange. But before the two started talking about the details, Pyle issued a demand that had to be met or he would stop the discussion: Halas needed to give him one-third ownership of the Bears.

Halas refused. No player was worth that much, he argued. Pyle hung up the phone and, a few days later, began planning to start his own NFL team—a team that would feature Grange. Based on the commercial success that Grange had enjoyed in New York during the tour, Pyle decided that his team should be based in the Big Apple. He contacted Ed Barrow, the general manager of the New York Yankees, and secured a five-year lease to play in Yankee Stadium.

Pyle then moved to gain admittance into the NFL. He traveled to Detroit to plead his case at the NFL owners' meeting. Tim Mara, the Giants' owner, feared that another New York–based team would ruin him financially, especially one with Grange on its roster. Mara had lost money in every game during the 1925 season except when the Bears and Grange squared off against the Giants at the Polo Grounds. When Pyle's request was put to a vote, Mara said no. According to league rules, a single dissenting vote could deny a new franchise from gaining entry into the NFL. Outraged, Pyle hatched a new plan: He would launch his own professional league to compete with the NFL. He fumed to Grange, "No blasted Irishman is going to keep me out of New York!"

A month later, in a meeting at Chicago's Morrison Hotel, Pyle announced the creation of his American Football League. The flagship team would be in New York. Its home would be Yankee Stadium. The team's name would be the Yankees, and it would feature Grange. There would be nine other teams based in cities as far east as Boston and as far west as Los Angeles. Sportswriters and radio broadcasters referred to it as "the Grange League."

Pyle was betting that Grange could single-handedly carry the new league on his broad shoulders. On the morning of the league's debut game at Yankee Stadium, the skies over New York opened up and unleashed a torrent of rain. Pyle counted on drawing 60,000 fans to watch Grange go against the Los Angeles Wildcats, but only 20,000 showed. Played in a steady downpour, the game was won by the football Yankees, 6–0.

Though poor weather seemed to follow the Yankees wherever they played, the team still drew 220,000 to its fourteen games—more than any NFL or AFL team. But by December, five of the nine AFL teams had folded. Grange had invested his own money to fund some of the franchises. To try to recoup his losses, Grange and Pyle organized another barnstorming tour at the end of the season, scheduling ten games in Texas and California against a team that would be led by George "Wildcat" Wilson. But the tour didn't possess the allure it had the previous year. Most of the games were played in half-empty stadiums because Grange was no longer a nationwide curiosity.

Realizing that he couldn't sustain his league financially, Pyle cut a deal with the NFL: He would disband the AFL in return for being awarded a franchise in New York. Pyle and Grange were named co-owners of the New York Yankees. To mollify Mara, it was agreed that the Yankees could play only four games a year in Yankee Stadium, and the contests couldn't be held on the same day that the Giants had a home game. This wasn't an ideal arrangement for Pyle and Grange—they would be forced to play twelve of the team's sixteen games on the road—but Grange viewed the Yankees as his financial nest egg. He believed that as long as the pro game continued to grow in popularity, the franchise would soon be among the league's most valuable.

The Yankees and Grange started the 1927 season strong. They beat the Dayton Triangles, 6–0, and then, a week later in front of twenty thousand at the University of Detroit's stadium, the Yankees topped the Cleveland Bulldogs, 13–7. This win set up the marquee game of the NFL season when the Yankees traveled to Chicago to play Grange's old team at Wrigley Field.

They were all back together on this gray October afternoon: Grange, Pyle, and Halas. A sellout crowd of more than thirty thousand flocked to the stadium, making it the NFL's most heavily attended game of the year. In the moments before kickoff, thousands of fans who had been turned away at the gate became unruly. Some stormed through the centerfield gate; others climbed the fences. There weren't enough police to control the lawless rampage, so thousands of fans who didn't pay for a ticket were able to stand along the sidelines—in some cases, three deep—and watch the action unfold. Pyle was furious.

Late in the game, with the Yankees trailing, 12–0, Grange intercepted a pass. Over the next few minutes, his old magic returned, thrilling the crowd with a pair of runs that covered about 20 yards each. The talents of the Ghost, who had been so beat up during much of his brief pro career, suddenly materialized: He ran as if it were his sole purpose in life, charging over defenders, spinning out of their grasp, cutting here, twisting there. He looked as natural as an eagle soaring through a blue sky. Even though he was on the visiting team, Grange won over the partisan crowd. After his second long dash, the fans stood on their feet and yelled in full throat.

Less than a minute remained. The Yankees, still trailing, were desperate. Quarterback Eddie Tryon received the snap, dropped back to pass, and hurled the ball in the direction of Grange, who was streaking down the Chicago sideline. He leapt as high as he could. But as he reached up for the ball, the Bears' George Trafton—the biggest, roughest player on the Chicago squad—lunged at Grange, smashing headgear to headgear. The ball sailed incomplete. When Grange crashed to the ground, his right cleat stuck in the turf. His leg twisted grotesquely as the weight of Trafton slammed on top of him. Grange shrieked in pain and rolled around on the grass, clutching his shredded knee.

The stadium fell silent. Pyle and Halas ran onto the field. Grange finally got up. He gingerly tried to put weight on his right leg, but tumbled awkwardly back onto the ground. Hundreds of concerned fans spilled onto the field, wanting to do something, anything to help their fallen hero. After a trainer examined his knee, Trafton and a few other players lifted him in their arms and began carrying him to the Yankees locker room. Two long lines of fans stretched from where Grange had lain in agony to the dressing room entrance, forming a double cordon that Grange was now being hurried through.

The fans in the stands rose one more time. Grange would never again be the same.

Pyle *told* the newspapermen that Grange was going to play again. Though Grange tore both a tendon and a ligament in his knee—an injury that today requires surgery but at the time was usually treated with rest—he returned to the field just seven days later. Pyle used the reporters to spread the word to the fans in Wisconsin that Grange would be fine for the Yankees' next game against the Packers. The ploy worked. More than eleven thousand, the largest crowd to ever attend a pro game in Wisconsin, turned out on a frigid autumn afternoon to watch the Ghost. Steadied by a cane, Grange walked cautiously to midfield before the game. He waved to the crowd, which greeted him with a roar. But then Grange hobbled off the field and watched his Yankees lose, 13–0.

Grange sat out three more games. Goaded by Pyle, he played against the Bears in a home game at Yankee Stadium on Election Day. Limping noticeably, Grange carried the ball only a few times for a few yards. Fearing that fans wouldn't come to the stadium if Grange wasn't in the lineup, Pyle told Grange to keep playing—otherwise they stood to lose a fortune. Grange begrudgingly followed Pyle's orders, just as he always did.

Grange played in each of the Yankees' last six games, but he was shot as a player. All of his magic had gone poof. In one game, he was in so much pain that he refused to carry the ball. In another, the Yankees home crowd booed him when he was repeatedly tackled behind the line of scrimmage.

Yet Grange kept lacing up his cleats. After the NFL season was over, he and Pyle embarked on another barnstorming tour of the Pacific Coast, as Grange believed he could "play" himself back into shape. He wound up further injuring his knee. It was so damaged that he would miss the entire 1928 NFL season.

Halas continued to coach the Bears, leading the franchise through the dark days of the Great Depression. Though several NFL teams couldn't remain financially solvent when the Depression hit with the crash of the stock market in October 1929, Halas carried on—barely. In the summer of '31, co-owner Ed Sternaman couldn't pay his mortgage on either his apartment or his gas station. His options limited, he asked Halas if he would buy his share of the Bears for $38,000.

Halas borrowed money from virtually everyone he knew. In return for cash, he offered stock in the team. His mother gave him $5,000, his friend Charlie Bidwell chipped in another $5,000, and George Trafton's mother sent Halas a check for $20,000. Halas eventually raised enough funds to buy out Sternaman. At the start of the '31 season, the Bears were his and his alone.

• • •

With *his star client unable* to play football in 1928, Pyle turned his attention to another sporting endeavor: a cross-country footrace. Dubbed the "Bunion Derby" by sportswriter Westbrook Pegler, the race would travel a 3,485-mile route from Los Angeles to New York City. Pyle charged contestants $25 to enter and promised to award $25,000 to the winner. He hired Grange to recruit prospective runners and promote the race in towns across America.

On March 4, 1928, a field of 276 runners took off at the sound of a firecracker set off by Grange from the muddy track at Los Angeles's Ascott Speedway. The event attracted a freak show of participants, including a Hindu philosopher who chanted as he ran, a man in red flannel underwear and an aviator's helmet, another man in overalls and logging boots, and another in moccasins. One runner carried a Bible as he jogged; another lugged a ukulele.

More than forty reporters followed the event across the nation, riding in a special bus that Pyle had customized for $25,000. Pyle called it "The America," and it featured a shower, enough beds to sleep ten, a kitchen, and a radio. Pyle also organized a sideshow that followed the runners and performed in several towns along the route. It included a fire-eater, a wrestling bear, a five-legged pig, and a mummified human cadaver.

By the time the competitors crossed the California state line and entered New Mexico, more than a half million spectators had witnessed the Bunion Derby. Grange, following Pyle's bus in his red roadster, sold programs for 25 cents to those who gathered along the race's route. By the time the cavalcade reached Oklahoma, Grange estimated that he had sold more than one hundred thousand programs.

As the race meandered along Route 66, it exacted an enormous physical toll on the runners. After eight days, the field had shrunk to 120, as runners dropped out with various foot ailments. In Illinois, a woman whose husband had been hit by a car attacked Pyle and scratched him on the face. A dozen other runners had to quit running after colliding with cars, motorcycles, and bicycles.

Near the midpoint of the race, two doctors who traveled with the runners wrote a report detailing what they were witnessing. "The general appearance of most runners after completion of the daily mileage was that of exhaustion, with cold perspiration, dyspnea, drawn facial expressions, hunger, thirst, and a desire to sleep," the report stated. " . . . As the race progressed, other complications in addition to those previously noted were as follows: boils, diarrhea, tympanites, sudden elevation in temperature while running, nausea, acute respiratory infections with fever of 100 degrees to 101 degrees F, loss of toenails, blisters of the feet . . ."

On the eighty-fourth day of the event, twenty-year-old Andy Payne was the first to cross the finish line at New York's Madison Square Garden. He had clocked a time of 573 hours, 4 minutes, and 34 seconds. Despite rumors that Pyle was broke, he paid the top finishers in cash. Payne, a farmer from Claremont, Oklahoma, used his winnings to pay off the mortgage on his father's farm. He never ran in another race.

A few weeks after the Bunion Derby, Grange and Pyle met to discuss a new contract. Grange's three-year deal with Pyle had expired. Pyle wanted to renew it, but Grange believed that his football career was over, and he told Pyle that he would never play another down. Grange severed his professional relationship with Pyle—he also relinquished his interest in the New York Yankees—and returned home to Illinois. It was time to move on, to let go of the game of his youth.

But the lure of football was too strong for Grange. After sitting out the 1928 season because of his injured knee, Grange received a phone call from Halas, who asked him to return to the Bears in the summer of '29. Though Halas knew that Grange would never be the player he was before the injury, he still believed that Grange could put fans in the seats. After consulting with his father, Grange agreed to play. His weak knee had robbed him of the ability to make sharp cuts, but he still possessed above-average straight-line speed for a halfback. For the season, he rushed for 522 yards on 130 carries.

Grange played six more seasons for the Bears. Though he never matched the magic of his barnstorming days, he earned first team All

Pro honors in 1930 and '31. But by 1933, he was only a part-time player—he gained just 297 yards rushing that season—and his speed had virtually vanished. The final game of his career was on January 27, 1935, at Hollywood's Gilmore Stadium against the New York Giants. The Bears were ahead, 21–0, when Grange, age thirty-one, entered the game in its final quarter. Halas wanted Grange to go out on a high note by scoring a touchdown. Halas hoped he could cross the goal line, drop the ball on the field, and then trot into the locker room.

With the ball on the Chicago 20-yard line, Grange took a pitch from the quarterback. He darted into the open field, crossing the 25, then the 30. There was no Giants defender in front of him, but just as it appeared he would break away, New York's Cecil Irvin, a tackle, lunged at Grange and brought him down. In his prime, Grange had rarely been caught from behind, but now, in the last minute of twilight of his playing days, a 230-pound lineman had outrun him. It was Grange's last carry. "I'm through," Grange told reporters after the game. "I'm getting out of the game before I get killed."

Grange and Zuppke finally reconciled. In 1937 Grange authored a book, *Zuppke of Illinois,* that was a tribute to his former college coach. Grange once again began referring to Zuppke as his closest friend and football mentor. The two frequently exchanged letters and phone calls for the rest of their lives.

Zuppke stayed at the helm of the Illini football program until 1941. He guided the team to four national titles (1914, '19, '23, and '27) and amassed a career record of 131-81-12. During his tenure, the average attendance at Illinois games rose from 4,500 to 60,000. He's credited with inventing the flea-flicker, the pass pocket, the screen pass, and spring practice. Today the surface at Memorial Stadium is named after him: Zuppke Field. He died in 1957 at the age of seventy-eight and is buried across the street from the field that bears his name.

Late in his life, Zuppke remarked on Grange: "They can argue all they want about the greatest football player who ever lived," he said. "I was satisfied that I had him when I had Red Grange."

. . .

George Halas coached the Bears until 1968. He had led his franchise to 324 victories—more than any other coach at the time—six NFL championships, and eight division titles. But when he looked back on all of his accomplishments, the Red Grange tour stood out. "I've always thought," Halas said, "it was the tremendous publicity generated by the Grange Tour that established pro football as a national sport."

Halas and Grange remained close up until Halas's death in 1983 at the age of eighty-eight. They frequently corresponded, enjoyed dinners together, and on the day of Grange's ultimate achievement—his induction into the Pro Football Hall of Fame—Halas rode with his former player in a car to Canton, Ohio. In front of an overflowing crowd outside of the Hall on a sun-baked summer afternoon in 1963, Halas introduced Grange, calling him "the eternal flame of professional football." Both Grange and Halas were members of the hall's first class.

Halas, who had struggled through the NFL's early years and flirted with financial ruin on several occasions, died a wealthy man. When he passed away, the Bears were worth $40 million.

Charles Pyle kept promoting. When he was rounding up runners to compete in the Bunion Derby, he met a Native American man on a reservation. "I complained [to him] about being too fat," Pyle told a reporter after the Bunion Derby. "The chief gave me some pills to take, and they reduced me in a week. I bought the patents on the pills, and when I get around to it, I'm going to give it to the public. I'm going to every town in the country, hire the fattest woman I can find, and put her in the drugstore window. I'm going to feed her those pills and let the public see her fade away. And I ask you, will the public buy those pills!"

As with so many of his grand plans, Pyle never followed through with his idea of selling weight-loss pills. He did promote another Bunion Derby in 1929, but it was a financial disaster. He couldn't pay the first-place and second-place runners their winnings, and he was sued and arrested. When reporters asked him what happened, Pyle replied, "Boys, I'm flat broke."

In 1930 Pyle started a radio transcription business. Three years later, at the Chicago World's Fair, he ran a freak show exhibit, which featured a woman who looked like a mule, a man who could swallow anything—including watches and toothbrushes—and a human goat who ate grass and rocks. Pyle boasted that it was the freakiest freak show of all time.

In 1937, at the age of fifty-five, he married Elvia Allman, a thirty-two-year-old radio star. But two years later, just months before he hoped to take his freak show to the New York World's Fair, he died of a heart attack. Newspapermen around the country—many of whom Pyle had spent his life courting—eulogized the first agent in NFL history. "Charlie no doubt had faults—as haven't we all, but how many of us had the virtues that were his?" wrote Bill Henry in the *Los Angeles Times*. "We all dream dreams, but few of us can couple with the hazy wishfulness, the initiative, and the courage that makes dreams come true. Charley Pyle could do that. He overreached himself at times, but that failing was not unique with him. It's the penalty that is paid—and rather gladly—by those who refuse to be shackled by conservatism, custom, and willingness to let well enough alone. Nobody could ever accuse Charley Pyle of that. He never quite found things so satisfactory that he was willing to quit trying to do something bigger and better."

When asked about his old friend and business partner, Grange said, "Charlie had more good ideas than any ten men about how to make a buck. He'd made and lost a million three or four times . . . But he was straight with me from the start."

Grange couldn't turn his back on the game. He helped Halas coach the Bears for three seasons and then, in the 1940s, became a broadcaster. For fourteen years, he called Bears games on radio and television, and he worked with announcer Lindsey Nelson on college games. Grange also enjoyed success selling insurance in Chicago, a job that Nelson said Grange was most proud of "because he felt he did that all by himself. Everything else was God given and team-work."

In 1941 Grange married Margaret Hazelberg, a stewardess he met on a United Airlines flight. They had no children. As the years went by, Grange remained in high demand. Whenever he talked— at a formal dinner, in front of business executives, at a graduation— people stopped what they were doing and listened intently to him as he spun yarns about the early days of the NFL. In 1969 the Football Writers Association of America chose an all-time team. Grange was the only unanimous choice.

Grange spent his golden years in Lake Wales, Florida. A few years before his death at age eighty-seven on January 28, 1991, he looked back on his life and at the tour that launched the NFL. "I don't have any complaints," Grange said. "I've lived the way I wanted, done what I've wanted. I don't owe anybody. I couldn't be this way if it weren't for football. But I wonder now and then how the other guys are doing, guys who helped make the pro game, guys who played even after I did.

"Pro ball in the early days got two or three inches on the third page. After we made those tours, it was getting top headlines. We spread the NFL across the country, taking it to the towns that never saw a pro game, doing anything to push the product. We played in Memphis one year, and after the game started, we were driving for a touchdown when the promoter came running on the field and told everybody we'd have to start over. The backer of the game was the founder of the Piggly Wiggly stores, Clarence Saunders, and he'd gotten caught in traffic and missed the kickoff. So we started over.

"They're benefiting today because of the things we did. And isn't it too bad that the NFL never took care of those players? I com-plained a few times because we had guys in hospitals, guys who had amputations because of football injuries. Guys who had problems that I thought the game could have done something for, but it never did.

" . . . I played football the only way I knew how. If you have the football and eleven guys are after you, if you're smart, you'll run. It was no big deal." And yet when Grange had the ball in his hands, it *was* a big deal. So much so that he fundamentally changed how the game was played and how it was perceived by the public. This, ultimately, is the legacy of Harold "Red" Grange.

Grange, Pyle, and Halas were the founding fathers of the pro game. Together they did something in the autumn and winter of 1925–26 that precious few at the time could have envisioned: They made it possible for the National Football League to survive. Together they laid the foundation of the National Football League.

ACKNOWLEDGMENTS

So many people helped me create what you now hold in your hands. I'm in debt to you all.

My editor at Random House, Mark Tavani, spent countless hours working on different versions of the manuscript. Mark's edits were always pitch-perfect and insightful. Any author would be hard pressed to find a more talented editor than Mark.

My literary agent, Scott Waxman, helped shape the idea for this project in its earliest stages and deftly edited the book proposal. This is the fourth book that we've worked on together; thanks once again, Scott. Wade Kwon, a Birmingham-based writer and editor, generously gave his time and talent in thoroughly editing two early drafts. Sean Kelley, a senior editor at Health.com, also pored over the manuscript and stamped his literary flourishes onto the pages. Karen Wingo, a former senior writer at *Southern Living,* greatly enhanced the copy with her graceful edits. And my stepfather, Gordy Bratz, a retired army colonel, painstakingly read several drafts and improved the final product immeasurably.

I'd also like to express my gratitude to the folks at the Wheaton College Archives and Special Collections in Wheaton, Illinois. Without the help of David Malone, David Osielski, and Keith Call, this project never would have gotten off the ground.

Finally, a big thank-you goes to Terry McDonell, Hank Hersch, Rich O'Brien, and the rest of the gang at *Sports Illustrated* for all the support they've given me in the fifteen years I've called SI my professional home.

NOTES

1. An Ambitious Plan

3 *Morrison Hotel:* George S. Halas with Gwen Morgan and Arthur Veysey, *Halas: An Autobiography* (Chicago: Bonus Books, 1986), p. 104.

4 *Room number 1739:* Gary Andrew Poole, *The Galloping Ghost* (Boston: Houghton Mifflin Company, 2008), p. 130.

5 *Short film clips:* John Underwood, "Was He the Greatest of All Time?" *Sports Illustrated,* September 4, 1985, p. 102.

5 *By '25, nearly three-fourths of Americans went to movie houses at least once a week:* Myra Weatherly, ed., *Living in 1920s America* (Farmington Hills, MI: Greenhaven Press/Thomson Gale, 2006), p. 11.

6 *Model Ts rolled off the Ford assembly line at a rate of one every ten seconds and cost only $290:* Arthur M. Schlesinger Jr. and Fred L. Israel, eds., *Touring America Seventy-five Years Ago: How the Automobile and the Railroad Changed the Nation* (Philadelphia: Chelsea House Publishers, 1998), p. ix.

6 *Professional football in 1925:* Underwood, "Was He the Greatest?" p. 104.

7 *Called by Jim Thorpe, who was the league's first president, the meeting:* Michael MacCambridge, *America's Game: The Epic Story of How Pro Football Captured a Nation* (New York: Random House, 2004), p. 7.

7 *Pyle and Halas negotiated through the night:* Gene Schoor, *Red Grange: Football's Greatest Halfback* (New York: Julian Messner, 1952), p. 107.

8 *They took periodic breaks:* Richard Whittingham, *The Chicago Bears: An Illustrated History* (Chicago: Rand McNally & Company, 1979), p. 42.

2. Something Not Seen in Football Before

9 *The caravan:* Associated Press, October 18, 1924, Wheaton College Archives and Special Collections.

10 *WGN executives expected thousands:* John M. Carroll, *Red Grange and the Rise of Modern Football* (Urbana, IL: University of Illinois Press, 1999), p. 70.

10 *"The eyes of the Middle West turn to Urbana [Champaign] Saturday"*: Poole, *Galloping Ghost,* p. 17.

11 *"Mr. Grange will be carefully watched"*: Ira Morton, *The Red Grange Story* (New York: G. P. Putnam's Sons, 1953), p. 50.

11 *That Michigan expected to "romp over us"*: Morton, *Red Grange Story,* p. 49.

11 *"Victory in football is forty percent ability and sixty percent spirit!"*: Red Grange, *Zuppke of Illinois* (Chicago: A. L. Glaser Inc., 1937), p. 47.

12 *"Hurry up! Speed it up!"*: Kenneth L. Wilson and Jerry Brondfield, *The Big Ten* (Old Tappan, NJ: Prentice Hall, 1967), http://bigten.cstv.com/sports/m-footbl/spec-rel/092607aaa.html.

12 *Weighed more than fifty pounds:* John U. Bacon, "Building a Sports Empire," *Michigan History Magazine,* September-October 2000, pp. 28–33.

12 *One time Ring Lardner:* Bacon, "Building a Sports Empire," p. 31.

14 *One reporter estimated:* Article, Wheaton College Archives and Special Collections, dated October 18, 1924.

14 *More than twenty thousand people had unsuccessfully tried to obtain tickets:* Morton, *Red Grange Story,* p. 52.

15 *"Without those heavy socks, you'll feel a lot fresher and cooler"*: Morton, *Red Grange Story,* p. 53.

16 *"Kick off to Grange!"*: Schoor, *Red Grange,* p. 59.

18 *"Grange had torn Michigan to pieces"*: James Crusenberry, *Chicago Tribune,* October 19, 1924.

19 *Yost, who invented the fake field goal:* Bacon, "Building a Sports Empire," p. 31.

19 *In the standard "Grange play"*: James A. Peterson, *77: Grange of Illinois* (Chicago: Hinckley & Schmitt, 1956), pp. 17–18.

21 *"I'm so dog tired I can hardly stand up"*: Morton, *Red Grange Story,* p. 56.

22 *"Shoulda had another one, Red"*: Morton, *Red Grange Story,* p. 57.

23 *Calling it "Western football"*: Carroll, *Red Grange and the Rise,* p. 67.

25 *Grange continued to walk leisurely through the dusk, wearing a cap and sweater:* Peterson, *77: Grange,* p. 22.

25 *He slipped into his room, changed clothes, and, with a friend, sneaked out a back door and headed to a small downtown restaurant for dinner:* Peterson, *77: Grange,* p. 22.

3. A Hard Life

26 *Newsmen shifted their focus, devoting more space to sporting news:* Carroll, *Red Grange and the Rise,* p. 67.

28 *At the turn of the twentieth century, Lyle Grange was as tough and country strong as any man in Forksville, Pennsylvania:* Morton, *Red Grange Story,* p. 5.

28 *One of his favorite games was played with his dog Jack:* Morton, *Red Grange Story,* p. 4.

29 *One day he broke off a branch from one of the towering hemlock trees:* Morton, *Red Grange Story,* p. 4.

29 *The bleeding was so profuse that she bled to death before her husband could rush her to the nearest doctor several miles away:* Poole, *Galloping Ghost,* p. 5.

30 *He needed their help in raising Red:* Carroll, *Red Grange and the Rise,* p. 13.

30 *Worried that his daughters needed a strong female figure in their lives, Lyle put them on a train back to Pennsylvania:* Peterson, *77: Grange,* p. 4.

31 *Ernest worked Red tirelessly on the farm:* Red Grange, untitled document, Wheaton College Archives and Special Collections, p. 1.

32 *Mayor H. Ward Mills appointed Lyle the new marshal:* Carroll, *Red Grange and the Rise,* p. 14.

33 *He opened a window at the back of the locker room and leapt out to escape:* Carroll, *Red Grange and the Rise,* p. 18.

33 *The two boys initially divided the tasks in the evening:* Carroll, *Red Grange and the Rise,* p. 19.

33 *Emma Dollinger, the wife of Charles "Doc" Dollinger, who owned a corner drugstore in town, was literally the neighborhood mother:* Morton, *Red Grange Story,* pp. 17–18.

34 *Lyle told his son that he would give him a quarter for every race he won:* Morton, *Red Grange Story,* p. 8.

35 *One day he told his dad that he was thinking about giving up football for good:* Morton, *Red Grange Story,* p. 8.

35 *Once he started dominating these games, he had his first inkling that, perhaps, he could someday play on the Wheaton High varsity team:* Carroll, *Red Grange and the Rise,* p. 34.

36 *The only thing that mattered once the fists were raised was not winning or losing but how one fought:* Morton, *Red Grange Story,* p. 8.

36 *When he was eight, he developed a severe cold:* Morton, *Red Grange Story,* p. 8.

36 *But instead of forbidding Red to play sports, Lyle, without even consulting the doctor, said to go ahead and participate:* Morton, *Red Grange Story,* p. 10.

4. The Wonder of Wheaton

38 *In some states it was as high as 40 percent:* Willis F. Dunbar and George S. May, *Michigan: A History of the Wolverine State* (Grand Rapids, MI: William B. Eerdmans Publishing Company, 1995), p. 462.

38 *The nation's top military brass encouraged high school principals to push their students into sports such as football:* Carroll, *Red Grange and the Rise,* p. 34.

39 *"What positions are open?":* Morton, *Red Grange Story,* p. 12.

39 *Pucky told Grange that the only position that wasn't filled by a returning starter was right end:* Peterson, *77: Grange,* p. 3.

39 *Clear the field of apples that had fallen from the trees:* Morton, *Red Grange Story,* p. 13.

40 *Although the cleats didn't fit—in fact, during his freshman season, Grange would never wear cleats that matched his actual shoe size—he kept his sore feet a secret:* newspaper article, Wheaton College Archives and Special Collections.

40 *As he galloped into the end zone:* Morton, *Red Grange Story,* p. 12.

41 *Castleman then moved Grange to left halfback:* Peterson, 77: *Grange,* p. 3.

41 *Though Castleman had no experience coaching football—he was the manual training teacher—even he could see that Grange was a rare player, maybe the best in the state, even as a sophomore:* Morton, *Red Grange Story,* p. 13.

41 *Grange and his gang liked to chase the horse-drawn ice wagon when Thompson came by, hoping to snag a coveted ice chip:* Underwood, "Was He the Greatest?", p. 129.

42 *Thompson handed over a silver dollar to Grange and asked him if he'd like to work for him during the summer at a weekly wage of $37.50:* Morton, *Red Grange Story,* p. 22.

43 *Then one of them would raise the remaining cake of ice back up on a shoulder and move to the next apartment or house:* Poole, *Galloping Ghost,* pp. 71–72.

43 *The next time Grange dropped off ice at their house, the wife loudly implored her spouse to "teach the young punk some manners":* Morton, *Red Grange Story,* pp. 24–25.

44 *The* Wheaton Illinoian *named Grange to its all-county team, calling him "the star of the selection" and noting that he often "spilled three to seven men" on runs with his stiff-arm: Wheaton Illinoian,* December 5, 1919.

45 *He feared the very worst: that he might not even walk again, much less play football:* Morton, *Red Grange Story,* p. 23.

46 *As Grange lay on the examining table while the doctor conducted a more detailed examination, he was cold with fear:* Morton, *Red Grange Story,* p. 23.

46 *The doctor bills could have bankrupted the Granges, but Thompson covered all of the expenses, and he continued to pay Grange his weekly salary:* Morton, *Red Grange Story,* p. 34.

47 *Earlier that summer, before he had injured his leg, Grange had hauled ice in the morning and competed in a track meet in the afternoon. He participated in six events—and won all of them:* Underwood, "Was He the Greatest?" p. 129.

48 *After wins like this, Grange and a few of his teammates would hop in the back of Doc Dollinger's Buick:* Morton, *Red Grange Story,* p. 18.

49 *Against Batavia High, for instance, he scored 52 points and rushed for 504 yards on 21 carries. Later in the season, against Naperville, he tallied 59 points in a decisive Tigers victory:* Wheaton High School Football Record, 1918–1921.

49 *"The greatest player Wheaton has ever had": Wheaton Illinoian,* October 22, 1920.

50 *And at least one team, Scott High in Toledo, Ohio, resorted to dirty tactics to stop Grange:* Morton, *Red Grange Story,* p. 19.

51 *He started at center in his first three seasons, but now he switched to forward:* Morton, *Red Grange Story,* p. 14.

52 *Carl Johnson, a track coach at the University of Michigan, traveled with several alumni 350 miles from Ann Arbor to meet Grange and tell him why he should attend their school:* Morton, *Red Grange Story,* p. 19.

53 *After Grange had finished those events, Zuppke approached him:* undated, unnamed newspaper article, Wheaton College Archives and Special Collections.

54 *Near the end of their walk, Zuppke told Grange, "I think you have a good chance of making the football team":* Morton, *Red Grange Story,* p. 20.

5. A Marked Man

56 *There was no way on God's green earth he was going to play football at Illinois:* Grange, biographical essay, Wheaton College Archives and Special Collections.

56 *Grange's neighbor in Wheaton, George Dawson, was a brother there, and he helped Red make arrangements to follow in his footsteps at the fraternity:* Grange, biographical essay, Wheaton College Archives and Special Collections.

57 *But on the first day of freshman practice, he was overwhelmed by what he saw: The players were even bigger in real life than in his imagination:* Schoor, *Red Grange: Football's Greatest,* p. 4.

57 *He wasn't going to play:* Grange, *Zuppke of Illinois,* p. 87.

57 *"Football makes a lot of sense to me":* Underwood, "Was He the Greatest?" p. 131.

58 *As Red ran toward the end zone, Zuppke couldn't take his eyes off him:* Grange, *Zuppke of Illinois,* p. 87.

58 *The player in front of him was given number 76; the player in back of him was issued number 78. Grange was handed jersey number 77:* Morton, *Red Grange Story,* p. 34.

59 *Zuppke was the first college coach in history to conduct spring football practice, and he believed these extra training sessions were crucial to developing his players:* Mark Tupper, Decatur (IL) *Herald & Review,* September 9, 2007.

60 *"The debut of Zuppke's new back will be anxiously awaited. Harold Grange has trotted through the freshmen ever since practice opened":* Urbana-Champaign *Courier,* October 4, 1923.

60 *During pregame warm-ups, he'd gazed across the field at the Nebraska players:* Morton, *Red Grange Story,* p. 35.

61 *"Let's make it a football game," Dawson said to Zuppke:* Chicago *Tribune,* October 7, 1923.

61 *"You're leaning, Red, and giving away the plays!":* Morton, *Red Grange Story,* p. 35.

62 *"A spectacular piece of work, the sort expected of a player with the speed of the former Wheaton star who has all the earmarks of developing into a wonderful player":* Chicago *Tribune,* October 7, 1923.

63 *"To hell with Iowa":* Morton, *Red Grange Story,* p. 37.

63 *That final drive proved to Zuppke that Grange wasn't just a gifted runner, he could also catch the ball as well as anyone on his team:* Grange, *Zuppke of Illinois,* p. 90.

65 *Officials at radio station KYW in Chicago, sensing the spiking regional interest in the game, decided to broadcast the contest:* Carroll, *Red Grange and the Rise,* pp. 56–57.

67 *"Here was a moment fitted for the climax of a novel":* Wheaton College Archives and Special Collections.

67 *"Grange has absolutely no lost motion":* Wheaton College Archives and Special Collections.

68 *"Keep away from professionalism," Zuppke often told Grange:* Carroll, *Red Grange and the Rise,* p. 95.

69 *Based on what he saw, he wrote a report on the Illini that the Buckeyes coaches and players used to prepare for the game:* Morton, *Red Grange Story,* pp. 43–45.

71 *"I'll squeeze your hand on this, and I'll squeeze your hand harder next fall":* newspaper article, Wheaton College Archives and Special Collections.

72 *So, at left halfback on the first team of his 1923 All-America squad, Camp named Grange: New York Times,* December 18, 1923.

6. The Education of George Halas

73 *Apartment at 4356 West Washington Boulevard in Chicago:* Jeff Davis, *Papa Bear: The Life and Legacy of George Halas* (New York: McGraw-Hill, 2005), pp. 71–72.

73 *But just a few months into the campaign, several teams had quietly folded, unable to pay their players even $50 a game:* Whittingham, *Chicago Bears,* p. 30.

74 *To get paid, the players passed a hat through the crowds:* Davis, *Papa Bear,* p. 50.

74 *In 1922 Walter Lingo, the owner of the Oorang Indians of LaRue, Ohio, a town of nine hundred, staged lavish halftime shows:* Jim Reisler, *Cash and Carry: The Spectacular Rise and Hard Fall of C. C. Pyle, America's First Sports Agent* (Jefferson, NC: McFarland & Company, 2008), p. 67.

74 *They discussed several issues: how to deal with escalating salary demands of star players; how to prevent players from jumping from one team one week to another the next; how to dissuade college players from using fake names and playing in professional games; and the potential threat of other growing pro teams in different areas of the country:* Joe Ziemba, *When Football Was Football: The Chicago Cardinals and the Birth of the NFL* (Chicago: Triumph Books, 1999), p. 69.

74 *"The purpose . . . will be to raise the standard of professional football":* Canton Evening Repository, August 21, 1920.

75 *Many college athletes played under assumed names in order to keep their amateur eligibility intact:* Davis, *Papa Bear,* p. 50.

76 *After 60 yards, Halas lunged and caught the player's leg:* Halas, *Halas,* p. 32.

76 *"Halas, stop loafing!" Zuppke screamed:* Halas, *Halas,* p. 34.

77 *Zuppke put Halas in charge of the team's supply room and paid him $300 a semester:* Halas, *Halas,* p. 34.

77 *"Just when I teach you fellows how to play football," Zuppke said:* Halas, *Halas,* p. 35.

77 *"George," Jones said, "I want you at basketball practice tomorrow":* Halas, *Halas,* p. 35.

78 *He was twenty-two years old and knew that he would soon be drafted:* Davis, *Papa Bear,* p. 44.

79 *"Son," she responded, "the navy knows much better how to win the war than you do":* Halas, *Halas,* p. 38.

80 *"Tackle him, tackle him!" shouted Navy coach Gil Dobie:* Chris Serb, *Chicago Tribune,* January 2, 2004.

80 *"I said it was a touchdown," Eberle told the official:* Halas, *Halas,* p. 40.

81 *That a defender caught Halas from behind on the interception would bother him for years:* Davis, *Papa Bear,* pp. 45–46.

81 *"Well, if that is so, how did you happen to break your jaw and leg at Illinois?":* Halas, *Halas,* p. 42.

82 *"Punk," Cobb yelled at Halas, "I'll see you after the game! Don't forget":* Halas, *Halas,* p. 46.

83 *As Halas sat behind his desk and worked in the quiet of his office, he would vividly recall Zuppke's lament, "Just when I teach you fellows how to play football, you graduate, and I lose you":* Halas, *Halas,* p. 50.

84 *One time he hit a Hammond player so hard:* Halas, *Halas,* p. 51.

84 *It had covered 80 yards:* Halas, *Halas,* p. 52.

85 *One cold morning in February 1920, Halas was in his office examining the drawing of a bridge when his telephone jingled:* Davis, *Papa Bear,* p. 51.

87 *"Two hours each day?" Halas asked:* Halas, *Halas,* p. 55.

89 *On each page, he diagrammed one play, which he would then write out for his team on the chalkboard in the meeting room:* Halas, *Halas,* p. 59.

89 *Halas was a ruthless coach, schooling his men in the fine art of dirty play:* Davis, *Papa Bear,* p. 55.

89 *He wrote several letters to coaches of semiprofessional teams around the Midwest asking to schedule games, but the replies he received were noncommittal:* Halas, *Halas,* p. 60.

90 *Halas and a few others sat on the cars' running boards:* Whittingham, *Chicago Bears,* p. 18.

91 *Eventually a passing motorist drove Trafton to safety:* Whittingham, *Chicago Bears,* p. 17.

92 *Even though the games typically drew five thousand to ten thousand fans, the gate receipts didn't cover expenses. Halas expected that the team would fold at season's end:* Davis, *Papa Bear,* p. 59.

93 *Halas loudly disputed the play, arguing that fans had interfered, but the referee*

didn't overturn his call, afraid that he would cause a riot if he did: Whittingham, *Chicago Bears,* p. 21.

93 *Since both teams had lost only one game to a league opponent, they agreed to a re-match for what they called "Midwestern honors":* Davis, *Papa Bear,* p. 60.

94 *"George," Staley said, "I know you are more interested in football than in starch":* Halas, *Halas,* pp. 69–70.

95 *He wouldn't charge any rent, but he requested 15 percent of the money earned at the gate and at the concession stand:* Halas, *Halas,* p. 71.

97 *"And now along comes another serious menace":* Whittingham, *Chicago Bears,* p. 22.

97 *The doctor gave him some life-changing news: He had contracted syphilis:* Davis, *Papa Bear,* p. 66.

98 *Halas ripped up the letter of agreement he had signed with Harley and his brother, terminating the deal:* Davis, *Papa Bear,* p. 66.

98 *For the year, the Staleys ended up in the red, losing $71.63:* Whittingham, *Chicago Bears,* p. 25.

99 *He had one request of the landlord:* Halas, *Halas,* p. 79.

99 *"It might be amusing to wonder what would happen":* Halas, *Halas,* p. 86.

100 *"George, go back to the railroad, dear":* Halas, *Halas,* p. 86.

100 *Halas was so concerned about his lack of money that he started selling cars during the off-season. His co-owner, Sternaman, ran a gas station:* Davis, *Papa Bear,* p. 69.

7. Worth Coming Thousands of Miles to See

101 *Riding in an open-air Hudson automobile:* Halas, *Halas,* p. 102.

102 *He'd written several letters to Grange:* Halas, *Halas,* p. 102.

103 *In 1924 an estimated sixty million Americans—more than half the population—attended theaters each week:* Carroll, *Red Grange and the Rise,* p. 69.

103 *Demand was so great that on game day, $2 seats were selling for as much as $100 on the scalper's market:* newspaper article, Wheaton College Archives and Special Collections.

105 *"It was worth coming thousands of miles to see," Camp told a reporter:* newspaper article, Wheaton College Archives and Special Collections.

105 *"Harold Grange is the marvel of this year's backfield":* Morton, *Red Grange Story,* p. 68.

105 *"It is seldom that a player's fame":* Carroll, *Red Grange and the Rise,* p. 76.

106 *When he made his rounds on his ice route, he frequently posed for pictures with his customers:* Carroll, *Red Grange and the Rise,* p. 79.

106 *He did take a screen test in Milwaukee with producers from Universal Pictures Company:* newspaper article, Wheaton College Archives and Special Collections.

107 *Zuppke had been firing up his boys for the contest since late in the '24 season:* Morton, *Red Grange Story,* p. 72.

108 *"[It would take] great football to beat this Nebraska team":* Grantland Rice, *New York Herald Tribune,* October 3, 1925.

8. Cash and Carry

110 *The visitor announced himself as Frank Zambreno:* Davis, *Papa Bear,* p. 76.

111 *Grange strolled into the Virginia Theatre in Champaign:* Robert S. Gallagher, "The Galloping Ghost: An Interview with Red Grange," *American Heritage,* 26:1 (December 1974).

111 *The note read:* Morton, *Red Grange Story,* p. 91.

112 *"How would you like to make one hundred thousand dollars, or maybe even a million?":* Morton, *Red Grange Story,* p. 91.

112 *"You'll have to get someone else":* Reisler, *Cash and Carry,* p. 22.

113 *William changed the spelling of the family surname:* Geoff Williams, *C. C. Pyle's Amazing Foot Race* (Emmaus, PA: Rodale, 2007), p. 131.

113 *He was sixteen years old when he promoted his first sporting event, a bicycle race between Barney Oldfield and a local kid named Holden:* New Yorker, December 8, 1928.

114 *At the age of sixteen, Pyle developed pleurisy:* New Yorker, December 8, 1928.

114 *Pyle quickly talked his way into a job selling time-service clocks for Western Union:* New Yorker, December 8, 1928.

115 *Pyle then found an elderly man who agreed to fight him:* Williams, *C. C. Pyle's Amazing Foot Race,* p. 68.

116 *He could flatter people like few could:* Reisler, *Cash and Carry,* p. 49.

116 *He even wrote puffy, superlative-laced reviews of the shows, which he then sent to newspapers in California and Oregon, where the articles frequently appeared:* Williams, *C. C. Pyle's Amazing Foot Race,* p. 70.

117 *Pyle wondered how many miles Great Falls was from other cities around the globe:* Reisler, *Cash and Carry,* p. 50.

118 *He started his own acting company and became the star of several traveling shows:* New Yorker, December 8, 1928.

118 *He organized a big tent show:* New Yorker, December 8, 1928.

118 *He went into partnership:* Reisler, *Cash and Carry,* p. 50.

118 *Pyle had come up with a unique concept to entice the public:* Reisler, *Cash and Carry,* p. 50.

119 *"Come with me," Pyle said:* Williams, *C. C. Pyle's Amazing Foot Race,* p. 94.

121 *"Red, I think you should move to quarterback":* Morton, *Red Grange Story,* p. 71.

124 *"Skeptical Pennsylvania consequently sits back with an expression that says plain as words, 'Well, big boy, strut your stuff. We're watching' ":* newspaper article, Wheaton College Archives and Special Collections.

125 *"On the third play, line up strong on the short side of the field":* Morton, *Red Grange Story,* p. 73.

126 *With white puffs of breath coming out of his mouth, Grange gazed up into the*

grandstands, and he could see everyone in the stadium staring at him: newspaper article, Wheaton College Archives and Special Collections.

126 *John O'Hara, a reporter for a paper in Pottsville, Pennsylvania, noted the scene:* Carroll, *Red Grange and the Rise,* p. 90.

128 *One writer, after pacing back and forth in the press box for several minutes, simply threw up his hands and cried:* Carroll, *Red Grange and the Rise,* p. 91.

128 *"Grange of Illinois is three or four men and horse rolled into one for football purposes":* Morton, *Red Grange Story,* p. 76.

129 *"We want Red and Zuppke! We want Red and Zuppke! We want . . . ":* newspaper article, Wheaton College Archives and Special Collections.

129 *"We, er, had a fine visit down East," Grange stammered:* newspaper article, Wheaton College Archives and Special Collections.

130 *Several reporters also decried the idea:* newspaper article, Wheaton College Archives and Special Collections.

130 *Tim Mara, the owner of the New York Giants, made a special cross-country train trip from the Big Apple to Champaign to meet with Grange late in the 1925 college season:* Peter King, "The Path to Power," *Sports Illustrated,* August 30, 1999.

131 *When asked what he'd tell his son to do, Lyle responded:* newspaper article, Wheaton College Archives and Special Collections.

132 *Halas asked who would make the arrangements:* Halas, *Halas,* p. 105.

134 *Grange flatly denied it, prompting Kinley to tell reporters:* Halas, *Halas,* p. 106.

135 *"I'm all mixed up," Red told the reporter:* Ziemba, *When Football Was Football,* p. 120.

135 *"They have nothing on me," Grange told the writer:* New York Times, November 20, 1925.

136 *A reporter from the* New York Times *wrote that if the train carrying Grange:* Carroll, *Red Grange and the Rise,* p. 94.

139 *"Keep away from professionalism":* Carroll, *Red Grange and the Rise,* p. 95.

140 *He donned a black wig and stuck a cigar in his mouth, both given to him by a friend:* Halas, *Halas,* p. 106.

140 *After waiting a few hours:* Howard Roberts, *The Chicago Bears* (New York: G. P. Putnam's Sons, 1947), p. 63.

9. A Plunge into the Pro Pool

141 *He was ready to dole out that amount for every game he played for Rochester:* Halas, *Halas,* p. 107.

142 *"Why, I cannot see that there is any difference":* newspaper article, Wheaton College Archives and Special Collections.

143 *He paid $500 for a raccoon coat:* Whittingham, *Chicago Bears,* p. 43.

144 *The mayhem delayed the game for several minutes:* Ziemba, *When Football Was Football,* p. 121.

145 *Grange, dressed in a necktie, had appeared on the cover of* Time *magazine a few weeks earlier:* Reisler, *Cash and Carry,* p. 13.

145 *The radio station issued a press release:* Ziemba, *When Football Was Football,* p. 123.

146 *Neighborhood kids charged:* Reisler, *Cash and Carry,* p. 70.

147 *They were "glad to see one of our boys get in on the big money":* Reisler, *Cash and Carry,* p. 70.

148 *"They are two great teams, the Bears and the Cardinals," Grange said:* newspaper article, Wheaton College Archives and Special Collections.

149 *He told his wife that he thought the crowd had been too rough on Grange:* Ziemba, *When Football Was Football,* p. 125.

150 *He simply rose from his chair at the end of the banquet, put on his hat and coat, and left the building, not even grabbing the letterman's sweater:* Poole, *Galloping Ghost,* p. 139.

10. The Barnstormers

153 *It didn't take long for the players to give their private railcar a nickname: the Doghouse:* Poole, *Galloping Ghost,* p. 158.

154 *Francis Donnelly, a St. Louis mortician, had hastily assembled:* Whittingham, *Chicago Bears,* p. 44.

155 *At nearly every depot where their train stopped, they would escort Grange off the train and the trio would speak to reporters, contacted ahead of time by Halas:* newspaper article, Wheaton College Archives and Special Collections.

156 *The best-known sportswriters in America—including Grantland Rice, Damon Runyon, Ford Frick, and Westbrook Pegler:* Carroll, *Red Grange and the Rise,* p. 110.

157 *"The fickle football public is not unlike the jams":* newspaper article, Wheaton College Archives and Special Collections.

158 *Before he left, Grange was one of the few players:* Roberts, *Chicago Bears,* p. 66.

158 *Pyle grinned and told Halas, "This tour":* Carroll, *Red Grange and the Rise,* p. 111.

11. My Worries Are Over

160 *Dressed impeccably in a $200 tailor-made suit and his derby and spats, Pyle would put his hand:* Reisler, *Cash and Carry,* p. 68.

161 *Before he arrived back home in New York, he sent a telegram to his family:* King, "Path to Power," August 30, 1999.

161 *He began to believe that pro football wasn't economically sustainable:* Dave Anderson, *New York Times,* November 26, 2000.

161 *Tim Mara's son Wellington often stuffed his pockets full of tickets to hand out to his friends in grammar school:* King, "Path to Power," August 30, 1999.

162 *New York governor Al Smith told Mara to cut his losses:* King, "Path to Power," August 30, 1999.

163 *Surrounded by a special detail of fifty police officers, Grange entered the stadium:* *New York Times,* December 6, 1925.

164 *"I'll have to sue that bum," Ruth joked to one of his friends sitting nearby:* Dave Anderson, *New York Times,* November 26, 2000.

166 *He was overcome by the moment:* Underwood, "Was He the Greatest?"

168 *His fist connected to the back of Grange's headgear, slamming Grange's head to the ground:* Westbrook Pegler, *Chicago Tribune,* December 7, 1925.

169 *Seeing that number 77 wasn't on the field, the fans started chanting, "We want Grange! We want Grange! We want Grange!":* newspaper article, Wheaton College Archives and Special Collections.

170 *He sprinted down the sideline, running past his teammates:* Morton, *Red Grange Story,* p. 110.

172 *Grange and Pyle visited radio station WEAF:* *New York Times,* December 7, 1925.

12. The Most Harassed Young Man in America

173 *Holding his razor out before him:* Carroll, *Red Grange and the Rise,* p. 113.

174 *Grange invited Ruth inside:* Gallagher, "Galloping Ghost: An Interview."

176 *The senator escorted the group to 1600 Pennsylvania Avenue:* Richard Whittingham, *What a Game They Played* (Lincoln, NE: University of Nebraska Press, 1984), p. 20.

176 *Without even looking at the woman or offering the slightest trace of a smile, the president replied flatly:* Reisler, *Cash and Carry,* p. 86.

177 *When reporters approached Grange on the train, Pyle would often intervene, telling the reporter:* Poole, *Galloping Ghost,* p. 173.

177 *He laid out a bold vision to Grange for a new kind of stadium:* Reisler, *Cash and Carry,* p. 88.

179 *As soon as Grange entered his office, Kennedy chatted on and on about his young boys:* Halas, *Halas,* pp. 109–110.

180 *"Hiya, kid. How you doing?" Ruth asked:* Poole, *Galloping Ghost,* p. 179.

181 *Even before the ball came to a rest, the crowd turned on him:* Carroll, *Red Grange and the Rise,* p. 115.

182 *The Bears were so short of able bodies that Halas asked team trainer Andy Lotshaw, who had never played organized football, to suit up for the Pittsburgh game:* transcript of an interview with Red Grange, Wheaton College Archives and Special Collections.

185 *Conzelman, who had hoped to net more than $20,000 from the Grange game, didn't know what to expect:* Ziemba, *When Football Was Football,* p. 128.

185 *The highlight came during halftime, when one of Grange's friends grabbed a megaphone and, near midfield, yelled:* Poole, *Galloping Ghost,* p. 183.

186 *On their way back to Chicago for the final game of the tour:* Roberts, *Chicago Bears,* p. 69.

13. The Ladies' Man

189 *For Garland, Grange bought a roadster:* Morton, *Red Grange Story,* p. 108.

190 *The newly wealthy Pyle lavished his money on the team:* Whittingham, *Chicago Bears,* p. 52.

190 *He opened up an office in New York:* Reisler, *Cash and Carry,* p. 74.

190 *Halas signed four more players before leaving for Florida, increasing the roster from eighteen to twenty-two:* Morton, *Red Grange Story,* p. 108.

191 *Expecting a large crowd, Halas verbally lashed out at the game's promoter and then quickly made a few phone calls:* Halas, *Halas,* p. 112.

192 *The night before the game, Grange lit a blue streak through the hottest Tampa nightspots:* Carroll, *Red Grange and the Rise,* p. 121.

193 *Late in the game at West Point:* Lars Anderson, *Carlisle vs. Army* (New York: Random House, 2007), p. 290.

194 *Halas called Nevers:* Halas, *Halas,* p. 112.

194 *Once O'Brien had secured Nevers on his roster, he contacted Pyle:* Whittingham, *Chicago Bears,* p. 53.

196 *Halas had the train parked in a remote area of the New Orleans railroad yard:* Halas, *Halas,* p. 113.

196 *Grange would come to call "the greatest ladies' man that ever lived":* Poole, *Galloping Ghost,* p. 135.

196 *Grange and Pyle weren't the only Bears having fun in New Orleans:* Roberts, *Chicago Bears,* p. 70.

197 *Grange visited the Fair Grounds Race Course:* Whittingham, *Chicago Bears,* pp. 53–54.

14. The Storming of Los Angeles

200 *The first night in the City of Angels:* newspaper article, Wheaton College Archives and Special Collections.

200 *Grange was so beloved in California:* Morton, *Red Grange Story,* p. 111.

200 *Grange and a few of his teammates stood on the roof of the thirteen-story Biltmore Hotel:* Whittingham, *Chicago Bears,* p. 54.

201 *Grange rushed to his old coach:* Carroll, *Red Grange and the Rise,* p. 124.

201 *Pyle was rarely far from Runyon:* Reisler, *Cash and Carry,* p. 76.

204 *At the team hotel, Sternaman, the Bears' quarterback and team captain, told center George Trafton that he wouldn't be starting against the Tigers:* Carroll, *Red Grange and the Rise,* p. 125.

Epilogue: The Founding Fathers

209 *The total costs of the tour:* Halas, *Halas,* pp. 115–117.

210 *After a brief discussion, the owners agreed to a resolution that would ensure there would never be another Red Grange tour:* Halas, *Halas,* p. 119.

212 *He started throwing his money around:* Underwood, "Was He the Greatest?"

212 *The movie was such a success that Joe Kennedy:* Carroll, *Red Grange and the Rise,* p. 131.

212 *Pyle issued a demand that had to be met:* Halas, *Halas,* p. 121.

214 *Pyle cut a deal with the NFL:* Carroll, *Red Grange and the Rise,* p. 143.

215 *When Grange crashed to the ground:* Morton, *Red Grange Story,* pp. 134–135.

216 *His options limited, he asked Halas if he would buy his share of the Bears for $38,000:* Halas, *Halas,* p. 147.

219 *Late in his life, Zuppke remarked on Grange:* Underwood, "Was He the Greatest?"

220 *He met a Native American man on a reservation:* Williams, *C. C. Pyle's Amazing Foot Race,* p. 287.

221 *Grange also enjoyed success selling insurance in Chicago:* Underwood, "Was He the Greatest?"

222 *He looked back on his life:* Underwood, "Was He the Greatest?"

INDEX

ABOUT THE AUTHOR

LARS ANDERSON is a *Sports Illustrated* staff writer and a weekly columnist for the magazine's Web site, SI.com. A graduate of Columbia's Graduate School of Journalism, Anderson is also the author of five books, including *Carlisle vs. Army* and *The All Americans*. He lives in Birmingham, Alabama.

ABOUT THE TYPE

This book was set in Granjon, a modern recutting of a typeface produced under the direction of George W. Jones, who based Granjon's design upon the letter forms of Claude Garamond (1480–1561). The name was given to the typeface as a tribute to the typographic designer Robert Granjon.